The Plural I
—and After

The Plural I
—and After

WILLIAM E. COLES, Jr.
University of Pittsburgh

Contains the full text of
THE PLURAL I
as originally published
and two additional essays

BOYNTON/COOK PUBLISHERS
HEINEMANN
PORTSMOUTH, NH

Boynton/Cook Publishers
A Division of
Heinemann Educational Books, Inc.
70 Court Street, Portsmouth, NH 03801
Offices and agents throughout the world.

ISBN 0-86709-217-3

Cover design by Jennifer Ann Coles.
Printed in the United States of America.
92 91 90 89 88   6 5 4 3 2 1

ACKNOWLEDGMENTS
J.D. Thomas, *Composition for Technical Students*. Reprinted by permission of Charles Scribner's Sons from *Composition for Technical Students*, 3rd ed., by J.D. Thomas. Copyright 1949, © 1957, 1965 Charles Scribner's Sons.
Sir T. Clifford Allbutt, *Notes on the Composition of Scientific Papers*, 3rd ed. By permission of Macmillan London and Basingstoke.
From a letter written by Nicola Sacco, August 18, 1927. From *The Letters of Sacco and Vanzetti* edited by Marion D. Frankfurter and Gardner Jackson. Copyright 1928, © 1956 by The Viking Press. Reprinted by permission of The Viking Press.
"I Saw a Peacock" (anonymous) from *A Little Treasury of Great Poetry* by Oscar Williams (copyright 1947 Charles Scribner's Sons) is reprinted by permission of Charles Scribner's Sons.
Edward Gorey, *The Willowdale Handcar*. Reprinted by permission of Candida Donadio & Associates, Inc. Copyright © 1962 by Edward Gorey.
T.S. Eliot, From "Little Gidding" in *Four Quartets* by T.S. Eliot; copyright 1943 by T.S. Eliot, copyright 1971 by Esme Valerie Eliot. Reprinted by permission of Harcourt Brace Jovanovich, Inc., and Faber and Faber Ltd.

For My Daughters,
Rebecca and Jennifer

good students
good teachers
good guys

FOREWORD

The Plural I is a book to be pondered by teachers of English composition —active and prospective.

But it is not the usual book of advice to teachers about how to teach. It does not propose a curriculum for others to adopt, unthinkingly. It does not describe for others' use methods of teaching that are either validated by research or supported by a few enthusiastic users' easygoing claims of success. It does not advance a new rhetorical theory, on the basis of which a curriculum design and teaching materials can be developed. It does not offer a model for annotating students' papers or a dependable scale for grading varied kinds of essays. It does not tell the director of the writing course or the chair of a department of English how to evaluate the teaching staff in composition. Those who come to it seeking a neat prescription— or some explicit suggestions—for their own behavior will be disappointed.

And yet *The Plural I* is about all of these elements in the teaching of writing. It shows how one instructional plan was employed at one college in one recent semester by one instructor in his teaching of writing. In showing the process of that teaching, the book dramatically represents the enactment of teaching techniques. In showing that enactment, it implies— though it never states overtly—a theory of discourse that might be the basis of a unifying rhetoric. And in showing, at the completion of the process enacted, how far teacher and students have progressed in their learning, *The Plural I* implies a standard for evaluation of the teaching of composition that is different from, and higher than, any standards that students or supervisors can apply by checking items on a rating scale or answering multiple-choice questions. *The Plural I*, furthermore, offers an implicit definition of "competence" in writing that retains the humane values often lost in ordinary enumerations of goals for courses in composition.

The Plural I, then, is a dramatic representation of the experiences that one teacher had with one group of students to whom he was teaching "composition." It is not a verbatim report, not the printed transcription of sounds preserved on a tape recorder. Instead, it is a recreation of a series of events —the events that took place in thirty successive classes of instruction over the course of a semester. The encounters between teacher and students, and between students and students, are recorded as they might have happened, or (to borrow Susanne Langer's term for fictional creation) "virtually" as they happened. Because the author was an actual participant in the events he recreates, there is much of the fictional "omniscient author" between the episodes of drama. Since the subject of the book, and of the course being reenacted, is writing, there are numerous examples of writing by the students in response to the teacher's invitations, along with samples of writing that the teacher himself produced in that course that one semester. If reliving, through this dramatic or fictional representation, the experience of this course at that time turns out to illuminate for readers the fundamental experience of teaching—to reveal what that experience might be—as good drama and good fiction illuminate for readers the experiences they represent, I think that William Coles will believe his book to have been worth the writing.

The experience being enacted—that portion of the lives of the speaker and of those spoken about—is a course of instruction in writing. Not a course in "how to write" or a course in the writing of people other than those in the particular classroom or a course in the reading of nonfiction or a course in grammar or a course in rhetoric or a course in civics or a course in any of the countless other subjects that—William Coles believes —substitute for and interfere with learning to write. It is a course in writing. The teacher plans, and (more important) the teacher writes. The students write, and teacher and students talk together about what they have written. They talk seriously and intensively about each piece, almost as if that piece were a work of literature. In so doing, the students learn to read, without being taught "how to read." They learn to look freshly and more perceptively at their work, as if they are part of the audience for their own writing. They learn to rewrite. They write for every class, every day of the course. Sometimes subjects are specified and questions are asked about those subjects. But nothing else is specified in the assignments: no rhetorical patterns, no techniques of argument, no syntactic structures, no modeling on professional prose. And at the end of the course, as at the end of a play, the characters—students and teacher—are different people from when they started.

The subject of *The Plural I*, then, is growth in and through language: growth in students' power to understand a subject, in students' power to find a "voice" suitable to the work they wish the writing to do, in students' power to detect and resist postures and superficial attitudes (what

Coles and his students call "Themewriting"—a tendency many teachers encourage and students easily follow), and growth in students' ability to know who they are as they confront a subject for writing. The growth takes place gradually, as one might expect; it cannot be charted (as psychologists and sociologists are wont to do) in precisely defined steps or stages; it cannot be directly identified as it occurs. Yet by the end of the course represented in *The Plural I*, the students can see themselves, their subjects, their responses to these subjects, and their own language more fully and more richly than when they started the course. The evidence for this growth is that students enact in successive papers their enlarged awareness of themselves; that they talk about their progress, deliberately and wisely; and that in their talk about what has happened to them (Coles asks students, as their final writing activity, to say what has happened to them since they wrote their first papers) they embody their increased sensitivity to their uses of language and their awareness of how language can shape their lives.

The process by which William Coles' teaching promotes this growth is hardly that of the ordinary composition classroom. There are no lectures, no discussions of readings from an anthology, no exercises on syntax, no workbook drills on usage, no assignments to library research. Instead, instructor and students write and interact. The questions that students confront in their writing look disarmingly easy: "Where do you stand on this issue?" "What do you understand by the terms . . . ?" "Do you respect one [of these figures] more than you do the others?" And so do the directive verbs: "define," "describe a situation. . . . "

But they soon turn out not to have been so easy. At each class after the first, there is some student writing from the previous day's assignment to discuss. And Coles, far from being the easygoing inquirer, the genially supportive listener, the ebullient catalyst for lively, freewheeling discussion, demandingly investigates the students' responses to the papers before them. Instead of accepting whatever the students offer and blandly inviting additional reactions, he insists on explanation and support for students' comments and aggressively derides thoughtless or superficial responses that acquiesce in "Themewriting." The air in Coles' classroom is often tense and charged, the interchanges between teacher and students swift and blunt. Students and teacher develop—and use with gusto—metaphors and key phrases that describe weaknesses in students' writing and talking; these metaphors and phrases become the vocabulary for analysis, class by class, of students' writings. The writing activities themselves, instead of being addressed to random topics or organized about someone's theories of rhetoric, are subtly arranged so that students explore, in successive writings, the many complexities in seemingly obvious subjects, such as "advice" and "nonsense." As students complete their explorations of one subject, Coles leads them to another—different on the surface, but related to the previous subject in its focus on language and its uses—and the intense discussion of language and of students' writings continues.

As the students get to know their instructor and come to see the superficiality of much of their thinking and the flatness of much of their language, and as they come to recognize the complexity of apparently artless questions, the tension in the classroom relaxes somewhat, and the spirit of discussion modulates from sometimes bewildered give-and-take into collaborative inquiry. It is from such inquiry, conducted still with relentless honesty, that growth comes in William Coles' writing class.

Some of what is distinctive in the drama recorded in *The Plural I*, however, comes from the fact that it is not only the students who grow in their interactions with the teacher. The teacher grows, too, in Coles' class. He grows in ability to perceive and express his students' difficulties, to analyze the sources of their problems, and to find language, for question and comment, that will help the students examine their language and their feelings more perceptively. More important, perhaps, is that the teacher increases his power to devise effective teaching instruments—writing assignments— from seeing how students respond to his earlier instruments. Several times during his course Coles notes that it was his instructions that helped to mislead, or that failed to lead, students to develop their ability to use language. Sometimes he does more than comment on this recognition; he rephrases the troublesome assignments and offers the revised version at a strategic moment when his way of giving an assignment comes up in class discussions. From seeing where their teacher fell short of asking the questions he wanted to ask or of inviting the activities he hoped to elicit, students increase their recognition of the connections between language and reality, and between language and action. And the teacher sharpens his ability to anticipate *his* readers' problems, as he makes clear in subsequent assignments, so that next time he plans a sequence of writing activities, we may suppose, Coles' invitations to his students will guide them more effectively to the considered, multidimensional responses that for him constitute a large part of good writing.

For that, fundamentally, is what *The Plural I* is about—and why the title of the book is a precise description of some of Coles' values in the teaching of writing. What Coles argues, as I read him, is that writers can have many selves, and that being aware of these varied possible selves, and of the self enacted at any given moment by one's style, is the beginning of wisdom. Coles does not define what he values—the point bears emphasizing—simply in terms of the number of ideas the student can generate or the neatness and order of an organizational plan or the coherence of a paragraph or the frequency of figurative expressions or the fecundity with which a student produces free modifiers or embedded constructions. These terms and concepts may occasionally come up in discussions, but they are not featured in Coles' course. What *is* featured, instead, are these questions:

Who is the writer in a given piece? Where does he stand in reference to his subject? Where does he stand in reference to his readers? Where, finally, does he stand in reference to himself? Early in the course students write as if unconscious of who they are and where they stand—and as if oblivious to the importance of such matters. They adopt conventional roles and postures—those of flat and ponderous preachers of generalized values, for example—that have been encouraged, directly or indirectly, by successive teachers of writing. It takes time for students to learn that they should examine, and can usefully discuss, the perspectives from which they are viewing their subjects, the ways they initially incline to treat those subjects, and the questions that need to be asked about the value of these commonplace approaches. Coles does not tell students what to examine; he makes them discover for themselves what they need to consider in responding to a subject presented, and what qualities in a piece of writing deserve serious attention. As the course proceeds, students learn to step away from their customary assumptions about language and about themselves and, as a consequence of their experiences in writing and their discussions of that writing, they begin asking who they are, why they react to situations and subjects in particular ways, whether different ways of confronting subjects might be preferable, and how their language or another's language is affecting their ways of seeing. What Coles praises, as we go on through the course, is this awareness that it is possible to *choose* a self with which to confront experience, and that it is possible to ask whether the self that was chosen is the best that could have been chosen. Ultimately the students come to see the choice of a self and a stance, in any writing situation, as the ultimate creative decision, and the choice of a style with which to embody that choice as the act most fundamental to writing. They come, indeed, to see the choice of a self as a decision to be made in almost any human situation, and thus as a decision that will, each time it is made, affect the course of their lives.

In short, Coles' course succeeds when students can enact, and also discuss, their perception that one's "I" is not flat, single, and regulated by earlier experiences, but can be rounded, multiple, and within the control of the writer. When these ideas behind "the plural I" become part of the way a writer looks at and records experiences, Coles' course has come to its desired conclusion.

How the students and the course reach that conclusion cannot be described; it can only be recreated. Nor can teachers be instructed directly in new methods of bringing about comparable conclusions in their courses, though Coles does comment occasionally on his procedures and strategies in running individual classes and connecting assignments to each other. Furthermore, although Coles is reenacting the experience of his course, I do not think that he is writing to be imitated. (Perhaps no one who is not Coles could teach exactly as Coles does.) Nor is he writing "teacher talk" (often distressingly comparable to "Themetalk") to fellow teachers. He is instead, I think, enlarging our experience of teaching and challenging our values in teaching; he is forcing us to reconsider our definitions of growth in writing and even our conception of the uses of writing. From his dramatization of his course, we can all come to a reexamination of our own courses, of our conceptions of teaching, and of ourselves as teachers—perhaps even, quite simply, of ourselves. The value of *The Plural I*, finally, is not in any direct advice it gives us to follow in our own work, but in the incentive, and help, it gives each of us to consider who, as teachers, we are. Each of us is a "plural I," and each of us must choose, every time we teach, which "I" we will present to our students and to ourselves. From that choice will follow what we teach, how we teach, and how our students will learn.

—RICHARD L. LARSON

Herbert H. Lehman College,
City University of New York

I wish to express my appreciation to the following, who read the manuscript and made constructive comments: David Higgins, College of the Holy Cross; William F. Irmscher, University of Washington; Richard L. Larson, Herbert H. Lehman College; Joseph Sperry, Ohio State University.

—W.E.C., JR.

CONTENTS

The Plural I
—and After

INTRODUCTION

The ambiguity of the title of this book is deliberate, for my concern is with both writing and the teaching of writing as processes of making or building that can be seen as processes of moment and worth. Neither of these activities is something that anyone can claim to know how to do except in the same more or less general way that one may claim to know how to be decent or what it means to grow up. It follows therefore that when it comes to someone's helping someone else to write or to teach writing, the most that would seem possible is for the someone to enact his notion of what is involved in the activity in such a way as to demand that others respond with an enactment of what for *them* is involved in it. Which is to say that when it comes to the teaching of art, what teaches finally is style. Learning, the other end of the activity, would seem to be connected with a stylistic response to style. This, I am convinced, is the heart certainly of the teaching-learning process involving a creative activity, maybe of the teaching-learning process period. Let me cheerfully admit that there is a great deal about it that I do not understand. I can only speculate, for example, on why exactly the calculated confrontation of style with style results in the mutual refinement that I know it can. And how it is that through such refinement there is personal growth I find even more mysterious. The important thing, however, is my knowing that such things happen, because it gives me courage to keep doing what I do to make them happen—for my students, for myself. And I hope for other teachers. Because this book is a way of offering other teachers of writing something similar to the best I think I have to offer my students: a style performed in such a way as to enable others to make for themselves, or to make better, styles of their own.

The book is an account of a freshman composition course I taught in the late 1960s to a group of science majors (all male, as it happened) at an institute of technology. So far as what I am doing in the book is concerned, it wouldn't matter whether I were talking about a writing course offered last fall for seniors at a liberal arts college for women—a teaching situation with which I am also familiar. For what I am interested in, what I think the book has to offer, is a presentation of my situation as a teacher at a certain time and in a certain place, which can serve as an illuminating metaphor for the situations of all teachers in all classrooms dealing with writing as a creative process—whatever may be going on there as a result of whatever techniques or approaches a particular teacher happens to be using. My intention, in other words, is to illuminate what is involved in the teaching (and learning) of writing *however* one approaches it, in hopes that this will enable other teachers to take a fresh hold on whatever they choose to do. Beyond suggesting that a course in writing ought to focus on the writing of the members of it (rather than on something else), and that teachers of writing ought to develop a methodology with the subject that is an extension of themselves, I have no desire to tell anyone else how he or she ought to go about handling the subject. The effectiveness of my way, finally, is that it is my way.

But the paradox here is that no one develops or maintains for himself an approach either to writing or to the teaching of it all by himself —not one that is or that stays effective at any rate. Though we confront a mystery when it comes to how to evolve a style for the teaching of writing (just as we do when we teach writing to our students), that we confront this mystery together can make a difference. The barriers to learning I have to face in myself, for example, may not be those that are faced by another teacher, but we both face such barriers—just as, though the problem reshapes itself as the arteries harden, I do not know a teacher working at having a life as a teacher who finds it easy to maintain an approach to his subject that is neither a procrustean bed nor an excuse for indifference. And so on. The point is not that such a context suggests the need for A Fresh Awareness of Fundamental Questions, or the Value of Various Points of View, or that We All Have Things to Share; it is rather that unless a fundamental question is being seen freshly it isn't being seen as a question at all, that as a consequence various points of view on such questions are all we have, and finally that a teacher shares as a teacher in order to avoid dying as one. What, for example, is the Answer to such questions as the following: Where do you begin with the teaching of writing? What do you move to and by means of what steps? What should students write about? What, that is, is a writing assignment? What's the difference between a good assignment and a bad one? How do you read a student paper? How do you read fifty of them? How do you mark what you read? What do you do in class with what your students write? And above all, what sense do you invite your students to make of what you do with the subject of writing? Where do you want to come out with a writing course? Where do you expect your students to come out?

How would we respond to a teacher of composition who claimed to know the Answers to such questions?

How would we respond to a teacher of composition who saw no reason to keep asking them?

In that betweenness is what I see as my opportunity with my subject.

By opportunity I mean that if I am right in locating the center of the teaching-learning process where I do, then there is a peculiar (and ironic) disproportion of emphasis in most of what there is available for teachers and learners to read on the subject of how to teach writing. In fact the very thing from which such teachers and learners have the chance to learn most—a style enacted as a demand for style—is the very thing on which next to nothing has been done. On how to do it and on what to do it with, on principles and goals, on teaching as a calling, on all this a great deal, and a great deal that is valuable, has been written.* But on the actual doing, on how a given theory of rhetoric or approach to the teaching of writing feels as an action, on the teaching-learning process as a process, involving the presentation of (decidedly)

---

* It is, of course, talk in which I have had my share. Readers interested in a more direct expression of the underlying philosophy of the course described in this book may wish to see: "The Teaching of Writing as Writing," *College English*, November, 1967, pp. 111–16; "Freshman Composition: The Circle of Unbelief," *College English*, November, 1969, pp. 134–42; "The Sense of Nonsense as a Design for Sequential Writing Assignments," *College Composition and Communication*, February, 1970, pp. 27–34; and *Teaching Composing* (Rochelle Park, New Jersey: Hayden Book Company, 1974). Those interested in my notions on the function of a teacher may see: "The Unteachables," *Journal of Higher Education*, February, 1964, pp. 76–78; "An Unpetty Pace," *College Composition and Communication*, December, 1972, pp. 378–82. I have also written a text for the teaching of writing: *Composing: Writing as a Self-Creating Process* (Rochelle Park, New Jersey: Hayden Book Company, 1974).

4   nonmythic teachers engaging with equally nonmythic students in a continuing dialogue at least as undramatic as it is dramatic in its workings, repetitive often, seemingly circular, inevitably messy, on the sheer dirty work of teaching and learning day by day, in this time, of that place—on this there is surprisingly little, and what little there is, perhaps not so surprisingly, is almost entirely fiction. What is wanted, however, is less a novel about teachers or learners of writing than a novelistic account of teaching and learning, an expression of someone in the midst of the activity of dealing with students who are themselves in the midst of the activity of expressing themselves in writing. It's that sort of book that this book tries to be.

Since certain readers will wonder, perhaps I should say here that in this fictionalized account of life in the classroom I have reproduced all the student papers we worked with and all the writing assignments for the course just as they were written. But it should go without saying that the dialogues of the book are not verbatim transcriptions of what was said in class. (Tape recordings of classrooms—aural, video, or both—have about the same relevance to the meaning of what goes on there as sex manuals do to what it means to make love.) I don't mean that I've simply made up the conversations; the student writing I reproduce should serve as proof that I haven't. The dialogues of the book have about the same relation to what went on in class as, say, van Gogh's *Sunflowers* does to sunflowers—when I am successful with them. When I am not successful with them, the relation doesn't matter.

IN-CLASS WRITING ASSIGNMENT

A change of mind

There were no guidelines given any of us who were involved in the teaching of Humanities I, as the required freshman composition course at Case Institute of Technology was called in the 1960s, no set texts that any of us were expected to deal with, no minimum number of papers the students had to write. In developing a plan for my two sections of the course, therefore, I was free to imagine that I was being original—which is to say no more than that I was free to work only with what I wanted to. This could, of course, have been a disaster, as most of the time, with most teachers new to the teaching of composition, it is. Not that anyone would have called it that or cared very much even if he'd been able to—and this not because I was teaching in a school that was different from other schools in the United States. The real reason, I think, now no less than then, that no one is particularly bothered by the fact that most teachers new to the teaching of composition don't know that they don't know what they are doing (and that as a consequence composition courses so seldom turn out to be courses in composition at all) is that very few teachers have had the experience of seeing how either the students' writing or the activity of working with it can be made into something to be believed in.

I had been so privileged. I was fresh from having taught five years at Amherst College where, in working with Professor Theodore Baird, I had experienced an approach to the teaching of writing that I had

6   seen enable teachers to find themselves as teachers. The approach—it
sounds so simple—was one based on making the students' writing (and
not something else), and the students' writing as a form of language
using, the center of a course. Also, as an undergraduate at Lehigh
University I had been, as were all my students at Case, a science major.
The advantage I had over the teachers who were working in the Program with me was not so much that I had had such a past but
that I believed in it—for the worst of reasons in a lot of ways I see
as I look back, but with one very happy effect. It was that belief,
partisan, raw, and desperate as it may have been, that gave even to
the crudely grandiose side of my approach to things a very special cut-
ting edge. It protected me not from making mistakes but from having
to pay what then would have been the wrong kind of right price for
those I did make. And it is the best insulation there is against the besetting sin of a teacher: unacknowledged self-contempt. I had been
privileged then, and I was blessed. I was nothing if not committed. My
sections of Humanities I were going to be mine.

I decided that the students were going to write a lot, in fact a paper
for every class meeting of the term. In order to create a subject for
the students to address this writing to, one which could serve as a kind
of theme for the term, thereby giving our course a shape and direction,
somewhere for us to begin and somewhere to come out, I devised a
set of assignments that I thought would have relevance not only to
where the students and I were at the moment, but to where, in some
sense, we might be said to be headed. A student who entered Case in
those days had already committed himself to at least the outline of his
future; there was no nonscientific curriculum in the school for him to
move to. I was still nervously at work on a Ph.D. thesis which was going
to certify me as an Expert in Nineteenth-Century Literature. Though
the real subject of our assignments was going to be language—what it
is, how it functions, why it is important—for their nominal subject I
decided on the concepts of amateurism and professionalism. For even
the dictionary definitions of the terms were relevant, though in a totally
different way, to the most central concerns of our immediate situation.

On the first day of class I came in with three batches of mimeographed materials. I first passed out copies of Writing Assignment 1,
which I told the students to address in a paper that they were to bring
to class to turn in next time we met. I then passed out copies of "Humanities I," a statement describing the course which I told the students
to read hard at home (I think my term in those days was "study")

before writing their papers for Assignment 1. This description they were to annotate and bring to class to talk about that same next period. Finally, I distributed the following in-class writing assignment and gave the students the rest of the period to write about it:

IN-CLASS WRITING ASSIGNMENT

This assignment is for the purpose of enabling me to sort you out as individuals.

I will read your paper as soon as you have written it, but will not return it to you until later in the term. (Why is this, do you suppose? Have your English teachers in the past always returned your work to you right away? Do you find yourself at all suspicious of my saying that I am going to read your paper "as soon as you have written it," particularly when you hear that you are not going to get your paper back for a while?)

You have not been in college very long, but even so you have certainly speculated on why you are here to begin with and not somewhere else, on what it is you imagine you are doing here, on the meaning of a college education in the context of your own life. Doubtless, too, you have changed your mind about some of these matters, perhaps more than once.

(Do things sound familiar so far? How do you account for this?)

Take the rest of the period to address yourself to something about your college education of some importance to you on which you have changed your mind. Make clear what it is that you once believed, and what it is that you believe now. What is it, exactly, that brought the change about, and where do you locate yourself at the present time on the basis of it? The answer to this last question, by the way, is not "at Case Institute of Technology," is it? Why not?

Do you think you are being asked here why you came to college?

I didn't expect very much in the way of a response to that Assignment, not any more than I supposed that the students' papers were going to enable me to sort them out as individuals—and not because I think the Assignment is extraordinarily difficult. It's complex, of course, when it is seen as other than a Themetopic (which I do my best in the parenthetical nudgings to suggest that the students do); but no in-class (or for that matter, out-of-class) writing assignment given a group of freshmen at the beginning of a term will be seen as anything other than a Themetopic—no matter what its subject, no matter how it is phrased. This, presumably, is one of the reasons why courses in writing are necessary to begin with. I used the Assignment mainly to provide each student with a paper for future reference, an unmarked paper

8 (for though I read over what the students wrote, I did not comment on it) that I hoped would, at the end of the term (see Assignment 30), give each student a way of seeing his twelve weeks' experience with the course as more than a sum total of classes attended.

The students behaved like Students. What I heard from was not individuals but The Committee, The Perfect Student, Mr. Corporate Identity, which informed me that he had come to college to be Educated: to be guided, steered, directed, formed, shaped, molded, and so on by teachers (that is, by Teachers) whose sympathy, tolerance, understanding, and unfailing goodwill he was sure could be depended upon to throw the switch that would painlessly complete the circuit of knowledge. (I was also assured, however, but with no sense of the contradiction involved, that of course it was the Student's responsibility to "digest" or "incorporate" his Knowledge into his Own Life, thereby learning to Think for Himself.) The heart of the Assignment: What "brought the change about, and where do you locate yourself at the present time on the basis of it?"—involving as it does a connection between a change of mind and a change of identity—no one, predictably, even got near.

But though the students did not talk about what they cared about in the way that they cared about it, they demonstrated very clearly their ability to learn to do so. Most writers, for example, recognized that the decision to enter an institute of technology rather than a university had already closed out a number of educational options. And whereas the attempt to see this as an advantage rather than a liability was sporadic and defensive, there was also evidence of the kind of devotion to a subject that suggested the germ of an interest in seeing it as more than a subject, an interest in how the literalness of a discipline might be enlarged into a metaphor for handling other areas of experience. Thus one student, who was intending to major in physics, wrote:

When I ask the question "What am I?" the question becomes "How honest am I in dealing with myself?" Problems arise that are similar to the linear equation in three mysterious unknowns; each unknown becomes a variable of the complete range of numbers both unreal and real.

Another in mathematics said:

The physical world and its many components intensely excite me. What is space? Where am I in the world? Where is the world in the universe? What exactly does *I* mean, with life having gone on for hundreds of thousands of years. Am *I* a significant creature?

And here is a statement from a student who was going into biochemistry:

I was doing a biology paper on the differences between living and nonliving matter. The more I thought, the more confused I became until I realized that there really is not much of a difference between that which we call "alive" and that which is nonliving.

Most of the students who talked about science made an attempt to establish a relationship between science and the world of experience, but at an abstract level. What I admire in those excerpts is each writer's attempt to establish a relationship between science and his *own* experience. The quotations have in common a suggestion of a certain metaphysical habit of mind, a readiness to see a discipline in terms of other disciplines, which (since every self is made up of a number of selves living in a number of different worlds simultaneously) is emblematic of a readiness to see a discipline in terms of the self. No learning, so far as I'm concerned, no learning that means anything, can take place without such a way of seeing. It was my hope that our course would enable the students, including the writers of those sentences (who, to judge from the context of them, were largely unconscious of what they had done), to understand why this is so—which is to say, to become good enough for that understanding.

STATEMENT: "HUMANITIES I"

At the opening of this, our second class meeting, before turning to the statement about the course, I collected the papers the students had written for Assignment 1 and passed out copies of Assignment 2. From this point on, I explained, the course would provide its own materials. At the third meeting, they'd turn in papers addressing Assignment 2, I'd pass out copies of Assignment 3, and in class we'd consider examples selected from the papers the students had turned in for Assignment 1. The period following they'd turn in what they'd written addressing Assignment 3, I'd pass out Assignment 4, and in class we'd consider some papers addressing Assignment 2. And so on. I also made clear that the students could expect, always, to get their papers back right away (I hadn't built that first parenthetical remark into the in-class writing assignment for nothing). Then, even though I'd told the students to read it carefully on their own, I read through the following statement aloud:

HUMANITIES I

The relation of the student to his education, of the student to his teacher, of the teacher to his subject, must be defined at the outset of this course, for, until we can think clearly of what we are all doing, misunderstanding and dissatisfaction are inevitable. The subject, the content, or however you want to describe it, of this course is writing. Writing is an action. It is something you do. It is not something you know about, except in the same more or less ineffective way you know about health, or you know about the symphony. You do know, for example, that Good Writing should be Clear, Coherent, and somehow Pleasing to the reader. But how to make your writing clear, coherent, and pleasing is another matter altogether. All of us know various rules, for the use of the comma, even perhaps for constructing a paragraph —as if it were a building made of building blocks. And all of us know that such knowledge is useless beyond a point, or that it may sometimes even get in the way. The fact is that the teaching of writing as writing is the teaching of writing as art. When writing is not taught as art, as more than a craft or a skill, it is not writing that is being taught, but something else. To teach writing as something else, to teach art as non-art, is to make impossible the conception of art as art. On the other hand, art because it is art, cannot be taught. What is wanted then, for the teaching of writing as writing, is a way of teaching what cannot be taught, a course to make possible what no course can do.

It would be, certainly, reassuring if I asserted that you are about to take such a course, and if I added that I can finally tell you whether or not you succeed in what you have done when you turn in your paper. But if writing is seen as writing, we ought all to understand at the beginning that no one knows how to teach another how to succeed; no one knows enough to pronounce finally that this or that example is a success. A teacher may praise something that the student has written. Another teacher, conceivably, might make a different judgment. This may not seem fair, but such is the world once you leave childhood behind. Lawyers, no matter how clearly they present their cases, do not always win. Medical doctors sometimes make wrong diagnoses. As for literary judgments, there are critics who do not praise *The Faerie Queene* by Edmund Spenser (1552?–1599). There is a wide difference of opinion about Henry Miller, Samuel Beckett, and so on. These are the facts of your situation—of my situation—in this section of Humanities I. Writing, even for undergraduates at Case Institute of Technology, is an art. You may feel at times that you are not being taught what you ought to be taught, that I do not seem to give you the answers you seek, but you actually are in a situation where no one knows the answers. The best we can do is treat writing—and the writer—with respect and imagination, and in our conversations about writing and the writer hope to say something. In the classroom we shall have good moments and moments not so good. Do not expect too much. On the other hand, be sure you expect enough.

This section of Humanities I might best be described by the single word "Composition." It is a course in composing, selecting and arranging, putting together, and it could as well be called Puzzle and Problem Solving. Our medium of communication will be largely the English language—largely, though not entirely, for you may wish to use colored pencils and crayons to make sketches or you may sometimes choose to express relationships in mathematical notation or with equations. Most of the time, however, you will be expressing experience by means of words, sentences, paragraphs, and we shall try to see how the composer, the problem solver, the writer in English goes about it. What does it mean to form a sentence in English?

Do not expect the usual course in expository writing (often seen as the polar opposite of "creative writing," whatever that phrase may mean) where the student writes book reports, essays on international affairs, research papers, reads everything from *The Reader's Digest* to *Paradise Lost* to William Golding and in general goes on doing what he has already done in school. Nor should

12   you think of this section of Humanities I as the introduction to other courses given by the Department of English. Our course is a part of the University Curriculum which is concerned with your general education, a training in method and certain basic skills. No matter what department of knowledge you are concentrating in, this course will have, it is hoped, relevance.

At certain levels of education the substance of knowledge—that which we are to think about—is supplied by the teacher; and the term paper, the quiz and examination, serve to measure how much has been retained by the student of what has been transmitted to him. In this course you will find that the burden of knowledge usually falls on the student. Thus, in this section of Humanities I, you supply for your writing your own information, material, whatever you want to call it. After all, you have held various jobs and have played games, and you have had your own thoughts and feelings for eighteen years, more or less. This is your "experience," and from this seemingly shapeless, yet entirely individual, source, you will derive whatever it is you have to say. If on first looking at an assignment you do not immediately recognize how you should proceed, you need not be unduly alarmed, for this is normal, expected, intended. Upon reflection, however, you ought to be able to find something in your own past experience to talk about. If you wait for me to tell you, you will be disappointed.

You supply the material for your own discourse, while the Assignments are contrived both to define a way of thinking and writing about something and to direct our general movement from day to day throughout the term. There is nothing perfunctory about them, and you are deceived if they look easy. Every year I make a new sequence of Assignments, dealing with a new and different problem, so that for all concerned, teacher and student, this is a new course, a fresh progression in thought and expression, a gradual building up of a common vocabulary, a more precise definition of terms. I ask the questions I do, not because I know the answers to them, not even because I do not know the answers to them, but because, though I know that they do not have answers in the conventional sense of the word (what kinds of questions do?), it is only the dead who cannot be brought to see as alive a subject through which there is the possibility of self-definition. For this reason, though I have never repeated an Assignment, every Assignment I have ever worked with, every question I have ever asked, involves the same issues: Where and how with this problem do you locate yourself? To what extent and in what ways is that self definable in language? What is this self to judge from the language shaping it? What has this self to do with you?

I wish to make clear that the self I am speaking of here, and the one with which we will be concerned in the classroom, is a literary self, not a mock or false self, but a stylistic self, the self construable from the way words fall on a page. The other self, the identity of a student, is something with which I as a teacher can have nothing to do, not if I intend to remain a teacher. That there is a relation between these two selves, between writing and thinking, intellect and being, a confusing, complicated, and involving relation indeed—this is undeniable. This relation, in fact, is the center of both the course as a course and the course as more than that. But the nature of this relation, that of the self to the roles or styles in which it finds expression and through which it grows, is one that only an individual writer or thinker has the right to work out, and it can hardly become the province of any public intellectual discourse without a teacher's ceasing to become a teacher, a student's ceasing to become a student. Ideally, hopefully, primarily, our concern is with words: not with thinking, but with a language about thinking: not with people or selves but with languages about people and selves. If I refuse, therefore, to be moved by tears idle tears, either to sympathize with or condemn a self outside our subject, apart from the words it has chosen to have shape, it is because I believe that my students are people as well as students, that they have lives as well as roles, and lives with which I have no right to interfere. I am neither equipped for nor ready to assume the responsibility of posing as a parent, a priest, a psychoanalyst, a pal. I am a teacher of writing. No more and, I hope, no less.

The Assignments, you will find, usually put you in a position to isolate a bit of your experience, and then ask you something about what you have just done in this act of separating one thing from another, of arranging what you know in some sort of pattern. As the term advances you will make increasingly complicated statements about your own activities as a composer, problem-solver, writer. Whatever continuity you construct from one paper to another, from one class discussion to the next, will be your continuity, and yours alone. It can only be as good as you make it, no better, no worse. In the actual day-by-day conduct of the course, this section of Humanities I can become, at its best, a dramatic dialogue, where you and I exchange remarks, you and your fellow students converse with a certain amount of common understanding. This is enough to expect, and it is really a good deal. There will be no verbal formula to memorize, and, although there is, as in all courses, a vocabulary we will develop together, you will within a relatively short time, a few months, a year or two, be able to say only what you can say for yourself. Whatever you learn, *you* learn. This goes for all formal education, when looked at from any distance.

As for me as your teacher, I do not exist to give you the answers. My function is to ask questions, and if by inadvertence I should ever chance to tell you something, you should immediately turn the questioning on me. Whatever answers you reach in this course, they will be your own. You will do your own learning.

Of course I will attempt to control the direction the discussion takes in the classroom. I will also read your papers. (You will write one-, two-, three-page papers for each class meeting. Specimen papers will be mimeographed and brought to class for us to talk about. Everyone will have his work mimeographed for discussion at least once over the course of the term.) Much of our conversation in class will be about ideas, techniques, meaning, but it should be emphatically said that conventional literacy will be taken for granted.

My regular policy is to invite the student to rewrite—as many times as he wants—any paper he is disappointed in. This is a standing invitation, and I will read as many versions as you have energy to produce. When you hand in a rewritten paper include with it the original.

I will keep a record of your work, but grades will not be placed on individual papers. Nor will grades or any loaded question pertaining to them ever be a subject of conversation between us, any more than will the sequence of the Assignments or the matter of how you can improve your writing. So far as grades are concerned, I can say that no one will fail the course. If without reason you cut class or don't turn in your papers on time, you are simply not taking the course with the rest of us and I will ask you to withdraw from it. As to how I grade a subject such as writing, I never knew anyone who claimed to know. It is, let's face it, finally a subjective matter.

So far as the improvement of your writing is concerned, if it were possible for anyone to tell anyone else how to do this, courses in the subject would not be necessary.

The subject for our writing and discussion this term is amateurism and professionalism. We shall see what we can say about it.

Finally, some practical matters. Provide yourself with a snap-back binder. Put in it the mimeographed specimen papers, the Assignments, and your own papers and bring it to class regularly. Use ink or typewriter (and then use wide-lined paper or double space), write on one side of the paper, and leave a margin on the left-hand side of your paper for possible comments. Plan to attend class regularly and to turn your work in on time.

That statement (a modification of a statement developed originally by the teachers of English 1–2 at Amherst College) is my attempt to be as honest with the students as I know how about where we are, what our situation is, and what we are going to try to do together. Few students at the beginning of the course have trouble with it: first, because they have very little in the way of history to enable them to understand what it means; and second, because what they do understand of the statement they don't believe. After all, not many students entering college have had the experience of having their writing seen as a subject, of having taken it very seriously themselves or of having had it taken very seriously by anyone else. Therefore, to say to a group of college freshmen about to begin a course in writing that writing is an action, that it is something people do, is not even to get so far as to confuse or baffle them. That writing is an action most students hear in about the same way they hear that good manners are important; they simply are not aware that what it means to form a sentence in English can be a question. And when it comes to remarks such as there being no formula in the course to discover and make use of, no answers in any final sense to the questions being asked, few students can hear what is being said at all.

This explains, I think, not only how little response the statement provokes initially (my second class meeting still lasts no more than about twenty minutes), but the nature of the responses it does provoke; for the students' primary concern in "discussing" the statement has less to do with it than with how to bring comfortably home to roost on it the very conditional responses to the subject of writing and the conduct of English classes it is constructed to question. No one that day asked me to explain, for example, what I meant by a stylistic self. Will we be doing any creative writing, one student wanted to know, as though nothing outside the novel or the heroic poem could engage the imagination—and in spite of my carefully contrived irony about just that sort of talk. Another, positioning himself, asked: "Then there are no books for this course at all?" But it wasn't really a question. And then, after the feelers, they got to what they were really interested in. Do you care as much about form as you do about content? How long *exactly* do you want these papers to be? Should we use titles? Do neatness and spelling count? And inevitably: About this business of grades. . . .

What are you *really* after? That's what the students really want to know. What kind of a game is it this time? What is it you want, anyway? Just let us know where the sidelines are, the ground rules of your particular ball park, and how soon we can call it a day. That the students do not *know* this is what they really want to know, let alone the meaning of the assumptions from which the desire takes shape, is precisely what makes the attitude so difficult to deal with. The best way I know of coping with the situation is to make available to the students what I do: a statement that the course can give them a way of understanding more fully as the term goes on, that can grow in meaning to them as they grow with our procedures and our subject. The second class meeting, like the first, is for the future, but a future that I hope the course will enable the students to make into a past that is present as well.

ASSIGNMENT 1

The meaning of "professional" and "amateur"

Here is a statement:

A professional, whether paid or unpaid, is the man that counts. An amateur is a clumsy bastard.

Stanley Woodward, *Paper Tiger*

Where do you stand on this issue?

Begin your paper by explaining what you understand to be meant by the terms "professional" and "amateur." Do you respect one more than you do the other?

That assignment is typical of the sort of thing with which I still like to open a writing class. For the first couple of weeks of the course I like to have us play around with the problem of definition, with the problem of finding, as Wittgenstein would put it, "a substance for a substantive." I come at things slowly with a pattern of assignments that is deliberately both repetitive and incremental. This is partly to allow time for the necessary street-cleaning that has to be done before anyone even begins to think about writing anything, and partly because the notion of definition as a way of seeing, as a description of the definer rather than the defined, while it can be revolutionary in its implications for a student, has such implications only if a student is given time to discover them for himself.

I also like to use some seemingly simple terms (such as "honesty," "machine," "problem") to work with in order to be able to use the students' taking their meanings for granted as a way of standing for a great many other things they are also taking for granted without being aware of it. To make students aware that they may know very little of what they mean when they use terms such as amateur and professional, or when they say that they sympathize with someone, or change their minds, or get the point, or remember something, or solve a problem, is not just to involve them in the Wordsworthian recovery of the familiar made strange, but to suggest that the use of language may play a larger part in what they see and the way they behave than they might have imagined: that a subject is not simply there, but is inseparable from the language shaping it; that it is made by a maker who makes himself in the process; that experience, in fact, is based on language and not the other way around.

The wording of this sort of initial assignment, of the first five or six really, I keep as lean as possible because I've never had much luck in building into the wording of them ways of stopping the students from doing on their papers what they seem determined to do no matter what I say and no matter how I put it. Please try to bear in mind that the issue in this paper is what *you* think, where *you* stand, what *you* have to say. Please don't turn yourself into a Board of Directors. Please don't tell me about Man, or about a view of Him that by some has been contended. Please don't speak with a megaphone. Please don't write a Theme. In the first few sets of papers of a term students have a tendency to sound the way they think they ought to sound, the way they think English teachers want them to sound, the way they think they have been taught to sound. Whatever subject they are given (or that they choose) to write about they will shape with an eye to what they believe is going to be expected of them, and any attempt before the fact to suggest that they can or might or ought to see things differently I find they have a tendency simply to ignore. On the other hand, knowing that the students will probably choose to do no more than what they already know how to do with a writing assignment is different from seeming to suggest that I expect it, so the best I know to do is to give the students what will very clearly give them a choice. To make clear how someone sounds on the basis of how he has chosen to sound is my way of enabling someone to develop the motivation to change.

None of the students with this first writing assignment behaved any

18   differently from what I expected. Triumphs of self-obliteration the papers were, put-up jobs every one of them, and as much of a bore to read as they must have been to write. I found myself being talked to as though I were a rube ("Now it may, perhaps, be thought by my reader . . ."), unoffendable ("It has probably never been a matter of concern to the reader") or a confederate, someone in on the joke of why none of it mattered ("of course, we, in a college classroom, can hardly hope to settle the question of . . ."). No observation was too trivial to escape oratorical pronouncement ("It is unfair to call the amateur a 'clumsy bastard!' "); no moral stance too obvious to assume ("After all, professionals are not necessarily good people"). So far as the proposition was concerned, the students handled it in the way that a Themewriter traditionally handles the Themetopic, as a moral issue (on about the level needed to condemn the man-eating shark), which is to say inside a moral vacuum from which all living concerns are carefully excluded. Hence Professionals were Good and Amateurs were Evil. Or Amateurs were Evil and Professionals Good. Or there were those who put two bucks on every horse in the race and found a Place for both. There was a heavy reliance on nullifying qualifiers ("usually," "perhaps," "probably") and of course on the dodge of the synonym, in which an equation is solved for x with the assertion that x equals y ("A professional is skilled; a skilled man is a professional"). Of course, it was implied again and again, the issue was a closed one anyway; the dictionary, with a little help from the sortilege of something called Logic, made that Perfectly Clear ("Since Webster's *Collegiate Dictionary* defines professional as . . . then obviously . . ."). I didn't read a paper in which anyone wrote a sentence that bore any relationship to any two minutes of who or where he was. There wasn't one student who convinced me that he had a modicum of interest in anything he was saying.

The phenomenon is one with which any teacher who has more than a term's experience teaching writing is more than familiar—at any level in college and probably at many levels in high school. Different teachers deal with the phenomenon differently, but no teacher teaches anything about writing without in some way dealing with it first. For the problem is more than a problem of skills (as indeed, the whole problem of skills is more complicated than Back to Basics sloganeering would allow). It's one that I get a lot of mileage out of seeing as a problem of attitude. It is axiomatic to say at this point (and so I will say it), that different teachers will name the phenomenon here differently, that there is no One Way of dealing with it, and that (in fact) the biggest mistake a teacher can make is to imagine there is only One Way of dealing with anything when it comes to teaching. All of which is axiomatic because it's true. But it is just as big a mistake, I think, for a teacher to imagine that there are a *number* of ways for *him* to deal either with this phenomenon or with anything else connected with teaching. Part of what it means to develop a style as a teacher is to begin to find ways for one's self. I, for example, am incapable of meeting the phenomenon of Themewriting other than head on. A matter of temperament. I want to make clear, therefore, that my way of dealing with what Ken Macrorie calls Engfish, Roger Sale calls Canned Talk, Richard Lanham calls Prose of the Books, and Jacques Barzun has christened, succinctly, Black Rot—may be only one way of confronting the problem, but it is my way for me.

I don't mean that I behaved savagely with the students' phoniness when I marked their papers, but I did try to make my final comments on them raise the question of just how stupid I'd have to be to believe that they were stupid enough to believe what they were saying. "Who do you think you're kidding, talking this way?" I'd write; and then, "Who are you really kidding?" Or: "Come clean now—didn't writing this bore hell out of you?" Or: "Look at it this way: what did *you* learn from writing this paper?" Or: "How much interest would you have in someone who claimed to be interested in what you say here?" I wrote such comments knowing that I wasn't going to pass the papers back to the students until the end of our first regular working class and in hopes, therefore, that I could shape the class into the context necessary to make such questions felt as more than rhetorical wisecracks.

I planned to work closely with only one paper in class, but I mimeographed three of them because it's a bad policy to try to make a case for a collective cop-out with what might give the students a chance to imagine privately was no more than a single sacrificial goat. The three papers I chose, therefore, were very obviously three registers of the same voice, three varieties of the same trick, three assembly line products the parts of which are completely interchangeable. Each of them was as suggestive of training, capability, and intelligence; as flawlessly organized; as free from conventional errors—and as depersonalized, as empty, as ultimately meaningless as this:

In Defense of the Ambitious Amateur

The question of the amateur's place in a society of professionals is one that has greatly been changed by the scientific and cultural revolutions of the nineteenth and twentieth centuries. The amateur, who was

20   formerly criticized as a bungling idiot, today has gained the status of a
      person who is capable of advancing by improvement of his own primitive
      institution, without the glorified educational and financial backgrounds
      which have made the professional man a symbol of intellectual and
      vocational superiority. Although the amateur may sometimes lack the
      spit and polish which distinguish the professional, it is somewhat
      irrational for him to be referred to as a "clumsy bastard." The amateur is
      definitely entitled to more respect than he is obviously receiving from
      such people as Stanley Woodward, who apparently does not realize the
      contributions which amateurs have made to society.

      Amateur athletics, for example, offer as much intrinsic enjoyment as
      the professional games which are widely publicized and acclaimed. The
      number of interested fans at college and high school competitions would
      readily testify that amateur athletics are as exciting, if not more so,
      than many professional sports.

      Another example would be the field of scientific research. Many of
      the basic experiments which later led to important discoveries were for
      the most part completed by amateur experimenters who made their
      own equipment, wrote descriptive reports, and kept accurate records of
      their findings. Although many lacked formal education, they compensated
      with long hours of intense and formal study.

      The fine arts are by no means restricted to professionals, as the many
      fine examples of art, music, and photography which are produced
      annually by aspiring amateurs will show.

      Another important aspect of the question of amateurism as opposed
      to professionalism is the fact that many professionals in their chosen fields
      were probably amateurs at one time. Among scientists, for example, it
      would probably be noted that many professionals were amateur
      experimenters prior to their college careers. Engineers of today are
      probably the boys of yesterday who were known to have tinkered with
      radios or automobiles. Most professional athletes began their careers as
      amateur athletes in college or high school.

      By assuming that most professionals were at one time or another
      actually amateurs in their fields, it would be possible to reason by
      transitivity that at one time even the professional was a "clumsy bastard"!
      The efforts of the amateurs with respect to both contribution to society
      and to future professionals are not to be disparaged, due to the fact that
      the clumsy amateur, through his own efforts, could easily become the
      man that counts.

      I began, as I generally do, with the question of voice, not as a way
      of suggesting that writing is speech, but to get students used to the
      idea that sensitivity to words on a page is analogous to one's response
      to the tonal variations of the spoken word—a response that for all of

us, whatever difficulty we may have in describing how we hear what we do, is immediate and full. The concept of voice, then, involving as it does the *feel* of words, can, after a time, become an appropriate metaphor for the life of writing—or for the lack of it.

What sort of voice speaks in this first paper? I asked after reading it aloud with the students. How do you characterize it? What's your response to what you hear?

No one, of course, had any idea of what I was talking about.

"I think he proves his point pretty well here."

"Yep," I said. "No question. It's well-organized. It's Clear, Logical, and Coherent. It's neat. Is that what you mean?"

"Well, yes."

"OK. But could we let that kind of talk ride for a minute? Would you mind taking up the question of who's talking in the paper?"

He just looked at me.

"Or isn't that part of the game?" I said.

"I don't know what you mean."

"I didn't cross you up, did I? I didn't get out of the mold with all that business about voice? You know, The English Teacher mold?"

"I'm not sure . . ."

"Look. Read the last two sentences of the first paragraph out loud. Just read them out loud."

He did.

" 'It is somewhat irrational,' " I said. "How much is 'somewhat,' would you say?"

"I guess he could be a little more concrete there."

" 'A little more concrete.' My God. Look, how old do you think the writer of those two sentences is pretending to be?"

"How old?"

"Well how big then? Do you think he's really the size of the Jolly Green Giant?"

He looked at me with a puzzled, queer half-smile.

"What would you say to Jim here, if he slid up to you in the snack bar and said: 'You know, Sam, the question of the amateur's place in a society of professionals is one that has greatly been changed by the scientific and cultural revolutions of the nineteenth and twentieth centuries'?"

They looked at each other and snickered.

"How about it, Jim, do you talk that way?"

"Not me."

"Do you know anybody who does?"

"Well, this guy seems to."

"Come on, man. You mean you really think the writer of this paper sounds this way when he isn't writing English papers for an English class?"

"I guess not."

"You know damn well not. There's nobody in this class three hundred feet high or a hundred and fifty years old for one thing. And what, by the way, does all that declarative wisdom of his amount to? What *is* the point that Sam says he makes pretty well?"

He leaned forward to look back at the paper.

"Without looking at the paper again, Jim, just for a minute, just for fun. What's it about? What's the point of it?"

"I think he says that maybe amateurs aren't as good as professionals, but they're still OK. I'd have to look at the paper again to be sure, though."

"Look, Jim. We just read it out loud. Was it too complicated to get on one reading? Or do you mean something else when you say you'd have to look at it again?"

"It wasn't too complicated exactly. I just didn't . . ." He stopped.

"Of course you didn't, Jim. I didn't either. And I had the same trouble with the whole damned set. Not with just these three. All the papers. I couldn't tell one from another—particularly after about the fifteenth time I was handed talk like 'most professional athletes began their careers as amateur athletes.' As though I were being given the Hope Diamond.

"But most professional athletes did, didn't they?"—this from a student who saw that one of the other two papers I'd mimeographed to deal with was his, and who could see what was coming. They were smart all right.

"It's true you mean. I suppose so. *My* point, if you like that sort of language, is the question of how you feel about writing where somebody uses the last trumpet to tell you that water runs downhill."

"But isn't a writer entitled to his own opinion?" Smart and seasoned. They also knew the game.

"Whose opinions would you say characterize that first paragraph?"

"His."

"All that supermarket pseudo history? Come on, man. I don't mean to cross things up again, but in the first place, whose position in society *hasn't* been changed by 'the scientific and cultural revolutions of the nineteenth and twentieth centuries'—whatever they were? Couldn't you just as easily say that of a child's place in a society of adults, of a woman's place in a society of men, of a Black's place in a society of Whites? Whose 'opinion' is that really? Secondly, couldn't you just as easily say of professionals what this writer says of amateurs and *vice versa*: that the professional's place in a society of amateurs has changed, that the professional was 'formerly criticized as a bungling idiot'? And by whom, incidentally; and even if you could dredge up a name, would that help much? Also, what's that jaw-breaking phrase 'improvement of his own primitive institution' mean anyway? That's his 'opinion,' that sort of thing, or is it in there just to wow Teacher?"

"But he does have examples supporting those views." Did they ever know the game.

"Specific and Concrete examples—except when you notice that for 'amateur athletics' you could just as easily read 'amateur-made bread' which contented eaters of homemade bread throughout the country would readily testify is just as successful as professionally made bread."

"What?"

"Take out the term 'scientific research' in the third paragraph. If you plug in the term 'medicine' or 'chimney-making' or 'textile development' do you have to change anything else in the paragraph to have it go right on seeming to make sense—particularly when you've got terms like 'for the most part' and 'many'? Do you think this writer ever gets a parking ticket? Do you think he ever forgets a quarter for the meter?"

"Then this is a bad paper—is that what you're saying?"

And there we were: good versus bad, correct versus incorrect, right versus wrong. Nor did talking about the second and third papers I'd mimeographed to work with help at all. Handbook language is what they stayed with. Englishclassese. The students could see what was wrong in the papers, but not what the trouble was really, not in any way that was going to be of any help to them. What's wrong with being "vague," with sounding like a phoney, I kept asking; what's in it for anyone to want to sound like anything other than a phoney? At only one moment did I sense anything more than faintly amused bewilderment at my persistence. The second paragraph of the third paper I had mimeographed read as follows:

An amateur, however, has a rather transient interest in the subject which he pursues. He is not dedicated to his field, and may give it up "if the going gets too rough." He may enjoy initial success, but he does not have the depth and determination to be consistently "on top."

I had asked the students what they could infer from that use of quotation marks. What were quotation marks, anyway? When did you use them? Why were they used here?

There was a good deal of flopping around with talk about how awful slang was and the importance of defining one's terms, in the midst of which one student took courage enough to ask why a phrase such as "if the going gets too rough" *had* to be defined, and he went on to claim that so far as he was concerned, in the context of the paragraph it was clear enough.

"I think you're right; in the context of *that* paragraph the phrase probably *is* clear; but 'clear' meaning what?"

"I don't get you. 'Clear' meaning plain, obvious. Is that what you mean?"

"Look, can you think of a situation where the phrase *wouldn't* be clear, the same phrase?"

"Nope."

We both knew he was ducking out.

" 'If the going gets too rough, you're going to fail this course.' If I said that to you, would you understand what I meant?"

"Well, I . . . No, I wouldn't."

"Would you care what I meant?"

"I guess I would."

"Or if your parents said, 'If the going gets too rough, Bob, you're going to have to drop out of school'; or if your girl said, 'Bobby baby, you're not the one anymore, if the going gets too rough'—would you care what the phrase meant in those situations?"

"OK. I would."

"Why?"

"Because those are all things I care about."

"But here, in this paper, it doesn't matter, as you said. How much then do you think that that writer cared about what *he* was talking about?"

"Not much I guess."

"As a reader, I don't even have to guess. It doesn't matter in the paper whether the phrase is defined, because it's simple to the point of being simple-minded."

"I see what you mean."

That, of course, could have meant just about anything.

"Do you? I thought Good Writing was supposed to be 'clear and simple.' Anyone ever tell you that?"

"Yeah, I've been told that."

"Do you think from what we've said here that writing can be 'clear and simple' at the same time? And be any good?"

He stopped and then said: "OK. But I'd like to think about it."

He could have meant no more than that he'd conceded the fact that I was bigger than he was. He also might have been thinking. And so might some others. We'd see.

ASSIGNMENT 2

Advantages and disadvantages of being a professional and of being an amateur

Make a list of some of those people you consider to be professional and of some of those you consider to be amateurs.

Using one or two people from your two lists as examples, explain what you see as the chief advantages and disadvantages of being a professional and of being an amateur.

The papers addressed to Assignment 2 were more of the same, abstractions about abstractions. Despite the injunction in my phrasing of the Assignment, which I'd hoped might urge the students into something like a look at a world where somebody lived ("make a list of those people"), they continued to play it safe by staying with what for years had not only gotten them by, but on. About a quarter of the students made no list at all; three quarters of those who did made lists of common nouns ("a carpenter," "an engineer"). Those few who made a pretense of dealing with proper nouns worked them quickly into a context which immediately neutralized their specificity ("Dustin Hoffman, like most actors . . .")—a technique which then enabled a writer either to settle for a Pavlovian recitation of the public achievements of public figures ("Winston Churchill came to the helm of England in her hour of darkest need") or to weave a rug of airy speculation ("Life would be meaningless to Fran Tarkenton if he didn't play football"). To judge from the way in which most students approached things, people were amateurs or professionals the way they were six feet tall or born rich. Professionalism was a state to be (and which could be) "sought," "found," "acquired" and so forth—the way one got a license to drive or a gold watch for so many years' service. Thus the majority of students talked not about *a* professional or *an* amateur, but about a profession, or rather an occupation—any occupation. The language for their papers, as a consequence, was as ready to hand as were the scissors and paste.

In all the papers I found only two sentences that seemed to have any possibility as sentences. I seriously considered not mimeographing them. The ability to write a good sentence is connected with the ability to recognize one, of course, but the two abilities do not always imply each other. I wasn't sure, in other words, that the student who had written the sentences was aware of how much he had said in them, and I had no confidence whatever that the rest of the class would, without help, be able to see them as in any way extraordinary. In such a situation, particularly at the beginning of a term, I have difficulty resisting the temptation to be of the kind of help that is finally no help. I was afraid that, if I worked with the sentences without being able to bring the students to see them for what they were, I'd be unable to resist *telling* them what at the same time I know is of value only when someone works it out for himself. But I decided to work with the sentences anyway, gambling that I could get things to break my way. It was a gamble I lost.

I opened class with the thumping obviousness of a paper that began as follows:

It is clear to me that the terms amateur and professional cannot simply be applied to people without the qualification of stating in what field or occupation the person being categorized is. In other words, John Doe, the carpenter, builds radios in his spare time as a hobby. Thus he is both an amateur and a professional. He is a professional carpenter and an amateur radio-builder. The difference between his two facets is that as a carpenter, he makes a living. If he suddenly became unable to do skillful carpentry, he would lose his job, and would probably face severe financial problems. If, on the other hand, he lost the ability to build radios, he might become unhappy, or even depressed. However, he would still be able to eat.

His carpentry is, no doubt, of excellent mechanical quality. He has been satisfying his boss, or his customers, and has stabilized on some practices which certainly represent the state-of-the-art of carpentry. Moreover, he has made such intense use of these practices that he probably goes about a job with a sort of a cold, machinelike, thoughtless attitude. He has developed his skills, they have crystallized, and there is no room for creativity. His methods are static.

I started with what it was possible for a reader to infer from the writer's use of "John Doe" in the paper by moving from the question of where one might expect to run into such a fellow (in a fifth-grade arithmetic problem, one student said) to the issue of what difference it might have made in our attitudes toward the generalizations he is being used to prop up had we been given a character who in some way conveyed the illusion of humanity. Would the writer then have been able to fob off as Universal Truth a sentence which implies that the development of skill means the loss of creativity? I reversed the procedure in handling the last half of the paper, the "I" of which is only "John Doe" abbreviated:

Last summer, I was both an amateur and a professional, and both in the field of communications-electronics. From eight-thirty until five o'clock each day, I was in the factory of the Weinschel Engineering Company, constructing, testing, and, in general, living amid all sorts of communications equipment. The most exciting part of each week, I am forced to admit, was Wednesday afternoon—when the man with the big cigar handed out the paychecks. In the evenings, during the summer, I generally spent from two to five hours a day working on communication-electronics—redesigning, actually *creating,* an automatic telephone system.

The paper concluded like the end of a geometric proof with the sentence: "On the job, I was a professional. At home, I was an amateur." What sort of "I" was a writer going to have to create in his paper to pass off stuff like that with a straight face?

"How about it, Bob, or do you think I was just playing a game with you last period?"

It took him a little off balance.

"What?"

"The 'I' of this paper. Is he clear? Is he simple?"

"Oh. OK, yeah. He's clear. He's simple."

"Does he fit the paper because that's what he is?"

He thought for a minute.

"I think I see what you mean. Sure he does. And that's why he *is* clear and simple. He's got to be a nobody, because if he weren't he *wouldn't* fit the paper."

"OK. A writer can be clear and simple, but when that's *all* he's being he can't afford to be anything else without blowing the game."

In the second paper we seemed to have something altogether different, and the class perked up as I read through it. This was Life, their manner said. This was Real. Here is the relevant part of that Real Life picked up after an introductory paragraph filled with the sorts of throat-clearing noises that I have the habit simply of drawing a large X through.

An amateur is, in society, generally looked down upon. Yet, such a prestigeless position can have its unique advantages. Take for instance the case of Jerry Lucas. When he was Ohio State's superstar of the hardwood, he played basketball—played because he loved it—played because the fans loved to watch him. He received pleasure and his own personal satisfaction from swishing a thirty-foot jump shot or making a left-handed hook from the key. He did what he wanted because he wanted to, not because he had to.

Lucas didn't have the prestige of the big "O" or "Wilt the Stilt," but he still played basketball. He didn't receive any real repayment that he could exist on for the rest of his life, yet as an amateur at college he could still survive. Finally, if he had lost his capacity for being thrilled by the sight of a perfect jumper or tip-in, he would have been finished. Hence, his amateur status did have certain advantages, but while playing for a school like Ohio State, who cared?

Jerry Lucas cared after graduation. He needed to earn a living. Professional basketball is a very lucrative livelihood, and pro basketball wanted Lucas. So he took the big step; Jerry Lucas turned pro.

Did Jerry Lucas play basketball, make lots of money and live happily ever after? Not exactly. Lucas rode the bench. He earned a few thousand dollars sitting on his . . . laurels (?). Did he retain the zest he had for the game? No, he rode the bench. Did he experience the thrill of the thirty foot jumper and varied experience of each new game? No, he rode the bench. He gained prestige all right. Now he was Jerry Lucas of the Cincinnati Royals. He could have cared less, he wanted to play ball. But, he couldn't, he had a contract, he was a professional.

We can see that, although a professional has much prestige and in fact earns his living from this, he is at a definite disadvantage as far as freedom, motivation, or relish for the work is concerned. An amateur may not be well known and may not earn a living from his work in this particular field, but at least he can choose to do what he wants to do without undue pressure. He must have a greater motivation in order to perform the same task as a professional, yet not be paid. The titillation and exhilaration with which he approaches each new facet of his chosen moil lends much to the enjoyment that an amateur affords from such work.

For all his racetrack glibness, the writer here, at least so far as I'm concerned, is no more someone writing, someone trying to forge a style of his own, than had been the writer of the paper we'd just been talking about. Alongside the mushroom pallor of the more obvious fakes that we'd been dealing with, the center of the paper (what the students called its Body) looks bronzed and supple, fast and fit in a well-trained sort of way. But its tan for me is cosmetic, the muscles silicone. Its grace, the grace of a card sharp. It's a hard-mouthed paper rather than a tough-minded one, with a voice and manner as easily imitated as that of the moralistic Theme. It is, in fact, no more than a Theme in mufti, a disguise with about the subtlety of a sheet that makes a Halloween ghost.

One of the easiest ways to see the phoniness of the paper is to focus on the writer's failure to marry the voice of the Moralist with that of the Candy Store Sports Buff, a failure that reveals both voices as poses, and the poses as no more than vocabularies enlisted for an occasion. It was with this notion, like the skull at the feast, that I moved into the students' celebration of the "liveliness" and "interest" of the paper. Were there any words in the writer's last sentence, I wanted to know, that anyone didn't know the meanings of. Once we had "moil" and "titillation" on the table, I asked whether there were, on the other hand, any phrases in the paper that sounded familiar.

"Well, 'superstar of the hardwood,' 'zest for the game': I've heard things like that before."

"Where?"

"From sports announcers. I've read them too."

"What about a word like 'moil'?"

"I don't know what it means."

"Not many people in here did, not any more than they knew what the writer of the first paper we looked at in here this term meant by saying we could 'reason by transitivity.' Why do you think the writer here uses 'moil' in this paper, right along with language you do know, that anybody would, and that anybody could scotch tape together the same way the writer does, from having heard it and read it, heard it and read it, over and over and over?"

"I don't know."

"Come on, man. Come clean. Did you ever speak of 'delving' into a subject?"

"I guess so."

"Where did you say that? Where did you use the word 'delve' that way? Would you use it to talk to Carl over there? 'Carl, I want to delve into a subject with you'?"

"No, I probably wouldn't use it that way with anyone I knew."

"Would you write it?"

"Sure. I have."

"To whom? Someone you knew? Or to some nit-wit of an English teacher."

He laughed.

"OK. So why do you think the writer here uses 'moil' in his paper?"

"OK. He wants to sound good."

"And does he? How do you put a writer together who sounds like Webster's *International* in one sentence and Bob and Ray's Wally Ballou in the next?"

"What do you mean, how do you put him together?"

"I mean what kind of character does the collision of those two vocabularies create for you? Is he clear and simple? Is this someone you'd trust in your home? Around the silverware? You say he wants to sound good. I'm asking you who you think he would sound good to."

He didn't say it, and neither did anyone else, but the air was thick with a sense of violation. We were in the middle of what Berne would call a crossed transaction.

"Or is this," I went on after a moment, "only intended to be another god-damned paper for another god-damned English course?"

No one said anything.

"Let's look at how this writer sounds in another place. 'Sitting on his dit dit dit laurels parenthesis question mark parenthesis.' What's he doing there?"

There was some shifting, a couple of sniggers, and finally I was informed that that was called Adding Humor. Its purpose was to Capture the Interest of a Reader. It was to make me want to Read On, didn't I see, to Find Out More.

"Find out more about what?"

"Jerry Lucas."

"Who's he in this paper?"

"He tells you who he is; he gives you the facts about him."

"Does he indeed? Specific and concrete examples again, eh? What are the facts?"

We kicked "facts" around for a bit until someone suggested that maybe the writer didn't really have any facts at all, not above what anyone could get out of a newspaper file. He had a lot of public information. The rest of what he had were no more than opinions that he was trying to make *look* like facts—as Walter Winchell used to, a student said. I did not at that time want to go into how all "facts," in the sense that we were using the term, were nothing more than interpretations of events, but I did want to dramatize the way in which the students' attempts to distinguish between facts and opinions in the paper were really ways of expressing their responses as readers to what the writer was doing with language.

"Where, exactly, does he give an opinion he's trying to make look like a fact?"

"Where he says, 'He did what he wanted because he wanted to, not because he had to.' How does this guy know what Lucas wanted to do?"

"What do you mean when you say he's trying to make that look like a fact?"

"I mean this is a snow-job. He's trying to make me think he knows everything about Lucas."

"Why don't you accept that he does? He's got all that evidence hasn't he, all those 'facts' about Lucas?"

"Yeah, but that's evidence anybody could get, like Jim said."

" '*As* Jim said,' you mean. And how much of what he says about Lucas could you make apply to any new basketball player in the league? Or seem to apply?"

"All of it practically."

"And with not much more than a change in the proper noun. Could you use any of this writer's language to talk about a second-string pro quarterback?"

"Sure. All you'd have to do is make it 'superstar of the gridiron.' "

"And you could do the same thing with a new pitcher in the majors. Which raises the question of whether there *is* any Jerry Lucas in this paper, whether the writer has any opinions *or* any 'facts.' As you say, he seems to be trying to make a reader think he knows everything. He's trying to sound like an authority, just the way he throws in 'moil' and 'titillation' to try to 'sound good,' just the way he adds that Humor, like a little pinch of oregano going into spaghetti sauce. But what's he end up sounding like? How *does* somebody sound who's trying to put on 'sounding good' that way? It's a snow-job all right—but where's the snow?"

There wasn't much time left to deal with paper three, and I moved to it without anything like a clear idea of how to contrive a question that would take them to the two sentences I admired in it. The paper was written about one of the writer's neighbors who all summer long had studied the stars from his back porch through a homemade telescope. Night after night the boy had seen him there watching, making notations, once in a while taking a picture. Now, with the advent of chilly weather, he'd packed his telescope away for the winter, which, as the writer saw it, the neighbor was free to do as an amateur in a way that a professional wouldn't have been. The sentences I admired were these:

> When the professional astronomer packs up his telescope he is unable
> to pack his astronomy away with it; astronomy has become a part of
> his life to the extent that he has become a part of his astronomy.

And the concluding sentence of the paper read: "The amateur brings life to the study and finds life in it."

Maddeningly, the talk drifted to whether winter was a better time for observing the stars than summer, and I got impatient. I read through the first sentence above and asked what the implications of "unable" were. It was a question that was open in all the wrong sorts of ways, but I was already into their responses to it ("Does he mean that the astronomer doesn't *want* to pack his astronomy away?"), and trying hard to avoid saying "No. That's not what I want you to say," before I figured out the question with which I should have started.

"Look. Move to the final sentence. If as an amateur you only *brought* life to the study, what, according to the writer of this paper, would you be doing as a professional?"

But it was too late. In seeming to ask as I had for the Answer to my first question, I'd lost the opportunity to have a conversation about a response to the second. Even if there had been enough time for me to work out of somebody the response that I wanted to have a look at the implications of, that a professional may be said to take life from the study as well as to bring it there, I think the class would have seen the response as the Answer, a place to stop rather than as something to go on with. When I end a class with a butcher's move like that one, it's a long time until the day after tomorrow.

ASSIGNMENT 3

Your aspirations in relation to professionalism and amateurism

What are your aspirations so far as professionalism and amateurism are concerned? Are there senses in which you would like to be a professional? an amateur? Are there senses in which you would not like to be a professional? an amateur? Professional what? Amateur what?

Even to the students, the green whiskers were beginning to seem a little the worse for moths, the putty noses a lot less durable than the manufacturer had promised. The doughy abstraction, the dictionary definition, the moral stance, the comic cartoon example, and above all the concept of a writing assignment as a mnemonic for some as yet undiscovered Right Routine—all this the students continued to seek some magic combination for in the name of the game they'd been taught that writing was. But their hearts weren't in the performance in the way that they had been; that kind of Show Biz itself had begun to sour.

I was not, of course, Making Friends.

Several students wrote me notes at the end of their papers: "Sir, it would help if you could tell us what you wanted." (To which I responded: "Us? I can tell *you*, William, that what I want of *you* is what you want for yourself when you're proud of yourself for having wanted it. Look back over what you've written. What, William, have you ventured?") Not many students wrote more than a page for the Assignment; most of these were indistinguishable from each other. Those who groped for something individual to say simply ducked dealing with the problems of the Assignment altogether—either by making cop-out leaps into doggerel verse on how silly the course was, or by making a subject for which they'd already canned the language (how *hard* it is to be a scientist).

Yes, of course it was Understandable.

I also draw a salary to do more than let my students bleed on me.

I started class with this:

I would like to be both a professional and an amateur and to be able to enjoy some of the advantages of each.

I admire the professional and would like to be one. I believe that a professional, whether paid or unpaid, is someone with a great deal of ability who can do a particular job or type of job quite well. But if I am to become a professional in all my fields of endeavor, I must limit the fields in which I will try to achieve success. I have only one professional aspiration—to become a physicist specializing in acoustics. I find a professional position desirable because of the respect and advantages that ensue.

On the other hand, a person needs some sort of pastime, something to take his mind off the humdrum of daily events. I consider amateurism to be solely the realm of the amateur, since the amateur owes allegiance only to himself or to those he wishes to serve voluntarily. I believe that his situation is as gratifying and enjoyable as a professional's. That is why I want to pursue various sidelines that would not necessarily be done for money.

My sights are set on the ideal situation. I would like to make the best possible contribution as an amateur and a professional, yet not be driven by my work.

In the sense that that is not a single paper written by a single student, the paragraphs above are a kind of parody, the paper itself a kind of trick. But since each of its twelve sentences is reproduced verbatim from a separate paper written by a separate student addressing Assignment 3—without so much as the alteration of a mark of punctuation—or the addition of a connective—in another sense there was no trick being played here at all—at least not by me upon the students. I knew that from the fact that such a trick was possible the class might have a tendency to conclude too much; but I believed it possible for us to be able to conclude more from it than that different students can sound alike. If writing was going to be seen as no more than a performance in the Theatre of the Absurd, we could at least have it clear what it was being seen as.

I read the paper through with as flat a tone as I could manage and the students took off with predictable solemnity about "facets" and "factors" that had never been mentioned and how the arguments needed "proving" and the fact that the paper didn't "seem to say very much." Was there anything familiar about any of it, I wanted to know. Well, yes, said a student from whose paper I'd taken one of the sentences, it *did* sound like stuff he'd heard before; the writer didn't seem to be "very original in his thoughts."

"No, I mean who in the class here do you think wrote it?"

He looked surprised. "I don't know."

"Aside from the fact that there's no name on the paper, why don't you know?"

"I don't know the people in this class well enough."

I turned to the fellow with whom I'd had the conversation about the paper on Jerry Lucas' being a snow job and asked him if he thought that that was the reason.

"No. I don't think it would matter how well you knew the people in the class."

"Why not?"

"Because anyone here could have written it. We all have sights 'set on the ideal situation,' for instance."

"How would you go about writing a paper like that, then, if anybody could do it?"

"Well, you just learn how to do it. Get a good shovel."

"A kind of a technique, then? A trick? A game you can learn to play?"

"That's it."

"OK, let's play it. Let's see whether you can play it with any subject and whether anyone can play. Let's play Themewriting."

I asked someone to give me a word, any word. "Man," he said to giggles. Then I asked someone else for another: "black." A third student gave me "TNT." I got them on the board and asked who could put them into a sentence that would write a Theme.

"The day that Man invented TNT was the blackest day in the history of humanity."

Then, out of "chicken," "arm," and "drugstore," we got "Any drugstore can arm itself against failure by selling chicken," and so on. How does one then proceed? Well, the opener, of course, set everything up. With the chicken sentence you'd go on to say that chicken was: one, delicious; two, nutritious; three, easy to prepare—devoting, say, a paragraph to each. With the sentence on TNT you'd talk first about peaceful uses of the explosive, in mining, railroading, etc., and then you'd turn to killing, particularly the killing of something called wimminenchilren, then to destruction by remote control, and finally to man's inhumanity to you know what with something like this as a windup: "In spite of the many benefits which the invention . . . great achievements . . . control of the environment . . . master of the universe. . . . BUT, when weighed against . . . hideous brutality . . . only conclude . . . not master of himself."

"But it gets you by," one student said; "you have to know how to do it."

I admitted that there was no question of this. Then I told the students the origins of the "paper" we'd just been looking at as a way of trying to complicate the notion of what "getting by" can mean. I was interested in their addressing the question of whether there is anything that could be said to get by the "you" who tries to get by that way.

"How many of you in here wrote one of the sentences from that portmanteau paper?"

There were seven from the class I was in, but twice that many hands went up.

I asked a boy who'd raised his hand (and from whose paper I hadn't taken a sentence) which one was his. I didn't have to lean on him very hard to make it clear that he really didn't know whether one of his sentences had been reproduced or not. Only one student, in fact, and this because of the topical reference to acoustics, could identify for certain a sentence he knew he had written. Did anyone have an explanation for this?

They had been confused by the Assignment, they said, and that was why they had all sounded alike. But no one could show me any confusion anywhere in the dead-level sameness of the sentences. Well then, maybe it was what they called the Topic. That was it; the Topic of the Assignment was too general, too broad. That had been their real trouble. How could anyone say anything specific about so broad a Topic? How could you even get interested in such a general subject?

"In other words, you're not interested in general subjects, right? Like sex or religion or politics. You never talk about things like that. Don't have time for bull sessions, I suppose."

And what did they think a writing assignment was anyway, I went on. Were subjects just there, found, the way Jerry Lucas had been by the writer whose paper we'd looked at last time? Or did they in some sense have to be made? And who was to do this making? Me? The teacher? Was it that *I* was obligated to supply them with a way of creating a subject which would have some meaning for them?

"No, it's not that exactly. But when you have to talk about amateurs and professionals, you can't talk about what you're really interested in."

" 'When you have to talk.' What happens when you use the first person in a sentence like that, Jerry: 'When *I* have to talk about amateurs and professionals, *I* can't talk about what I'm really interested in'? Do you see any reason why you didn't put it that way? And what would these things be? Man and TNT? Capital punishment? The evils of pollution? All those Themetopics for which you've got all that Themetalk cozily gathering interest in the bank?"

"OK, sex, since you mentioned that."

"I have your word for the fact that you could talk about sex without the language of *Playboy* or of popular songs?"

"At least I'd have a chance to talk about something I cared about. That's what you want, isn't it?"

"The question, pal, is what you want. To sound like the sentences here, in this paper, and for the rest of your life; is that what you expect us to believe? And who says you didn't have the chance on this Assignment that you're telling me you didn't have? Look at the terms of it. 'Are there senses in which you would like to be a professional? an amateur?' Do you really expect me to believe that you can't create a subject out of the terms that you care anything about? Do you think someone who claimed that would belong in college? What else wouldn't he be able to do, for Christ's sake? Do you mean to tell me even that you can't get from those terms to sex? You're a professional lover, are you?"

He'd gone sullen. He didn't answer.

"Are you? You raised the sex thing. You think you're an expert on sex or not?"

"No, I don't."

"OK. Then maybe you're an amateur. Maybe in some ways you're both, just like the rest of us. Maybe there are some ways you'd like to be professional with sex that you're not now. And the other way around. Why didn't you like it when I asked you if you were an expert on sex? I thought to be professional was something everybody shot for. Do you know the derivation of the word 'amateur'? Couldn't you have gone into some of this on this Assignment if you'd really wanted to?"

"I don't care to go into my personal life that way."

"Or is that just a cop-out? You started by saying that the Assignment didn't give you a chance to talk about your personal life, about anything you cared about. Is it that you didn't have a chance, or that after years of Themewriting, of getting by, as Bill said, the idea of taking a chance is maybe a little bit scary? And not just because sex is personal either. Maybe it's because the personal wouldn't come out sounding very personal at all. It would be scary to me to have to see that maybe I'd been playing a game so long that I couldn't do anything more than play a game, to have to see that another way from what you call 'that way' wasn't necessarily a lot of wide open doors."

We dealt with two other papers that period. One was another Perfect English Paper (Clear, Logical, Coherent, and Empty) that I used to demonstrate the technique of padding. In order to make clear to the class the trick by which the paper had been manufactured, I told them to imagine that it was their responsibility to make the paper twice the length it was without saying anything more in it than the writer had already said. We began with a sentence to which the writer had devoted only a short paragraph: "I would like to be a professional and have the opportunities which Rudolph Meyer has available to him." How was it possible to double or quadruple the length of that paragraph without going anywhere.

"Well the key word is 'opportunities.' You just elaborate on it."

"How?"

"You just make up a whole mess of good things that can happen to you and call them opportunities. You could say he gets a lot of money in grants, for example."

"What else?"

It was possible to go on for blocks, of course: Rudolph Meyer had a chance to travel ("visit foreign lands" in Themetalk), to meet other scientists ("come into close contact with the minds of other nations"), to become well-known ("gain the respect of the community as well as that of his fellow scientists"), and so on. You stopped when you

40   reached the end of your Word Limit. Or you stopped when you couldn't bear to go on any longer.

The last paper we worked with was a strange one:

Say you're this kid, see. And one sunny afternoon you're fishing with this friend of yours. You ask your buddy why fish bite, and he tells you it's because they're hungry. You ask him why they're hungry, and he tells you they want to eat. But if you were this kid, see, you wouldn't be satisfied with that. You'd want to know why fish like to eat. You'd want to know what would happen if they didn't eat. You'd want to know what they eat, when they eat, how they eat.

It's good you're not a stone. A stone can't ask questions. A stone can't know. *A stone doesn't want to know.* But you're not a stone; you're this kid, you see.

Sure, you're going to get a lot of wrong answers. You're just a kid. But that's not important. The important thing is that you want to know.

After a while, you'll realize that you don't learn much by asking your buddies. They don't know about the fish. But someone must know about the fish. Sure, the fish know about the fish. They know why and when they get hungry. So you start to study the fish. But you still make mistakes.

So what you do is to find out how to study fish. And meanwhile you might learn that other people have already studied them too.

So finally after many long, hard years of learning how to study fish, you can finally begin to answer those questions.

But now you're not just a kid anymore. Now you're a pro, a fish-man, or as your buddies call you, an ichthyologist.

Now, being a professional ichthyologist, you might go fishing one sunny afternoon as part of a research project, "Feeding Habits of Marine Life," or something like that. You're trying to find out what the fish eat and when and how and . . .

As I read it, that paper is simultaneously an attempt at something original as well as a fake, a put-up job. As with the paper on Jerry Lucas, at first glance it looks to have a voice of its own, and in its total impact is just enigmatic enough to appear profound. But so far as I am concerned there is not enough indication of knowing manipulation, not enough orchestration of tone, to create the illusion of a sensibility in control of a subject. Is the writer suggesting that trying to say something about the distinction between amateurism and professionalism is absurd because the distinction is so fine as to be nonexistent? This, maybe, is the reason for the easy mock-Salinger mode with its derisive, even sneery overtones and the explanation of how, juxtaposing the opening of the paper with its conclusion, we seem in it to have come full circle. But I can't square what I hear as the dismissiveness of the paper with the quasi-straight tone of such remarks as "So what you do is to find out how to study fish" and "you can finally begin to an-swer those questions"; any more than I can weld the flippancy of "this kid, see," "you're just a kid" to the notion of the paper as a serious metaphor for a subject. Something breaks either way. And seen either way, what the students called the "point" of the paper, its "message," is something to which the paper as a paper simply reduces, making the inclusion of details such as that of the stone largely gratuitous.

The students quickly split into those who said that the paper was gibberish and those who wanted to make it mean something. Without trying to resolve the question of What the Writer Meant, I tried to get them to play with the implications of their having taken the sides on the issue that they did, to get them to see what their lady-or-tiger quarrel could lead them to infer about how responsible the writer had been in his writing. Was this ambiguity we were dealing with, or confusion; what *kind* of originality was operating in the paper?

"Well, I could write a paper like this. Easily, too. Is that what you mean?"

"Do you mean you could imitate the technique here? The same way you can the technique of the Themewriter? The same way you knew how to puff up the paper on Rudolph Meyer?"

"I think I could. I'd just use a lot of short sentences and start them with 'sure' or 'that's right.' It doesn't look that hard to do."

"Particularly when you don't have to do any more than keep a reader guessing about whether you're getting at anything or not. Can you show me how you'd use the technique to take a girl to the zoo, say? How would your sentences sound?"

"OK. 'Say you're this broad, see. And one day you're at the lions' cage in the zoo. And you wonder how the lions stay in shape. You wonder and wonder. Then you ask the guard there, and he tells you . . .' I'd go on like that."

"OK. I'm with you. Now just tell it the way you'd tell it. Just use your own voice, not a manner or a style you've borrowed. Just be you, something somebody couldn't imitate, or couldn't imitate easily. Can you do that?"

He smiled. "I haven't been able to do it so far."

That was my chance to pick up what I'd fumbled away the period before.

42   "OK," I said. "You haven't been able to so far. So far you haven't been able to do much more than imitate the voice and manner of someone else, of some non-someone else. Remember the paper we had last time about the astronomer who was 'unable' to pack his astronomy away with his telescope? Might it be that at least in one sense you, too, like that astronomer, are a kind of professional—I mean as a writer—and that to judge from the portmanteau paper this might be true of everybody in here? Might it be that what you're 'unable' to pack away with high school is a set of attitudes that you worked very hard to accumulate? And in this sense, is it more professional you need to become with what you've been calling 'writing,' or is it something else you need?"

ASSIGNMENT 4

Describe yourself
as an amateur

Describe a situation in which you acted as what you would call an amateur.

Where were you? Who else was there? What was said and done?

On the basis of what you have written, define amateur.

Our discussions of the first three assignments gave me a chance to use the students' handling of Assignment 4 as a way of beginning to see the problem of definition as a problem of self-location, as the way in which a writer, through describing what he sees, describes himself as a see-er. I began with a paper which was a *sine qua non* of evasiveness:

Last year, I was a member of a dixieland band. The band played on various occasions, and was usually well-received. However, our first performance was filled with apprehension.

The band consisted of six aspiring musicians, a pianist, a trumpeter, a clarinetist, a drummer, a base player, and myself, a trombonist. We were to play at a school function, the Cavalier Collaboration, and this was to be our first performance before an audience. The two numbers we were to play were ad-libbed, and we had rehearsed only a few times.

The night of the performance we arrived early, warmed up, and

played some background music for another act. Then we were announced·
. . . I wasn't very confident. . . . My turn finally came. . . . We
finished and were a great success. [*my ellipses*]

In this instance I acted as an amateur. I didn't have the experience
a professional possesses. No one showed me how to play dixieland.
I wanted to play and learned how to play. I had no particular preparation
for this occasion. It was not a goal that I had to reach. It was secondary
to my interests, but I wanted it and tried to get it. The amateur can
live without his interests, but he strives to keep them.

"Well, that's a Theme," they said.

They seemed satisfied to leave it at that.

"Come on, now. Get some money up. If it's a Theme, it's a trick.
What's the trick here? What's the mechanism by which the paper is
written? Using that paper as a model, show me the easy way to dust
off this Assignment?"

When they stalled a little, I said maybe it would help to play another game. This one was called Situations from Cinders, and like the
Knock-Knock jokes it had a form, the mock-haiku of:

> Frog
> Pool
> Plop

Was there any way in which the paper we'd just read could be
seen to reduce to not much more than that sort of formula?

"Sure. About all he does in the paper is tell how they weren't prepared, and how nervous he was, but then everything went fine."

"Which boils down to a formula how? Could you write about The
Big Race this way, or how wrong they turned out to be in laughing
when I sat down at the piano?"

"Yes. You could write this same kind of thing for any situation
where you didn't think you were going to be able to do something
that you turned out to be able to do."

"OK. Or in the form of the mock-haiku:

> THE DIXIELAND BAND PLAYER
> I'm nervous and low
> Then I blow at the Show
> Ho Ho.

Now let's turn things around. I'll give you some formulas to which I
boiled down some papers. You tell we how you think the papers went.
Then I'll read you what the writers wrote."

I gave them two. The first I called The Fishing Trip:

> Dry Fly
> Pal's Eye
> Oh my.

And the second was The Candy Maker:

> Hot Taffy
> Kersplashy
> No laughy

Given these bones, with the flab they had no trouble, and by taking a sentence from one student and another from the next we came up with a startlingly close approximation of just what the writers of those papers had themselves come up with: The Tale of the Grief-Stricken Fishing Buddy; that of the fellow who to this day was unable to look a piece of fudge in the face. Did *this* make plain the easy way out of the Assignment? It did. You began by making "amateur" equal "unskilled" or "inexperienced" and then made that equal "stupid" or "totally incompetent." What about a situation? Well, you could use anything, from emptying an ashtray to getting a rocket in orbit, so long as you remembered to keep the "I" of your paper a square, a character with two left feet: "Alfred E. Newman Washes a Car," "Dagwood's Date." Believability? There were ways around that too: "The very *first* time I. . . ." You had to be particularly careful to keep your details at one with your conception of character and situation. Either you stayed with the predictably Tried and True ("I was scared. My knees shook, my hands trembled, my hair stood on end."), or you became a set of directions on a do-it-yourself kit ("I first removed the contents of the container, and placed them neatly on the table in front of me. Next, I . . ."). What you couldn't afford was to create a situation you couldn't name everything inside of or a definition that relied on anything other than simple equivalents. In their blandness, the situation and the definition had to be mirror images of each other; hence the clichés. If you gave your reader a scene to judge for himself, if you gave him anything like a real situation in fact, you were dead. Everything had to point to an unarguable generality the inevitability of which nothing could be allowed to interfere with: "Much to my embarrassment, I really made a mess of things"; "Of course I played very well/badly." A reader might find such a formula trivial or boring or unreadable, but he couldn't call it wrong. He couldn't say the writer wasn't entitled to his own opinion.

"In other words, all you'd say to yourself about somebody who told you that rocks were hard was that he wasn't wrong?"

Well no, but damn it all, the point was that that way of writing a paper *did* answer the Assignment. Besides, and there was more than a trace of pettishness here, who could define amateur and professional anyway? Everyone knew the difference was A Matter of Degree, of Personal Opinion. Words meant whatever we wanted them to mean.

I took off one shoe and put it on the desk in front of them. "All right," I said, "let's suppose I decide, out of Personal Opinion, to call this shoe a Buick."

My Buick needs repair. Go get my Buick. I shined my Buick. I hit him with my Buick—I went through all the possible sources of confusion I could think of and finished up by asking whether they thought that a fellow who behaved that way ought to be let run around loose. The alternative, that finding a definition is like playing "Button, Button," I came at through the question of when the meaning of words didn't depend on what they were calling (as though it were a dirty phrase) Personal Opinion, and what was meant by personal opinion anyway. Would the dictionary help them to discover the meaning of "fair" in the sentence: "Fair is foul, and foul is fair"? How was it possible for one person to call an action kind and another to call the same action cruel? Did they know any more of what "inexperienced" or "unskilled" meant than they did of "amateur"? Finally, and I took some time with this, when they defined a word, what else were they defining? I stand on a knoll and see hills like white elephants. Nonsense, says someone at my elbow, those are drumlins and what's more they are plastered over with triassic age arkose. A third comes on the scene in a flowered shirt, picking his teeth while claiming that what we see in the distance interferes with his television reception. We have all defined hills. But more important, we have all defined ourselves as see-ers at a given point in time. Perhaps it is not possible to say that a formula approach to an assignment is "wrong" in the way that the word is usually used in the classroom. But it is possible to say a good deal about the sensibility that chooses to define itself from that way of defining an opportunity to write, a good deal which might conceivably have a lot more bite and prove to be more of an incentive to change than does the vocabulary of right and wrong, correct and incorrect.

The possibilities of other ways of seeing the problem of Assignment 4 were what I tried to dramatize with two other papers—both of which, in their separate ways, made me understand that to talk well of oneself as an amateur necessitated conjuring the illusion of its opposite. What I admire about each of the papers is the way the concept of amateurism is created out of the sense of some standard of behavior that has been violated. Here is the first paragraph of the second paper we read:

It was a cool night, the stars were peeping through the trees, and the night air was holding its breath expectantly. There we were, just the two of us, standing at her front door. She had her hands behind her back and leaned forward encouragingly. I kept my hands behind my back and leaned backwards. She then smiled expectantly, waiting. I blushed back, waiting. She stared at me. I stared at my shoes. She made small talk. I mumbled. Then she said, "Well, Dave," sweetly and slowly, looking right into me. Quickly I retorted "Well, good-by," and me and my amateurism streaked for home.

I started discussion of the paper by asking whether we could play "Frog, Pool, Flop" with it; what about all those clichés? Didn't this paper reduce to no more than a matter of Young Boy on First Date?

As with the fish-stone paper of the period before, there were camps. One group in the class found it only another formula paper, but there were other voices:

"Sure, this is trite, but the point is the guy knows that. Here's a simple scene, night air and her waiting and all the rest. The point is that the guy knows what he's supposed to do, but he can't make it. He can't make the scene. That's why he's an amateur. I think he's using the triteness in the paper on purpose."

I did too and said so. And I went on to say that it was precisely that quality of "using," the writer's consciousness of a cliché as a cliché, which for me created the illusion of character. The clichés the writer uses he transforms syntactically into an expression of a convention which is broken again and again by his character's inability to fulfill it. Such phrases as "she leaned forward encouragingly," "she then smiled expectantly," and so forth, I read as more than trite because of the knowingness with which the writer places and utilizes their triteness. The dramatic juxtaposition of a convention then ("She stared at me. . . . 'Well, Dave,' "), with the comic incapacity of a character to realize himself through it ("I stared at my shoes. . . . 'Well, good-by,' "), is what produces the illusion of a person, someone trapped between two worlds, aware of two languages, but unable to handle

48   either of them. And the final line (with the exception of the arch "retorted") in capsulating as it does the conflict of fear and desire with that sharply distanced sense of exasperation, strikes me as very nice indeed.

I probably overpraised what the student had written—I generally do overpraise the first attempts at something other than Theme-writing that we share as a class—so I felt it only fair to say that I could also see an argument for the paragraph as a *tour de force*. I also wanted to underline for all of us how the conversations of our last two classes suggested that to conclude whether a piece of prose works or doesn't is less important than understanding how one reaches the conclusions he does.

Paper three I reproduced in its entirety:

There Are Times . . .

Last summer I worked as a systems programmer/engineer in the Computer Technology Section of the National Bureau of Standards in Washington, D.C. To avoid the distractions that happened during the day, I got into the habit of going back to work after hours and working from eight in the evening to two or three the next morning. I wasn't being paid for this unrequested overtime, but I was doing professional work. However, even a professional has off periods, times when it seems he can't do anything right—times when he acts like an amateur. For me, one of these spells came early one Friday morning, about one o'clock.

Having just successfully run a major program, I was in the process of dumping it on magnetic tape when I ran into trouble. I mounted my tape on the tape unit and tried to get the computer to write on it with no success. When I looked at the tape unit, I noticed that I'd forgotten to put it in the "ready" state, so I fixed that and tried again. Again the machine refused to cooperate, this time because I'd forgotten to put the write-enable ring on the tape reel. This time I had to rewind the tape, unthread it, and put on the ring. When I finished that, I reloaded the tape and tried to write on the tape, which failed when the tape leader snapped because I'd left the unit in the "rewind" position. Before the reels locked, eight feet of magnetic tape lay snarled in the innards of the unit, clearly visible behind the plastic doors of the unit. I groaned as I thought of the wasted tape, but the worst was yet to come. Mad at myself as I was, I remembered to take the unit out of "automatic," but I forgot to turn the power off when I opened the door —which meant that the huge fan inside the unit remained on. As I opened the door, the tape spilled out onto the floor, where it was immediately sucked up through the air intake of the unit. Before I could hit the power switch, nine feet of tape had become entwined around the vanes of the high-speed fan, and what was worse, I could smell the Mylar tape burning as it was digested in the bearings. There was also the disturbing "switch-click" over and over again as the macerated tape brushed the sides of the fan well. By that time it was two-thirty, and I decided to clean up and get out—the odds were too great that I'd wreck the whole computer complex if I worked any later.

From this example of behavior which I consider amateurish, it should be obvious what I think an amateur is. An amateur is, to me, anyone who doesn't know what he's doing while he's working at a job requiring experience and knowledge of the task and the equipment. In my case this lack of knowledge was caused by the meager nine hours of sleep I'd gotten in the past four days. In an amateur it is lack of dedication to a field that produces ignorance of things related to a field, not lack of sleep.

The students were ready to praise the paper for its specificity and humor, but they had difficulty in saying just what it was about the specificity that appealed to them and just where it was they located, and why they praised, the humor. I went to the subject-verb sequences of the second paragraph.

"You'll notice he switches in that paragraph from what English teachers call the active to the passive voice. 'I'd forgotten' becomes 'it was.' How is that important in determining your response to what's going on here, the shift from the writer's seeing himself as a subject to his seeing something other than himself as the agent of the action?"

"Well, that is what's happening, isn't it? He's becoming more and more helpless?"

"Yes, but in the face of what? Just a machine? What's the effect of his talking of the tape as being 'sucked-up' by the air intake, and then 'digested' by the bearings? He grows helpless, but what's happening to the machine?"

"It's getting bigger. Also it's like it's getting to be more than a machine, like a monster of some kind."

And the writer, we noticed, is careful not to end up with this technique's handling him. He keeps what happens believable by restoring his character to perspective ("I decided to clean up and get out") in the wittily hyperbolic "realization" he brings him to at the end of the paragraph: "the odds were too great that I'd wreck the whole computer complex if I worked any later." Specificity, therefore, as a dimen-

50   sion of character was more than filler here, just as the humor of the
      paper was not "added" or superimposed, but organic.

      There was just time at the end of the period for me to ask about
      the relationship of the last two writers' definitions of amateur to the
      situations they'd described in their papers. Was there anything in the
      situations the writers had created, I wanted to know, not covered by
      the definitions they had applied to them? In his last paragraph the
      writer of paper two had called himself a "phoney," for example: "I
      choked, buckled under pressure, chickened out, whatever you want
      to call it." Did such terms cover our responses to the idea of amateurism
      he had created in his opening paragraph? Similarly, would the defini-
      tion of amateur given by the writer of paper three as someone "who
      doesn't know what he's doing" be an accurate description of the be-
      havior of the character he had made? The students were hearteningly
      quick to see that in neither instance had the writers begun to do any-
      thing like justice to their own tonal complexity. The character of
      paper two was more than a phoney just as that of paper three was
      more than inept. It was the first example of writing we had shared
      which created the illusion of something like human beings involved
      in human experience. And in both cases the result was a "to be de-
      fined" for which dictionary terminology was not enough. Dictionaries
      define words; they cannot define word users who seek in their use of
      words to be someones as well.

ASSIGNMENT 5

Describe yourself
as a professional

Now describe a situation in which you acted as what you would call a professional.

Again, where were you? Who else was there? What was said and done?

On the basis of what you have written, define professional.

Most of the papers addressed to Assignment 5 I could take care of with one variation or another of a standard comment: "Man. Black. TNT. Remember the game? What do you lose when you win it?" But I was lucky enough not to have to make such stuff the focus of yet another class. It was only one Theme I reproduced for us to consider, and that, a Situation from Cinders, I chose to use primarily as a way of getting us to something else.

It was a paper that nosed and sniffed about for a couple of paragraphs before settling down to its subject, to what purported to be its situation:

Upon a friend's suggestion, a group of five fellows including myself went to the base's pool table room. Since I hadn't shown an immediate interest in participating, I watched as the guys played the first round. As they were about to start the second game, they started ribbing me about not playing and persuaded me to take one of the others' positions.

52   The game started slowly as each person in turn missed, but as it continued there was suddenly a radical change. Abruptly, I declared that I would clear the table and I did. They watched in amazement, wondering if I knew what I was doing or whether I was just lucky. They challenged me to do it again. I accepted the challenge and was successful. The truth was that in my own home I have a full-size pool table and that I had been practicing extensively just before the trip.

There I was a professional amongst the amateurs. Although I was not boastful or pretentious, I was able to present the high quality skill for which the professional is famous. People looked up to me because of my dexterity and ability, and the way I made practical application of knowledge and interest.

There isn't any situation here, of course, and that's what I mimeographed the paper to demonstrate. What *might* have been the situation is buried in two sentences: "Abruptly, I declared that I would clear the table and I did," and "I accepted the challenge and was successful." The rest is Themetalk ("an immediate interest in participating," "they watched in amazement," and so on) *about* what happened. Nothing is rendered. We're told not shown that the writer was neither "boastful [nor] pretentious," and that he was "looked up to." For both the situation and what is made of it we have to accept the writer's solemn word. The question was what that word, on the basis of that writing, was worth.

One student said that the voice of the paper reminded him of Little Jack Horner: Lo, there I was a professional; and what a good boy am I. Another nailed the functionless sprawl of detail leading up to the game (involving a bus trip across a desert, a flat tire, the disposition of a group of boy scouts at an army base, etc.) by pointing out that such talk could go on for pages (like the paper on Rudolph Meyer), and could be used as a preface to virtually anything.

But things opened up beyond this with one boy's saying of the paper: "You know, I don't believe this ever happened."

"What do you mean?"

"Well, you know the paper on Jerry Lucas when somebody said the writer there didn't sound like an authority? It's that way here: 'Clear the table.' I play a lot of pool. When you clear the table you run the rack. Anybody who played pool the way this guy says he does would know that. I don't believe he wiped out those guys this way."

"Maybe he just learned the game at home as he says, never went in a pool hall, never talked to a pool player."

"Maybe, but I still don't believe it. He says he practices a lot. He'd have *had* to know how pool players talk to be this good."

It was the first direct connection anyone had made between professionalism and the use of language, between professionalism and behavior.

"You don't mean that to be a professional you have to sound like a professional, do you?"

It was the sort of minor-seeming question that certain students love to climb with, and there were a lot of attempts made to convince the fellow I'd been talking with that you really didn't have to sound like a pro to be one. No one seemed to be making much of an effort to try to see what he might have meant, and he was about as far with what he'd noticed as he seemed able to go by himself. I came back into things by asking the boy if he'd seen the first Superbowl game on television. He had. I then recreated a moment in the postgame interview with Vince Lombardi, the moment at which a reporter had asked him whether the Packer's interception of a pass at the start of the second half was a "key play" in their winning of the game. With the same style that had got the Packers to the Superbowl to begin with, Lombardi replied, "I don't know what a 'key play' is." Maybe there was a way he could use that exchange to explain what he might have meant by saying that a professional also sounds like a professional. What, to begin with, was Lombardi saying to the reporter?

"He was saying that that's a stupid way to talk about football. All plays are key plays."

"Would you say that he sounded like a professional in saying it?"

"Sure. It was a put-down. He was saying that if you know anything about the game, you don't talk that way. I see what you mean now, I think. I'm not saying the guy in this paper has to come on with 'superstar of the hardwood' stuff. He doesn't have to sound like a pool-hall punk. But if you know pool, you just don't say 'clear the table,' you say 'run the rack,' right?"

"'If you know pool,' meaning if you respect it and respect also your ability with it, which it's hard to believe someone wouldn't if he had the kind of ability this writer says he has. I don't know whether to be a professional you have to sound like one, but it would seem that one of the things you know as a pro is what an amateur sounds like. You know at least the way you *can't* talk. Anyway, I think I know what you mean when you say that you don't believe this happened. It's the *paper* you don't believe, isn't it, the sentences this writer uses to represent what happened? The writer can't talk like an amateur about his professionalism that way and be very convincing."

I then turned immediately to the next paper as a way of continuing what we'd just been talking about.

> The football season was drawing to a close. Our high school "B" and "C" teams each had only one more game. On the day before these games were to be held, the yearbook sports editor decided that he wanted two pictures of each game. One was a home game at 3:15; it would be easy. The other game was away, forty miles away, and it started at 3:45. I complained. He, being a fairly typical editor, said, "Get them." I usually used an assistant for occasions like this. He worked in his dad's shop Fridays after school. The games were on Friday.
>
> Being sure that I had at least three gallons in my VW, I arrived on the home field at 3:15 the next day. About a half an hour later I got word that the opposition's team bus had had a breakdown. By the time the team arrived at 4 o'clock I was ready to have one myself. It took them another fifteen minutes to get the game started. I clicked off half a roll, four shots, on my Speed Graphic and headed for my car. The pictures didn't have to be good; however, luck was with me, and two of them were above average. I don't usually rely on luck. But then I don't usually spend only ten minutes at a game either.
>
> Out of town, the San Diego freeway wasn't very crowded. On the long straight stretches I managed around eighty-five miles per hour. I had to drop down to around sixty after the Laguna turn-off. Laguna Canyon Road is two-lane and twisting. When I arrived at Laguna Beach High School, our team was doing fine. The score was forty-five to twenty-something, with six minutes to play. In those six minutes I managed to get a good pass interception and a beautiful shot of Cadreau (our quarterback) breaking away from the crowd for a touchdown.
>
> When I turned in my prints, the editor said, "Thanks." The season was over.
>
> A professional is a skilled worker who enjoys his work some of the time, and is driven by it most of the rest of the time.

I admire that paper for the way its style enacts the expertise which is its subject; the way character, manner, and circumstance become one. The image it creates of its writer is of someone in whom the line between responsibility and compulsion has dissolved. This is why, in several sections (the end of the second paragraph and the beginning of the third), it becomes impossible for a reader to separate the dutiful from the enjoyable. And it's the reason why the "I" of the paper seems to be serving something bigger than his own ego. The success of the paper is born, in part, of its flirtings with failure. The shifting meaning of "luck," that ride in the Volkswagen—any editorial comment would have spilled them into crudity. As it stands, the paper is one which enables a *reader* to say about the writer he creates from the prose: he cares; he knows what he's doing; he's a professional, all right. It's a paper which enables a reader to make the phrases "enjoys his work" and "driven by it" mean something.

I used it as a way of continuing the conversation we had just been having by focusing on an argument between two groups of students over the character of the photographer. For one group the speaker was simply "conceited"; for the other he was someone "damned good who knows it." It had already been pointed out by a couple of people that someone who was *just* conceited wouldn't have said things such as "luck was with me" or that he was ready himself to have a breakdown. Also, he'd have done up his triumph with a lot more gingerbread than he does (" 'Thanks.' "). I was interested in the assumptions under the arguments.

"So, in order to be a professional, you have to be morally admirable?"

"I guess not. There are professional thieves."

"Can you admire a professional thief?"

"I admire the guys who pulled the Brinks' job."

"Why? It was stealing, and they didn't get away with it. Not finally."

"That doesn't have anything to do with it. It was a good clean job."

"You mean being a professional has nothing to do with morality—or with accomplishment either?"

He thought for a bit and then said: "Well, with the Brinks' guys it was the way they went through all those locked doors on just the right night. Nobody got hurt. There were no loose ends. Sure they were stealing, and I know they got caught. But it's how they did it; the whole thing was so slick."

"You mean it was their style you admire?"

"Yeah. I guess you could say style. They had class."

"Would this mean, then, that professionalism for you *depends* on somebody's showing something you'd call style or class?"

"Yes, I think it would."

"I think it would for me too. It would depend on *how* somebody expressed himself, on the language he used—whether that language was one of words, or actions, as it was with the guys who pulled the

Brinks' job. From this point of view, going back for a minute, do you see another way of talking now about what could be said to kill the paper on the pool game?"

"You mean it has no style."

"Which is why the question of *that* speaker's conceit or lack of con· ceit was never raised. Since there's no style, there isn't any speaker to talk about, really. So the only question that came up was whether the event had happened or hadn't, which as you say, Jerry, is irrelevant anyway. A pro would seem to be a pro on the basis of the *way* he goes at something, not on whether he throws every pass for a touch-down, or comes up with a royal straight flush on every deal. Or even on whether he runs the rack or doesn't."

"So to write about professionalism you're going to have to talk about the way somebody goes at something?"

"Except put that way that's just another Themewriter's formula, isn't it? It's more a question of finding a way to talk about the way somebody goes at something so as to enable a *reader* to say 'I see how somebody goes at something.' I was economical; I was careful; I was skillful; I was efficient. You could go on that way all night and how far would it get you? The pool player, for example, tells you how he went at things to be a professional. But what does 'skillful' mean in that paper?"

"Only that he won the game. He said he'd clear the table and he did."

"Right. And that's about all. But does 'skillful' in the second paper mean only that the guy got his pictures?"

"No. It's the way he did it, driving the car the way he did and all the rest."

"You mean even how he drives the car is part of his professionalism?"

"I think it shows his attitude toward what he's doing, yes."

"I do too, the same way that checking to see that he has gas does the same thing. A guy who didn't care about doing what he was re-sponsible for might not have done that, any more than he would have driven the car the way he says he did. He drives fast, but he's not just a lead-foot. He slows down when he has to."

"So when you're a pro, you're a pro all the way?"

"Well, at least in this paper I have difficulty separating the pho-tographer's skill from him. In the paper about the pool player, a skill is no more than something somebody uses. Here, the skill is who the character is. It's like the astronomy that can't be packed away with the telescope. It's part of the writer's whole character and something his whole character enters into. He's made the term "skillful" mean something that breaks him out of the circle of words where professional equals skillful equals winning the game equals professional. He doesn't say 'I didn't use not having an assistant as an excuse for not doing my job.' But I do. I say it because he's written a set of sentences that enables me to say it—to say that and to say a lot more too; that he didn't waste time feeling sorry for himself, for example; that he conserved his energy for what he had to do; and so on. He's found a way of talking about something that makes *me* say, 'I understand what being skillful and economical and the rest means to this writer.' I praise him for creating a meaning for such abstractions that I can't do justice to with a simple synonym—not any more than we were able to explain 'amateur,' as it was defined in the last two papers we looked at last period, with a dictionary definition."

I'd mimeographed one other paper to look at that period, a paper I knew to have been a real step for the boy who had written it. In many ways it is clumsy, but for its writer, a fellow who up to that point had only been lunking along inside the incantatory formulae about Man as a Rational Animal, it represented a reaching out that I wanted to praise.

Just for an Instant

It was the kind of Saturday morning that I wished I could spend in bed. A light rain was making short work of what little snow remained, and the cold wind was whipping through the brittle branches of the willow tree outside my window, strewing numerous small twigs over the patio and lawn. It just about summed up how I felt about making the long trip to school to help the basketball coach instruct the grade school kids who had aspirations of becoming varsity players themselves. After the terrible performance I had given the previous night in the game we'd lost against Park, I wasn't sure if I could set much of an example for them anyway. Besides, most of them were little brats who wouldn't listen or even try to imitate any of your moves. I always felt sorry for our coach when I saw him trying to teach a youngster how to make a chest-pass or to dribble the ball without staring at it like it was some kind of toy, but I could tell he was sincere in his work; I admired him for that. The sessions never lasted for more than an hour or two, but I still hated to get up. Oh well, it was for the good of the kids. Yeah, the kids!

As I pulled in the parking lot, I wished that I had just finished showering up and was headed for home. It just wasn't a day for basketball. I made the walk down the empty hall to the gym and headed across the court toward the locker room, when one of those little brats, I didn't even know him, stopped me.

"Hey, Rich, you played a good game last night. It wasn't your fault."

I looked at him and then glanced up at the empty basket suspended from the wall. For an instant, just for an instant, I felt like a professional.

"Come on, Rich," said the coach, "let's get going with these kids."

The crudities there are obvious ("little brats," "Yeah, the kids!") as are the regressive lurches ("instruct the grade school kids who had aspirations of becoming varsity players"). Also, the paper is written perhaps a little too obviously with a point in mind. On the other hand, the unwillingness, maybe the inability, of the writer to name himself at the moment he claims to feel like a professional, his effort to find language for a welter of conflicting attitudes through his description of the rain and the willow tree, his attempt to see professionalism as a way of seeing, of naming (traceable in how the term "kids" shifts in meaning)—all this suggests, if not a writer, someone grappling with imagining what he could do if he *were* a writer, someone on the way to making the activity of writing an extension of himself.

I couldn't get all this out of the class of course. There wasn't enough time for one thing, not to develop the concept of courage as applicable to a writer's engagement with the writing process, but the response to my question of how the term "professional" was to be defined in the context of the next to last paragraph at least made it obvious that the writer of the paper had created a character larger than he had the language to explain:

"It's more than just being looked up to, though. Maybe he feels like a pro because he knows that in a way maybe the kid is right, that he did the best he could and that that's all anybody can do."

"The game and playing it are more important than one win or loss you mean? Possibly. He may mean too that he comes to understand in what way yesterday is yesterday; that while a pro never forgets anything he needs to remember, he also has to have the ability to forget what it can get in his way to keep recalling—something like that?"

"Maybe. Maybe he means that the kid reminded him he was a member of a team too."

"You mean that in taking the blame for the loss against Park as he first does he was seeing himself as more important that he was—the way an amateur would?"

"It's a possibility."

"Sure it is. We've got a number of possibilities. Does that mean you're in the same position as a reader of this paper that you were in as a reader of the paper on the fish and the stone? There we had people arguing on the meaning. Here we have a question about meaning but nobody's arguing. How come?"

"With the fish paper we were arguing about what he was saying. Here we seem to be wondering about how much he's saying."

"That's a nice distinction. In other words, no one of the possible meanings we've raised for this paper excludes any of the others—which is to say the paper's complex rather than confused. I can't label the nature of the character's realization here any more than I can label the skill of the photographer, or than I could label the amateurism of the characters in the last two papers we looked at last time; that's part of what I'd praise this paper for. But as you say, the difficulty with it is that we can't say for sure how many of those meanings the writer is in control of, a control without which the paper loses focus, blurs. And, even more important, so does the experience. To rewrite a paper like this, then, might be to have a chance at more than the shaping of sentences; it might be a chance for this writer to find out something about himself that he doesn't now know."

ASSIGNMENT 6

Imagine a world of amateurs or professionals

Try to imagine a world in which everyone was either an amateur or a professional.

What would other people do and say?

Would you want to live in the world you have chosen to describe?

I wrote Assignment 6 with not much more in mind than the idea of giving the students a chance to play with the concepts of amateurism and professionalism as adjuncts of one another. I certainly didn't plan it as the kind of a trick it turns out to be, nor did I discover the extent to which it is one until I was reading the papers the students had written addressing it. It is not an impossible Assignment to work with, but it's a lot more difficult to address intelligently than it should have been. Its manner is wrong. As written, the Assignment constitutes a kind of skeptic attack upon the platonically idealistic notion of words as things, of language as actuality; but the attack isn't made openly. The trickiness of the Assignment, then, is a matter of a writer's having to recognize that its proposition is contradictory, impossible to entertain as a proposition because it is unimaginable. No one can imagine a world the sole basis for which is a statement denying the relationship between language and experience that enables us to begin to imagine anything. No one can imagine a world in which black is white or up is down, because terms cannot be coupled that way in the same language system without bankrupting the system as a system. A world in which everyone is either an amateur or a professional is as inconceivable as a square circle.

If I had it to do again I'd write the Assignment in such a way as to put this issue of the limits of language at the heart of it. Something like this would have been better:

> *You have no doubt had it said to you at one time or another: "What if everyone in the world thought as you do?"*
>
> *Perhaps you have even been momentarily stopped in your line of thinking by such a remark. Why might such a question be likely to stop anyone, at least for a moment? Is it a question you can seriously entertain?*
>
> *For the purposes of this Assignment, consider this question in relation to amateurism and professionalism. Suppose someone asked you "What if everyone in the world were an amateur?" or "What if everyone in the world were a professional?" How would you respond? Can you imagine such a world? What would life be like in it?*

But the problem then was then and what I was going to do with what I had to work with: a poor Assignment and a batch of student papers that had found very little in it to talk about. To have walked into class with an explanation of all this, into that class, then, would have been a mistake. It would have been to risk providing the students with just the sort of excuse I'm tempted to find for myself for being dull with a dull set of papers. And since I believe it is as criminal and enslaving for a student to imagine that what he does depends on his teachers as it is for a teacher to imagine the reverse (but students are students in part because they don't understand what no teacher ought to be forgiven for not understanding), I didn't see the risk as worth taking. Boys, you'll just have to make allowances for me today because I had a fight with my wife last night. How can you *expect* us to write anything good on an Assignment you admit is bad? There's no doubt that the Assignment provided the students with more of an opportunity to write Themes than it should have. There is also no doubt that the writing of Themes is a choice. For about thirty papers worth of reading I thought that that choice was all we were going to be able to have a class on. Then I came to a paper which made me aware that we could deal with something else.

62   It was an exception. For the most part, and without giving any indication of knowing what they were doing, the students seemed to see the Assignment as one in which anything went. I read paper after paper of talk about little green men, and trudged through the silliest imaginable generalizations about how horrible (or how marvelous) it would be if everyone . . . (There would be no wars, no laws, no sex, etc.). Over and over again the papers reduced to no more than a single sentence: one which through the rest of the paper was simply repeated in various phrasings, illustrated rather than explored or developed. The only interesting thing about such papers was the fact that the single sentences they were made up of, sentences describing life in an impossible world, were dead ringers for the sentences they had written earlier about what they then claimed was life in this one. (A world in which everyone was an amateur would be a world in which everyone had a right to his own opinion. A world in which everyone was a professional would be a world in which excellence was prized. And so on.) In dribbling out the same clichés they had in their first papers, then, the students were reverting, but given the problem of Assignment 6 as most of them were seeing it, the students this time were providing an unwitting comment on what they were reverting to.

I came at this with a paper that had a ring of familiarity the class picked up without any trouble.

If the world was populated by people who thought of nothing but their own jobs, it would be a stifling place. No one would want to stop and talk to anyone else, except for a few of his colleagues. Thank goodness most professionals aren't like that. Sam Huff is a pro line-backer, but he's also a TV commentator, card player, lover, and endless other things. He's a professional in one field and an amateur in many others. He's a well-rounded man. Sam Huff is the kind of person who makes life interesting; he knows more than just what he needs for his profession.

A society of amateurs would be chaos. I'd certainly hate to have an amateur President running the country, or an amateur doctor, dentist, electrician, or anyone else who has to do something that is important to my comfort and safety.

Professionals are vital to a society; without them the society is dangerous to all concerned and likely to slip into a low state of culture. I hope that our country always has enough professionals, but I also hope there are well-rounded professionals, and a few amateurs for variety.

The class went right away to the opening sentences of the paragraphs, each of which, as they quickly noted, positioned the writer to grind out as much nickelodeon rhetoric as he cared to produce. Yes, we'd seen that trick before, most recently in the paper on Rudolf Meyer. The voice of Little Goodie Two Shoes ("Thank goodness," "I'd certainly hate") on a moral crusade ("Professionals are vital to a society") was also no stranger, particularly in that it was speaking for a world view about as comprehensive and as complicated as that of *Goldilocks and the Three Bears.* The example of Sam Huff as "the kind of person . . . who knows more than just what he needs" took us back to the paper on Jerry Lucas, and so on. It was what the writer of the paper was assuming about the relationship of language to experience that I wanted to move to, however, the assumption which had made the trick of the paper (and all those for which it was the pattern) possible to begin with.

"OK, so we've seen all this before. The voice, the world being described, the bullet-proofed argument, the passing off of Themewriting as writing. But I'd like to look at the assumptions of it for a minute, what the writer seems to assume about the meanings of the terms 'amateur' and 'professional.' "

"He seems to assume that he knows the meanings of them."

"All right. That he knows the meanings of them and therefore that they have absolute meanings. Now, what's the absolute meaning of 'professional'?"

"That's what we're trying to find out, isn't it?"

"Well, is it? You make it sound like the end product of a paper chase, as though the meanings of such terms were simply there, somewhere, to be discovered, found."

"But there's got to be some meaning for the terms. Shoes can't be Buicks."

"Look," I said, "if I poured a handful of sunflower seeds onto this desk, what would you say we had on it?"

"A pile of sunflower seeds."

"And if I took one away, what would be there on the desk?"

"Still a pile of sunflower seeds. Minus one, maybe."

"And if I took all but three seeds, or two, or one—would we still have a pile? Even a pile minus sixty-eight?"

"It would be easier to say we had two seeds, or three."

"OK. Now what happened to the word 'pile'? When did the pile become something other than a pile?"

"You can't say."

"Of course you can't. There's no absolute meaning to a word that way. Words aren't things; they're the names we give to things. So to say my shoes aren't Buicks is not to say that the word 'shoe' has an absolute meaning or that it always means the same thing. Of course there has to be some meaning for the term, but—well, let me show you."

I then leaned over and picked a book off the desk of a student in front of me.

"What's this?"

"A book."

"OK. Now suppose this room were airtight and filling slowly with a poison gas, and here you were, you and the book and nothing else, and the door was locked. What would you do with the book?"

"I'd throw it through the window."

"Throw what?"

"The book."

"What would the book be when you threw it through the window? Still a book in one way, of course, but in another way it would have to be a thing you saw as something other than a book, that you renamed as an object which could break glass. You can't find that as a definition under 'book' in the dictionary, not any more than you could find it defined as a paperweight or a stool or a murder weapon. 'It' doesn't change, whatever it may be. But the way I name it does, and as a consequence so do I."

"We're back to those hills like white elephants."

"We sure are. We're back to language as a description of the language user, of how he chooses to see, of who he chooses to become. Somebody else could look at that pile of sunflower seeds we were just talking about and say 'There's the road to health,' or 'that's food for my parakeet,' or even 'that's the occasion of a lesson about the relationship of language to experience.' In each instance we could understand what the speaker meant only if we understood that he was using the verb 'to be' in something other than an absolute sense. *We're* back to the hills like white elephants maybe, you and I. But the writer of this paper, the Themewriter, is somewhere else with his assumption that amateur and professional have absolute meanings, evil and good, that words are things."

And then came the question I'd been waiting for.

"But on this paper, wasn't that the Assignment?"

"To write this way?"

"No, to describe a world where everyone was an amateur or professional. Didn't you have to assume an absolute meaning for the words to do that?"

"Meaning?"

"Meaning that you'd have to invent a world to talk about. That you couldn't write about this world."

"Does this writer do that?"

"Well, he does and doesn't," said someone else. "He does, but he doesn't seem to know that that's what he's doing. He just says that a world full of amateurs would be chaos and then he takes off."

At which point I turned to the first paragraph, the only one I'd mimeographed, of a thing that went on for pages:

On September 29th of the year 19___, the General Assembly of the United Nations unanimously agreed that it was a crime against international law and against human nature in general to be an amateur. From that date forward no one could engage in any activity without being issued a license by the U.N. Secretariat certifying that the bearer was a professional in said activity, nor could any person engage in a licensed activity without documentary proof of said activity being done in a strictly professional capacity . . .

"Is that what you mean by inventing a world to talk about? And that writer certainly knows what he's doing doesn't he?"

"Yeah, but it's a game. It's a joke."

"What do you mean it's a joke?"

"I assume this guy went on the same way."

"He did. For longer than I could bear to read."

"Well, it's a set-up. This is how I started my paper. It's a game because the guy could go on all night this way, about how all the amateurs were gunned down and none of the professionals would talk to each other. He could go on just the way the first guy did about chaos."

"You think he's about to describe chaos then?"

"Chaos or heaven. It doesn't matter. Because he could move it the other way if he wanted. He could describe paradise too, how great it is that we got rid of all the slobs. But chaos is easier."

"You mean you've got more stock language for it?"

"Sure. Innocent women and children, the way we said."

"But he does, this writer, know what he's doing?"

"Well, as Tom said about the other paper, he does and he doesn't. I mean I could write a paper like this, anybody could. All you'd have to do is assume that everything was going to be rosy or that everything was going to be lousy and then just let go with the stock language."

"What is it you think that the writer doesn't know then?"

"That his world isn't going to be another world at all. It's going to be a world just like everyone else's, at least when he sets it up this way. It's just like the world I started with."

"A world with which you called the shots in a completely predictable way, of which you were sole owner and proprietor. Another world only in the sense that the world of the Themewriter is another world. And it's this you're saying he doesn't know? You're saying he's behaving like a Themewriter without being aware of it?"

"He is a Themewriter. This is just another Theme, this second paper. It's just a different kind of Theme from the first one."

I then turned to the one interesting paper of the set as a way of trying to talk about the kind of knowingness on the part of a writer that the students had said was absent from the first two papers we'd looked at. It had been written by the boy with whom I'd had the last conversation above and, as I told the class, had been the turning point in my working out of the problem Assignment for myself:

Imagine a World

Imagine a world where poverty was wealth;
Imagine a world where sickness meant health;
Where death was birth;
Where last came first.

Imagine a world where love meant hate;
Imagine a world where six equalled eight;
Where inexperience bred skill;
Where it was legal to kill.

Imagine a world where peasants were kings;
Imagine a world where people were things;
And one couldn't tell—
Whether heaven or Hell!

The lines don't all scan, and there are lapses of ear ("inexperience"), but the tone of knowing playfulness suggests a natural inevitability to the form that I didn't want to write off as just doggerel. I came at the paper by picking up the notion of a writer's knowing what he was doing.

"Is this writer too just writing a Theme, just saying the same thing over and over?"

"Yes, but here that's the point, I mean that's what he's saying about the Assignment, that it's impossible."

"By repeating himself?"

"Well he is repeating himself, but he's doing it deliberately. He knows he's repeating himself."

"How do you mean he knows?"

"You remember the paper about Dave and the girl he couldn't kiss goodnight and the way he knew he wasn't being cool? Well, it's that way here; this guy knows he's repeating himself that same way."

"So that means he isn't just repeating himself, the way the clichés about Dave weren't just clichés because he knew that that's what they were?"

"Right. He's trying to make an effect with repetition. It's like he's saying the same thing over and over to show that he keeps coming up with the same answer."

"That he can't imagine a world that's impossible to imagine no matter how hard he tries to move into it. And so his form becomes the way he expresses this."

Which is what I too see happening in the poem. Its piling up of opposites is more than a trick, or perhaps a trick I'm willing to accept as more than a trick, because that's so openly what it is. The verse form, particularly in its rhythmical variations, becomes, incrementally, the image of an impossibility that the writer is simultaneously making possible as a subject and playing himself off against.

"If the Assignment is impossible," I concluded class by saying, "here at least is one writer who didn't let that impossibility tell him what he was going to have to do as a writer."

ASSIGNMENT 7

What is good advice
when it is given to you?

We are about to change the point of view from which we are seeing our subject.

For this assignment, describe a situation (outside your English class) in which someone gave you what you consider to be very good advice.

What was the occasion? Who was there? What was said and done?

To judge from the way you have written about it, what exactly is good advice?

I had originally planned Assignment 7 not on the notion of advice but as the first of a series of four on the concept of work and play. (What is work? What is play? Under what circumstances does one become the other? Can you describe such a moment of becoming? Are you an amateur at such a moment? A professional?) After our class meeting on Assignment 5, however, the period in which we had talked about professionalism as a matter of how something was done and of the how as a form of expression that could create the illusion of being, I wrote out a new series of Assignments, six of them, with a new nominal subject—that of advice. The allover structure I had devised to involve us in the real subject of the course, the nature and function of language, there was no reason to change. Assignments 1 through 6

I had written to be concerned in various ways with the problem of definition; the assignments following them (7 through 12 as it turned out), whatever their nominal subject, I wanted to provide a way of complicating the students' understanding of the role of a definer depending on whether he was the subject of an action, the object of an action, or both. Our classroom conversations, however, had given me an idea for a better nominal subject than the one I first thought to work with.

If, as I saw it, the key to professionalism was a *how* of some sort, and the *how* a form of expression from which the professional was inseparable, then the relationship of a nonprofessional to the professionalism of a professional would have to be established through a relationship made with his way of expressing himself, through some kind of coming to terms with his language as a metaphor of who he was. Seen in this way, the attempt of a nonprofessional and a professional to get in touch with one another as people involves the same problems as does the attempt of any one human being to reach another. What better way, then, to suggest such a connection and to examine the importance of language to it, than to focus on the language with which one person reaches for another, to concern ourselves with the question of what it means for anyone to try to avail himself of the knowledge or experience of someone else—or to try to make his available.

Advice. We all know *about* it certainly, but what is it exactly? What does one do when he gives it? Or takes it? Or rejects it? And how does one go about giving or taking it? I found myself thinking of the queer, often enigmatic ways in which professionals expressed their professionalism. Thoreau advised someone who would learn to write to learn to split wood. There was Nijinski's famous explanation of his grand jetés as something he simply paused in the middle of before coming down. Pavlova is said to have told a young dancer that the art of dance is all a matter of thinking of the earth as something to leave. My father, whose woodwork was beautiful, told me that the secret of a true cut was to make the saw part of my arm. I remembered a dog-handler I once helped trim the nails of a litter of puppies advising me to hold the dog so that he wouldn't think he was being held. And of course there are the more common, though no less mysterious enjoinders: Accept God's will. Keep your temper. Grow up. How totally available such remarks are from one point of view. How totally inaccessible from another. Like the professional himself? Like the humanities professor for the future scientist? Like any teacher for any learner? Like anybody for anyone else? Like advice? Or was advice no more than a matter of self-location? If so, then how did you describe the difference between one kind of self-location and another? What was good advice? What wasn't? Could you understand an explanation of self-location without understanding what the explanation explained? It seemed a rich and fascinating subject.

For me it did. The students, to judge from their performance with Assignment 7, didn't seem able to imagine any possibilities for the subject at all. In a way, I'd expected this. I'd changed the nominal subject of our dialogue, in fact, primarily to dramatize how the habit of Themewriting is more of a back-riding monkey than might first be thought. Still I was angry with the aplomb with which most students headed straight back to the wallow, back to begin all over again in the worst sense of the phrase. Their papers had no "someone's." They had no "you's." Advice was seen alternately as a copybook maxim ("work hard in college"; "play it cool"), a slogan ("Be prepared"), a Safety-First directive on the order of don't play with matches, or an after-the-fact generalization that could mean whatever a reader cared to make it mean ("he taught me to be myself"). Advice was "very good" because it "worked" ("and, sure enough, they did come home, wagging their tails behind them"), or simply because it was asserted to have worked ("Thus, I succeeded in becoming a much better bowler"). "What was said" the students smothered with the indirection of "he showed me," or "he taught me"; "what was done" they submerged in "I saw," "I learned," "I thought about it." To be given advice, most of the time, meant to be jerked on strings; to take it meant no more than to acknowledge the jerk. The "how" of everything simply got left on the shelf. No one made even an attempt to notice the sorts of sentences he was writing. There was not a paper of the lot I could praise.

I began with rock bottom:

It is unfortunate that good advice is not always recognized as such until it is too late. Some advice that I should have heeded was given to me by a buddy of mine about a year and a half ago. At the time, I had just turned sixteen and was able to drive a car legally. I had about a hundred dollars saved up and my parents agreed that I could use it to buy a car if I wanted.

The next day I was at the used car lot with my friend. We found a Ford that seemed in pretty good shape for $89.95. Steve, who is a much better mechanic than I, scrutinized the car to make sure that it was in reasonably good shape for a ten-year-old job. He pointed out two rusty bars

under the front of the car which he called the A-frame. Apparently it was
almost rusted through, and I was advised not to buy the car because
the A-frame was ready to break at any time. But I was so anxious to have
a car that I neglected to take the advice and bought it anyhow. You can
guess the outcome of this investment—just three and a half weeks later
the A-frame broke and I was out a hundred bucks for less than a month
of driving.

The puerility of that paper I came at by asking where we'd met
Steve and "I" before, and we got five panels and some stick figures
up on the blackboard. The panels I labeled Young Boy Decides to Buy
Car (with an "idea" light bulb above it); Young Boy Consults Steve
(who is smiling); Young Boy Buys Bad Car (Steve is no longer smiling); Pride of Young Boy Goeth Before a Fall (clunk); Young Boy in
Bandages. From the question of how much of the paper was unaccounted for by the cartoon sketch (none), I moved to the question not
only of what the writer had had to become to write as he did (nobody),
but to that of what a reader had to become to take such writing seriously. It was not the first conversation of the sort we had had by any
means, and I let them go through all the tricks of demolition they
knew before stepping in with a point of view that I hoped was going
to move us a little farther along the way. I had something very specific
in mind.

"Do you think this is the best this writer can do, then?"

"Oh, I'm sure he could do better than this."

"What makes you think so?"

"Well, nobody's this stupid."

"How do you know that from the paper?"

"Well, the way the thing is organized for one thing. It has a plan.
The sentence structure. Spelling. I guess it takes a certain amount of
intelligence even to write a Theme."

"What kind of intelligence? At this point? In this course?"

I didn't have to work at making it sound scathing. The boy shifted
a little and then said:

"OK. Maybe he was just screwing off."

"You mean the writer was perfectly aware that this was a put-up job
when he wrote it? He had a bad night, knew he had to turn a paper
in, and just thought he'd try to slip one by? By us? This class? After
the way you guys took that paper to the slaughterhouse?"

"Maybe it was like that. I'm sure he knew what he was doing,
anyway."

"And that he chose, freely chose, to do what he did?"

"Yes."

"Along with everybody else?"

"I don't follow you."

"I mean there isn't anybody in here who didn't do just about what this writer did on this Assignment. I'll prove that if anyone wants to call me."

Nobody did. There were thirty seconds of the kind of sullen silence that's as heavy as winter in a classroom.

"Look. I'm not interested in having somebody say how sorry he is that he acted like a horse's ass on this Assignment, or that the reason it happened is that the shift in subject caught him off guard. I'm interested in what being caught off guard means in this instance. I'm interested in what it means that the minute you get anything like what looks to be a new subject, what I get is another batch of goddamned Themes. Bill says everybody in here wrote a Theme out of choice. Did you?"

We had some more of the same kind of silence.

"How about it, Dan?"

"Are you trying to get us to say we didn't have a choice, that we're all puppets or some goddamn thing? Because I'm not going to buy that."

"You mean so far as you're concerned there's absolutely no connection between what that guy does in his paper about Steve and the A-frame and the way he sees the world? He just chose to do what he does there at the same time he really knows that things are more complex than that and *how* they're more complex than that?"

"I'm not saying there's no connection. All I'm saying is, he had a choice."

"OK. He had a choice certainly. I'm not saying that the only hope for this writer is to be born again. My point is that even though everybody had a choice, everybody chose the same way. What I'm interested in is what it can mean for someone to make that same choice the same way over and over again. Let's look at another paper."

Growing Up

It was Friday night, but not just any Friday night. This Friday night I was not at home but in a strange town; and I was not in high school anymore, but in college. There was a mixer coming that night with

Mather College. I had been out with girls many times before, but somehow this felt like my first date all over again.

The night began with a dinner, and slowly the Freshman class entered the dining hall to choose the table of girls they wanted to eat with. As we walked from table to table they stared at us and we stared at them. The dance which followed was a failure, and I was too. The action was so fast I failed to see it. The girls I had met left and so did every other decent one. I decided to try The Library and The Cask. On the way out my counselor sensed the situation. We talked for a while about how I had lost the girl and missed meeting a new one.

He told me how he had had the same thing happen to him, and soon realized the cool approach. Act quietly and somewhat disinterested, but don't let anyone else move in. Substitute "like to learn how to dance?" for "may I have this dance?" Never take "no" for an answer, because they're playing the same game that you are. I thought back over his advice and could think only of how upperclassmen and fraternity boys acted. I went to the Reserve rush parties and started again. That time I won. That first Friday was really my graduation from high school.

It was no trouble establishing the ways in which the writer of that paper turns human beings into objects and human relations into a game—equations which turn the "I" of the paper into what the students called a "bastard." But we were crowding the line that's all important not to cross with students in a classroom.

"Look. Let's be clear that it's not the character of the writer we're talking about or concerned with here. The subject here is writing, what these sentences represent this writer as. What the writer is we can never know and is up to him anyway. The question I'm interested in here, the question that this paper and the last one and all the other papers written for this Assignment raised for me is the cost of choosing to talk one way, to see experience one way, over and over again. What's the relationship, in other words, between an habitual way of talking or writing and the way one sees?"

"Do you mean if this guy keeps talking like this will he start to think like a bastard?"

"Is it possible for a way of talking to begin to determine what one sees? Yes. What do you think?"

"I don't think you could ever lose the power to choose, no."

"Maybe not. But let's see what the power of choice amounts to when you use only one way of talking over and over again. You know what the telephone dial looks like, don't you?"

This was the dramatization I'd been leading up to. A colleague of mine had told me about using it with his class to explode some of the more popular notions his students had had about the workings of the memory.

"The telephone dial? I guess so, sure."

"You can picture it in your mind?"

"Yes."

"Do you think you could draw it from memory?"

"I'm not sure. I think I could."

"OK. I'll bet you five bucks you can't, that nobody in the room can. In fact I'll *give* anyone who can do it five bucks, anyone who can draw the dial from memory without making a mistake."

It was better than a good bet. Most people who try it make on the average of two dozen mistakes. I told the class to go to work with paper and pencil. They weren't to worry about making perfect circles and the rest, but were to try to reproduce as accurately as they could the placement of the numbers, letters, holes, and so on. At the end of ten minutes I asked them to talk me through a sketch on the blackboard. Where was I to place the dialing holes in relation to the lines making the quadrants? Was there a hole directly at twelve o'clock? At three? Six? Nine? There was no absolute agreement, but we settled on there being a hole at twelve o'clock (which there isn't) without any violent opposition. Next came the placement of the letters. Did they start where the numbers did? Were they above the holes? In them? Under them? Were they parallel to a horizontal axis? On a slant? If slanted, slanted which way? Did the letters all read from left to right? If not, which ones didn't? And the letters themselves, were all the letters of the alphabet used? This was the first question to which I had an absolutely unequivocal response, and this from just one student:

"No, all the letters aren't used. There's no Q and no Z. All the rest are there."

"How do you know that?"

"I heard it on a quiz program."

As soon as the boy said that, I told everyone in the class to shut his eyes for a moment and to keep them closed. I then asked the same boy this:

"If you imagine a human head divided in half by a horizontal line would the ears on most heads be attached above this line, on it, or below it?"

He hesitated a moment, "Above it."

"Anyone know for sure," I asked, "the way Sam knew about Q and Z?"

Three hands came up and all three of the students agreed that the ears were most normally about on the line. Two of the three students had studied drawing and the other had had a course in art history.

What could be concluded from all this?

First of all, that no one had drawn the dial of the telephone or even his "mental picture" or "mental image" of the dial, because what got drawn was in every case inaccurate (no one won the five dollars) and in 95 percent of the cases could not have served as the model for an apparatus that would have reached across the street for a pizza. What the students drew was their *experience* with the telephone dial as made by their language for it. One "knew" there was no dialing hole at twelve o'clock, or that the letters Q and Z were omitted from the dialing system not on the basis of how often he had looked at the telephone dial or used it, but on the basis of what he had looked with, what language he had used to tell himself what he was seeing. Hence those who "knew" certain details knew not only that they knew them but how (as was the case with the boy and the quiz program). "Experience," at least as the term is ordinarily understood, did not seem to be of much help in explaining these phenomena. How many ears on how many heads had each one of us looked at, for example? Did it make any sense to claim, then, that one remembered what he experienced when confronted with evidence that there is a very real way in which no one even experiences what he experiences? Did anyone in the class have the power of choice in how he had remembered the telephone dial?

What I remember, the experiment seemed to demonstrate, what I experience, is not Isness, Reality, What Really Happened, but what it is I *tell* myself really happened, the way I represent to myself what I choose to *call* reality. I recall not events but the symbol systems with which I have shaped them—the reason, for example, that I know immediately the ages of my children but invariably have to figure the years in which they were born. I experience my children in a way to which their chronological age is relevant. Of course I *can* figure the years in which they were born, just as I can check a sketch of the telephone dial against the telephone dial. But where for me now are all those rich experiences I must have had in third or fourth grade? Where are all those lesser-known Shakespearian plays that I've read but was never "made" to write papers on? Why is it that when I go

76   tiptoeing back through a diary I kept my senior year in high school and come upon the entry: "With Marilyn tonight: the greatest yet"— I can no more remember the event than I can what was great about it? Did it make much sense to say that an event someone told himself about in the way, say, that the writers of the two papers we'd been considering that period had told themselves about what they had experienced, could be remembered as it "really was" for very long? Did "experience," shaped in the terminology those writers had used, really continue to exist in some throbbing human fullness somewhere outside that language, in contradistinction to that language? And to go through life Themewriting one's experience into bloodless abstractions —we had a swell time; it was a great trip; she was really cool—was to end up with how much of life having dribbled through one's fingers? Yes, the habit of Themewriting was a choice, I concluded class by saying. But maybe not always a free one, and maybe not one that remained open forever.

ASSIGNMENT 8

What is good advice
when you give it
to someone else?

*Describe a situation in which you gave someone else what you consider
to be very good advice.*

Again, what was the occasion? Who was there? What was said and done?

Again also, to judge from your paper, what is good advice?

There's no question that some of the students were beginning to
come along as writers, but the shift in focus in Assignment 8—from "I"
as the receiver of advice to "I" as the giver of it—in about half the
papers written involved no more than a mechanical reversal of equally
mechanical roles. Whereas in Assignment 7 the writers of such papers
had simply gone to vending machines, in 8 they turned themselves
into the vending machines they had previously gone to—ready, upon
the duly inserted coin of trouble, to dispatch anything from an Emily
Postism to the Tablets of the Law. It's true, of course, that nine papers
in three weeks can't work a miracle; it is just as true that there's no
faster way of stopping what can happen with a class than to be sure
what can't. At any rate, the edge I'd worked to hone on the students'
need to grow as writers I intended to keep there.

I didn't want to mimeograph, therefore, just in order to beat up,

another example of the sort of paper we'd looked at the period before—
Steve Explains How to Steal Second Base, or some such—not so much
because I had any fear of the students' going Sullen with Discourage-
ment—but because there comes a point at which the returns on the
beating up of bad writing can reverse as well as diminish. I, as teacher,
become crank; they become a "we"; class becomes a routine. For the
same reason, in marking the students' papers I took care to handle each
instance of Themewriting as though it were an individual aberration,
the only paper of its kind still being written by anyone in the class.
I'd read a Theme no further than was obvious that that was all the
paper was going to amount to; at that point I'd draw a slash line, write
"read to here" in the margin, and, at the end of the paper, following
the appropriate title (Steve as Miss Lonelyhearts, Steve Saves Lab
Partner from Electrocution, Steve for Coach of the Year), I addressed
each writer directly:

> Come on, Rick. Pack up the Greasy Kid Stuff, will you? You know better
> than this.

> Now look, Paul, which of us would be the bigger fool to imagine that this
> is the best you can do after what we've done so far this term?

> You were pretty good in class on the exposure of just this kind of trick—
> back on Assignment 4. Where are you now, Bill?

Because I was doing a lot of this, and because I wanted to be sure
that the students understood me as more than a smart-ass reader, I
started class with a paper that I thought we could use as a way of
talking about ways of talking about writing—an oblique approach, of
course, to the whole notion of advice:

I was talking on the phone with a friend who was going to take part
the next day in a march on the Capitol in protest of United States
action in Vietnam. The group was planning to march from the White
House, along the Mall, to the Capitol, carrying the usual banners
and singing or shouting appropriate slogans. They knew they were
committing an act of civil disobedience and would be arrested when they
came within a certain distance of the Capitol. Marching on the Capitol,
for any reason, is illegal.

My friend was planning to be in the front lines of the march and get
arrested. "Look at our insane President," she told me, "sending all sorts of
troops down there to torture and kill. They're all a lot of blundering
idiots up on Capitol Hill. They're letting their own people in Appalachia
starve while they waste more men and money on mistakes than on

actual combat, as if either was really necessary. What's wrong with just sitting down and talking with the Communists? They're human, aren't they?" I think she was ready to cry.

She wanted to be arrested, post no bail, and serve a thirty-day prison sentence. She was then going to begin classes at American University three weeks late as a result and risk being put on some sort of probation because of the prison term.

I convinced her that whether or not she went to jail, the Vietnam war would go on and that it would be better for her cause, in the long run, if she were to go on to the university (I believe her major was political science), where more powerful, lasting changes in society begin. I told her to go ahead and march and sing and carry her poster, but not to follow the relatively few members of the group who would cross the line and be arrested.

The trick of that Theme, like the one making use of John Doe written for Assignment 2, is a matter of the bullet-proofed consonance of character and situation. Given the characters of that paper, the advice cannot be other than simpleminded and vice versa. A touch either of complexity or humanity would have spoiled everything. I wanted to use what takes place in the paper between the second and third paragraphs, what the handbooks sometimes call "a shift in mode," not only as a way of talking about what goes wrong with the writing here, but also as a way of talking about how to name what goes wrong with writing.

I began with the paper by asking the class what they could say about the characters in it.

"This girl sounds a little crazy to me."

"Why, because she believes in something?"

"No. It's the *way* she sounds; she's all over the place."

"But isn't that the point? Maybe she's so upset she doesn't make any sense, and maybe that's what the writer's saying by representing her that way."

"Maybe. But I still can't see anybody sounding like this."

It was Jerry I was talking to, the pool player who'd talked about the difference between "clearing the table" and "running the rack." He was quickly put on the defensive by a couple of other members of the class who saw no fallacy at all in the imitative form of the girl's sentences.

"The writer here does say she was ready to cry. Besides, isn't she supposed to be a little crazy?"

"Yeah, but if all you have to do to make a character upset is write a bunch of sentences that don't go together, then anybody could do it."

Then I stepped in by asking Jerry if what he was objecting to wasn't really a matter of there being no character to the girl at all.

"How do you mean?"

To show him I picked five students at random and had each of them read aloud the first sentence spoken by "she." The first I told to emphasize the word "look," the second "insane," and so on with "President," "troops," "torture and kill." After the reading, I asked the class which way the sentence was written to be read. No one could decide, and no one could read the sentence and emphasize all the words at once without sounding ridiculous.

"That's what I'd use to argue that for me as a reader the character here has no center, fails to suggest anything recognizably human; that the character, in fact, isn't a character at all. You can't tell where she's coming from. All her sentences give you is a cliché about craziness—as you said, nobody would have any trouble creating a character if that's all there were to it. What the sentences don't give you is *someone* who is crazy or upset, a particular someone, 'a friend.' "

"What you get is a Suzie for Steve."

"And a way of making Steve sound like he's more than Steve when he isn't really. What's he say to Suzie in this instance, exactly? What's his advice?"

"Well, he tells her she could do more for the cause by going to school."

"Yep. Get thee to a university—where you can enroll in courses to begin 'powerful, lasting changes in society.' But what is it about *how* he says that that convinces Suzie?"

"You can't tell. All he says is that he did convince her."

"That my advice did the trick—just take my word for it. But you don't know how he sounded, what words he used exactly? He shifts his point of view there between the second and third paragraphs? Shifts his mode, as they say?"

"He quotes her but he doesn't quote himself."

"Conveniently. It makes a difference, then, how he said what he said? We're back to the how again?"

"Sure. How you say something is the whole problem of advice, isn't it?"

"It's the whole problem when it's something like a character that you're dealing with, someone with the illusion of a human personality.

When all you've got's an abstraction like Suzie, or like John Doe back on Assignment 2, it's an easy problem to look like you're solving at the same time you really cop out on it."

"Because you can say you said anything and then just say that she did what you told her to?"

"That, and even more importantly maybe, because you never have to say *what* you said in any way that a reader gets a chance to judge. All you have to do is to talk *about* what you said—when, as you say, the whole problem is how you tell another person to 'go ahead and march, and sing . . .'"

"Without sounding like the Jolly Green Giant."

"And at the same time you *do* sound like a friend and *are* convincing. OK. Now, if you were marking this paper how would you let the writer in on all this? How would you call his attention to what happens between the second and third paragraphs, the point at which he shifts the mode of his paper?"

"It is a shift in mode."

"Is! Like a book is a book? Like a pile of sunflower seeds is a pile of sunflower seeds?"

I then told the class about Ed Meadows, a thug in a football uniform who, in a Lions-Bears game in the 1950s had broken the wrist of Bobby Layne. Meadows had been caught at it, was thrown out of the game (later the league), and the Bears were penalized fifteen yards for something called unsportsmanlike conduct. But no one who commented on the play from the stands used that language. "Unsportsmanlike conduct" was not the name the fans gave to what had happened, nor was Meadows referred to as just "guard" or "player 62"— not by the boys with the bottles or the kids with Lions' pennants. Similarly, the technical name for what goes wrong in the sentence: "He's a nice guy for a nigger" is diction, but no one who knew the first thing about language would be willing to stop there.

"Could you think of anything to say about what goes wrong between the second and third paragraphs of that paper that would name what goes wrong for you there any more accurately than does the term 'shift in mode'?"

"That's where he dodges the whole problem. I could tell him that. I could tell him he copped out."

"OK. If you wrote 'cop-out' in the margin, you'd at least be telling him where you were with what he'd written. That's one thing that the phrase would have over 'shift in mode.' Could you think of anything to add that would tell him where you thought *he* was with what he'd written, particularly when you're both members of this class?"

"Well, you mentioned the John Doe paper. I could write 'Cop-out. Remember John Doe.'"

"Or 'Cop-out. Steve Stands for Law'n Order.' Do you think the writer would get what you meant if you talked that way? Do you remember the John Doe paper?"

"I remember that we went over it. I could look it up. He could too."

"You'd make this writer go all the way back to the beginning of the term to look up something just to understand you? You're a hard man."

"So are you. You made me do it. You wrote on one of my papers that I was right back to the first paper we worked with on Assignment 1. I had to look that up to see what you meant."

"Yeah. Me and my authoritarian fascist pig methodology." I turned to the next paper:

Scene: Study Lounge
Characters: Me and one other student. Deeply disgruntled.
"Did you have to do any of these dumb math problems?"
"I don't know. Let me see."
"What I'm particularly interested in is that number five. They're all bad but that number five is the worst."
"I can see what you mean; it looks like a Chinese nightmare. No, I didn't have to do it."
"Lucky you. Meanwhile I'm screwed."
"Maybe not. Why don't you try simplifying it a little."
"What do you mean 'simplify'?"
"You know, adjust the problem so that it's a little easier. Turn what you don't know into what you do know. In this one you might take all the sides of the figure as being equal; that way you eliminate half the variables in the problem."
"Yeah, but the problem specifically states that all the sides are unequal."
"Sure, but when all the sides are unequal is probably just a special case of a more general problem. At least this way you get a good general glimpse of the solution. Then you can figure out how to solve it with all those variables included."
"Well, I've tried every other way."
"Go ahead. I don't see what you're belly-aching about; you've solved rougher problems than that."
"You sure you don't know how to prove this?"
"Listen, I don't even want to know how to prove it."
(Ten-minute pause.)

"Oh, hey. I see it. If you take this thing as being proved, you can work it backwards to the information they gave you in the first place. Reverse the whole thing and you've got it solved."

"Sounds good. You can do it that way even with all those variables?"

"Well, no. But I simplified it like you said, and then I got this idea about working it backwards."

"Excellent. Now if you're finished with that thing, maybe you can help me with my physics."

I began our conversation with the paper by picking three pairs of students and having each pair read aloud two lines of the dialogue:

"You sure you don't know how to prove this?"

"Listen, I don't even want to know how to prove it."

I then asked the class as a whole what they'd heard in this reading and how they accounted for what they'd heard.

"They all read the lines the same way. Everybody emphasized 'sure' in the first sentence and 'want' in the second."

"So what?"

"So that's pretty good. The guy didn't underline the words even."

"Pretty good in what way?"

"Well, it isn't like Suzie or Steve all over again. He's got two different people here."

From there it was a matter of the students' attempting to find language for this twoness, for the separate voices from which it was possible to construct two states of mind which created the illusion of two distinct characters: one wondering, bemused, skeptical, maybe even pettishly suspicious; the other frank, disarmingly dismissive, restrained, detached. But no single descriptive term covers either voice in its entirety. The attempt to label the speakers crudely (someone suggested the first speaker was whiney and the second arrogant) was immediately complicated by reference to other sections of the dialogue: a whiner wouldn't have done for himself what the puzzled student does; someone arrogant couldn't have suggested he was glad he didn't have the problem to do, and couldn't have put "I don't see what you're belly-aching about" in the same sentence with the buck-upish "you've solved rougher problems than that." One student took exception to the phrasing of the final line by pointing out that even making allowances for the possibility of irony, its flippancy in the use of the somewhat superior "Excellent" ("Excellent, my boy" was suggested as better) didn't quite match the unimpugning knowingness of the character earlier. I said

84   I heard something analogous going wrong with the other character's lapse into stodginess—"What I'm particularly interested in is that number five"—at the beginning of the paper. But the certainty with which that student and I were able to locate such slips was a measure of how good the writer had been in the rest of the paper. What "pretty good" came to mean through our discussion then, was praise for the way the complexity of tones generated by the dialogue worked to create the illusion of human complexity. Also, because the writer conceives of the giving of advice as a process, and concentrates upon the how of it as determined by human relations, no one in the class could say for sure just what the advice of the paper was, or where it started, or where it stopped. Rather, what one student would try to exclude as part of the advice, another would reintroduce:

"But his starting out by saying 'let me see' *is* part of the advice; it's part of what he's giving; it's the *way* he talks that the other guy accepts."

" 'The way he talks.' His tone. Would you say his tone is a part of his personality?"

"I think it is."

"Do you mean, then, that the giving of advice is connected with the giving of the personality, of one's self?"

"It is here."

"And how about the taking of it here; is that connected with the same thing? Does the taker of the advice here have to give of himself?"

"Sure he does. The guy giving the advice just suggests a way of going at the problem. The guy taking it works out the idea of working backwards himself. The first guy never tells him to do that."

"So the receiver of advice here is the one who makes the advice advice?"

"He's part of it; it's a two-way thing."

"Just the way it was with my remark on Kurt's paper about being back at Assignment 1. I didn't 'make' him do anything with that comment. It didn't become advice until he did something with it, until he involved himself with it in such a way as to make it mean something."

"Right. It wasn't advice until he saw it as advice."

"Not any more than it was good or bad until he named it that way on the basis of how he used it, what results he got with it. And there's another connection that the writer of this paper made me aware of. Tom, you were the one who suggested that both the giving and taking of advice here involve the personalities, the selves of the speakers. Can you think of anything else we've looked at this term about which something like that was said, a paper in which you couldn't separate a character's actions from his personality or his self?"

"The paper on the photographer; the guy who took the ride in the V.W."

"Which was on the subject of professionalism. The question *this* raises, then, is whether that expression of professionalism, which was said also to be an expression of the self, can be seen as the giving of advice."

"I didn't see it that way then, but maybe you could see it that way. I don't think the guy is advising me how to be a photographer, though."

"I didn't see it then either. I didn't see any of this until I read this paper. And I think you're right that the writer of that earlier paper isn't advising me how to be a photographer—not any more than the guy in the paper on the math problem is telling his friend how to solve the problem. But maybe there's a way in which the photographer could be said to be offering me advice in the same way that the fellow in the study hall offers advice to his friend."

"You mean he gives you something you can make into advice, the way Kurt did with your comment on his paper?"

"In a way doesn't he do just that? He doesn't, in the ordinary sense of the term, advise me, tell me how to become a photographer; he gives me an image of himself at one with what he's doing. Now if I find that image compelling, maybe there's a way in which I can see his talk as a way of advising me to make what *I* do an image of *myself* in an analogous way. And maybe the ability to suggest that is part of what makes a pro a pro."

ASSIGNMENT 9

Self-given good advice
that you didn't follow

"Come, there's no use in crying like that!" said Alice to herself rather sharply. "I advise you to leave off this minute!" She generally gave herself very good advice (though she very seldom followed it), . . . for this curious child was very fond of pretending to be two people.

Lewis Carroll, *Alice's Adventures in Wonderland*

Describe a situation in which you gave yourself what you consider to be very good advice that you did not follow. Who was there? What was said and done? Did you pretend to be two people? Be sure to explain your answer.

For Assignment 9 I had high hopes that came to very little. The question "Did you pretend to be two people?," coming off the quotation from Carroll as it does, still seems to me a suggestive way of inviting students to deal with the paradox of multiplicity in oneness as a writing problem. And we'd had, I thought, enough conversation about tonal ambiguity as a metaphoric approximation of "real" states of mind experienced by "real" people to prepare them to handle it. But whether the gap between the ability to understand a distinction and the ability to make one was wider than the students could at that point bridge; or whether the Assignment for me and that class was simply the wrong one at that moment; or whether we'd hit one of those mysterious blank spots that every class sometimes comes to—what I saw as an opportunity for the students, most of them decided to play dead with. The core of the Assignment, when the students addressed it at all, was handled with close-out sentences: "Yes, I was two people," or "No, I wasn't two people." There things stopped. I found very little in the situations the students created that I could praise as the attempt to *render* the conflict of the simultaneity of opposite states of mind. The "two people" of their papers were either two totally separate voices ("You better get your physics done" versus "go to the dance and relax"), or they were wrapped in a oneness which totally obliterated all sense of dramatic opposition: "Even though I knew better, there I was out with the boys anyway." Steve was still around.

A great many students seemed for some reason to resent the suggestion that the self might be seen as other than one, entire, and whole. But in order to preserve the notion of the self as irreducible, and as a consequence to have to develop some alternative metaphor for "people," the students either ground out allegories on the nervous system (my logic told my emotions; my conscience told my reason) or leeched onto the vocabularies of language systems with which they had only minimal familiarity (my id told my ego). The difficulty in both cases was that the students had nowhere to go in explaining themselves. It was the problem of the papers addressing Assignment 6 all over again —though this time it wasn't in any way that I could see the fault of the Assignment. Again I was facing a set of papers most of which were only one sentence deep. Again the problem, though I wasn't about to talk this way in class, was one that involved an inadequate understanding of language as metaphor.

As a way both of acknowledging this linking and of giving us the chance to approach the concept of language as metaphor from a different angle, I began class with an example of what I would call a retreat:

Is advice a group of words,
　　That people like to use?
　　　　To tell me things that I should do,
　　　　　　That they, themselves, refuse.

Is advice what I sometimes seek,
　　When I don't know what to do?
　　　　If so it is a helping hand,
　　　　　　Organizing my point of view.

88   Advice can be so many things,
      I scarcely know where to begin,
        And after I have started,
          Where shall I come to an end?

    Since advice can be so many things,
      Myself, I've probably advised.
        But I don't know where or when or why,
          Or how—or what to call advice.

There were a couple of sharp slumpings and a few hisses as I read the poem through and then:

"What's this guy think he's trying to pull, anyway?"

"What don't you like about it?"

"Everything. He's just copied the other poem."

"How do you mean copied?"

"Well, it's the same idea for one thing, how the Assignment's impossible. This guy just stole the idea because he knew you liked the first poem."

"Isn't the Assignment impossible?"

"Not that way. Not this way. This guy doesn't sweat anything. He doesn't even try to find out anything about advice. He hears a poem praised, so he writes a poem. It's phoney."

"OK. I won't say I don't know what you're talking about, but so far all you've done is throw rocks at the writer. Tie what you're saying to the words on the page. How would you explain to someone who *didn't* see what you were talking about why you think this writer's trying to pull a fast one? Let's see you do it just with the poem as a poem."

"All right. Take a look at that third stanza." He read it through with a mincing, contemptuous tone. " 'Scarcely know where to begin.' He *doesn't* begin. Look at what he says about advice, that it's a 'helping hand.' That clears things up, eh? That's like saying a professional is skilled."

"But he puts it as a question, doesn't he?"

"Only because he doesn't have enough guts to just come out and say what he knows you'll shoot him down for. 'Advice can be so many things'—for Christ's sake I know that. Who doesn't?"

"It's a matter of platitudes then. OK. I follow that. I'm interested in what makes you angry about the paper though. God knows we've seen platitudes in here before."

"Right. But this guy just gives up. He quits before he starts. 'I don't know where or when or why/Or how—or what.' He's just lying; he knows a lot about a lot of those things."

"And that isn't what makes the problem of advice a problem anyway," said another student. "I always know where and when and why. He said this. I did that. I don't have any trouble that way. It's what *makes* the advice advice that I have trouble with."

"OK. So the paper's a dodge. But we've seen dust-offs before in here too. That still doesn't explain why you all sound so pissed-off."

"It isn't an honest dust-off, that's what bothers me. The way he imitates the first poem he's acting like he sees something when he really doesn't."

"He's pretending to be something he isn't? Do we have two people here then?"

"I knew you were after something. OK. I think we do see two people."

"Let's find 'em. On the one hand there's the guy whose observations reduce to clichés, as Dan said, or to irrelevancies. Who's the other person in the poem?"

"The guy who doesn't want to get caught at it, the one who's trying to fancy things up."

"And it's the collision of the two that makes *you* react as a person, with anger in this case."

With that I turned to the next sample, a section of a paper which is a paradigm of a number that had gone the same way, papers that in seeing the problem of the Assignment as one of location rather than action, had run out of language pretty quickly:

What is "good advice"? Is it possible for a sane person to "give" himself "very good advice"? I find considerable difficulty trying to imagine "giving myself" any kind of advice. Deep inside the brain, the "advice" is always there in the sense that material is stored in the memory and "giving" is the mind's attempt to find the particular answer to some problem by putting together pieces of this stored material.

"Very good" merely indicates that the application of the memory material has resulted in a greater compliance with my particular code of ethics which in turn produces a greater feeling of accomplishment than normally. Since I consider advice to be a revelation to the workings of the mind, it is impossible, therefore, for me to receive advice except from another person.

Since the writer of those paragraphs remains totally unaware that it is a metaphor he is dealing with, there is no way that his writing can help make him aware that the terms with which he seeks to deny the multiplicity of the self could, from another point of view, just as easily be said to be a demonstration of it: Mr. Code of Ethics does something with Mr. Mind's having processed some of the raw material shipped in by Mr. Memory. As the writer handles things, however, Mind and Co. are no more individuated or personalized than are the sections of a computer. I wanted the class to understand, first of all, that it was metaphors and not actualities the writer was playing with. Secondly, I wanted to have a conversation about how one judges the appropriateness of a metaphor: what makes one metaphor for a subject more or less appropriate than another?

I came at things by asking the students to locate and characterize the verbs connecting the actions of Mind, Memory, and Code of Ethics. They were quick to see that to speak of the activities of "finding," "storing," and "putting together" in order to "produce" something called a "feeling of accomplishment" was talk commensurate with a discussion of objects, things. What was the matter with that, I wanted to know. No one knew how the mind worked anyway. Why couldn't you see its working any way you wanted to?

"But I think there is something wrong with seeing a 'feeling of accomplishment' as a thing."

"What?"

"It's too simple that way. It's like something that comes out of a gum machine."

"Are you saying that how you talk about something's working makes a difference, even if the something is an unknown?"

"Sure. We do that all the time in science."

"Can you give an example of it?"

"OK. Take whether the earth goes around the sun or the sun goes around the earth, for instance. My physics professor said that the question was too complicated for him to begin to answer, but that if he imagines the earth going around the sun he can get rockets to the moon a lot easier."

"You mean you could get rockets to the moon in a universe conceived of the way Ptolemy saw it?"

"Sure. You'd need a computer the size of Australia maybe, but you could do it. All you'd need would be a different set of equations. See, as a scientist—my physics teacher said this too—I'm like someone walking into a pool room just after a game is over. 'How did the balls get into the pockets?' someone asks me. I give the simplest explanation I can think of. I say, 'Someone put them there.' That's right in a way

I guess, but it doesn't tell you anything about sticks or cushions or carom shots . . ."

"Or running the rack?"

"Or running the rack."

"So in other words in science you don't work with actuality, you work with constructs."

"That's all we work with. Constructs. Models."

"What makes one model better than another?"

"Simplicity."

"But I thought you said that seeing a 'feeling of accomplishment' as a thing was *too* simple?"

He sat thinking for a minute, and then I went on.

"Look. Maybe by 'simplest explanation' the way you just used it you mean something pretty special. There's a simple explanation of the how of the universe in Genesis, but how workable it would be in getting someone from Mars to Venus is another thing. 'Simplest explanation' the way *you* used it has to do with what you want to use the model for, doesn't it, with how useful it is in getting done what you want to do? I 'know' that the world is round, for example, but how many hours of a day do I live on a round world? I don't consider the curvature of the earth when heading for the snack bar for coffee. The concept isn't useful that way. When I worked physics problems in college we were told to forget about the curvature of the earth."

"We are too."

"OK. When I say the world is round, then, I say that as someone who at that point is interested in roundness as opposed to the flatness or squareness of heavenly bodies. For a moment I'm taking an astronomer's point of view; I become, for a moment, a kind of primitive astronomer. Most of the time, though, I'm not saying so, really; at least I'm acting as though I assumed the world were flat. In other words, whether my model is a good one or not depends on what I want to do with it. Even more importantly, what I want to do with a model is, at least for the moment, going to depend on who I'm choosing to be."

"The way the guy talking about hills like white elephants was choosing to be poetic. A poet."

"Right. And how right *that* identity would be would depend on the situation. I can't imagine a geologist's writing up the white elephant line for a firm that had sent him out to prospect for oil. Not if he wanted to keep his job."

"So this guy in the paper has the wrong model."

"In this situation I'd say so. And to say it's 'too simple,' meaning too simpleminded, is really a way of saying that the writer has made himself too simple. Like the voice in the poem that Dan objected to, the writer's voice and manner here says it's all in the bag, that he's explained everything. He even implies that you'd have to be insane to see things another way. But he's done this by saying that people work like steam engines or, as you put it, gum machines. Maybe for a TV ad about a headache pill the model would work, but it's no more a model of how he works or you and I work when it comes to the question of advice than is the diagram of the guy in the aspirin ad with all those little A's and B's rushing through the body to bring speedy and lasting relief. Maybe that's where he got the model, I don't know. And maybe the model sells a lot of aspirin . . ."

"But it wouldn't get you from Mars to Venus."

"Or reach across the street for a pizza. Right. Would this writer have been any better off had he chosen to see the self as multiple the way Carroll's Alice does do you think? As multiple and as made up of persons or people? Suppose 'mind' in this paper had been Mr. Mind, for example, and 'memory' Mr. Memory instead of circuit 74. Would it have made any difference?"

"Yes, I think it would have. He couldn't have been this simpleminded about things for one thing."

"Why not?"

"Well, he'd have had to show Mr. Mind *acting* like a person, putting things together the way a person would."

"He'd have had to show the process of 'sorting,' 'sifting,' 'arranging' you mean. And would that have shown him he was just talking bull?"

"It would have if he'd gone on the way he does here."

"Is there another way to go on? Would imagining the self as being made up of people give you a chance to move in a direction that you can't move in very easily with this writer's language?"

"I suppose so, but I have a feeling you have something in mind I'm not following."

"I do have something in mind, yes. Look. Have we looked at a paper in here in which someone tried to describe advice as a process of 'sifting,' and 'sorting,' and 'arranging'?"

"Yes," said another student. "The paper about the guys in the study lounge doing that math problem."

"OK. What I had in mind was whether you could write about giving yourself advice that way? Could you show Mr. Code of Ethics and Mr. Memory having a conversation?"

"You could, but it would be hard to do."

"Why?"

"Because you'd have to know a lot about yourself to do it."

"And which if you didn't know, but had to come up with if you didn't just want to bull, you'd have to find out, wouldn't you? You'd have to use your writing as a way of learning. I grant you, it would be hard. But to judge from this paper, what do you get for yourself when you make it easy?"

The last paper I reproduced in its entirety:

"Keep off the grass." "Study hard." "Stay in school." These are all pieces of "advice" that I've been hearing all my life. There are thousands more like them. Many of them I've heard and have thought were good advice. Now I can see that they are just a group of words that threaten to slap your wrists if you disobey them, or they are statements that can be twisted in one's mind to mean whatever one wants them to.

Now I'm faced with the problem of writing about good advice. I am not sure that such a thing exists. At first, I was tempted to concoct some dramatic situation where I was stumbling along and suddenly said to myself, "Pull yourself together." This of course would end with my coming out of the situation with flying colors. Anyone could write a hundred Themes like this.

I could also write that when I saw the stop sign I stopped. Again I'm taking some very good "advice." Sure I am, but if that's all there is to the subject, I might just as well hand in a "No Parking" sign. Well, all the times when I gave myself some good advice have become a meaningless equation of x plus y equals 0. I don't think I would know a piece of meaningful advice if someone hit me in the face with it.

Right now I'm in the embarrassing position of not being able to think of a time when I have done anything but reword the meaningless. I'm not going to write about that; I don't think my stomach could stand it. On the other hand, the real or imaginary animal, "good advice," has been leading me around in circles. Therefore, rather than write an x plus y equals 0 type of paper, I'm just going to hand you this, and keep on looking for some advice that really means something.

In a way, that paper also dodges the problem of the Assignment, but not in the way most of the papers did, certainly not in the way that the other two we looked at do. It was the only paper of the set that had

had to it anything like the ring of frustration faced as frustration, and was for this reason a paper I wanted to see as relevant to the problem of the Assignment, even if it didn't address that problem directly. Whether I could bring the students out there with it, particularly after moving to it from what we had done with the first two papers, I wasn't sure.

I read the paper through and then for a while simply got out of the way. This was such a dust-off, the conversation ran on the one side. Look at that last sentence. Anyone could write a hundred Themes like *this* one, too. Oh come on, ran the argument on the other, he isn't saying the Assignment's impossible the way the guy in the poem did. He levels about things. He's not a know-it-all. Maybe not, went the hard line, but it's still clichés about clichés. And how honest is someone who says he couldn't know a piece of meaningful advice if someone hit him in the face with it? Do you think he really believes he's done no more than reword the meaningless? The Assignment asked for a situation. Where's his?

At that point I stepped in with the question of whether the paper itself could be called a situation.

"I don't see how."

"Well, can you locate two people in the paper?"

"You mean the way we did with the poem. Yes, they're the same two people here. One of them is copping out, the other is covering up for it."

"That's not the two people I hear," said someone else. "I think the paper is a situation, but I don't see the guy covering up or copping out the way the writer of the poem did. I think the situation is that one part of him is saying 'go ahead and write a Theme on advice,' but another part of him is saying 'I don't want to just write another Theme; I don't want to say stupid things.' "

"Where's he say 'go ahead and write a Theme on advice'?" the first student asked.

"In a lot of places. He doesn't come right out and say it; it's between the lines. He keeps saying over and over I could do this and I could do that."

"I know, but he doesn't do it, that's why the paper's a dodge."

"He says he can't do it, can't stand to do it. That's different. He could do it all right."

I asked the group defending the paper which "he" they were talking about. " 'He' says 'he' can't do it, can't stand to do it." Were those "he's" the same? Was there more than one "I" in the paper?

"Well, the guy talks about himself as being 'tempted' to write something to steal home with, is that what you mean?"

"Yeah," said someone else, "but that's not another person. He just says, 'I was tempted.' He's still him."

"I know, but when the guy was tempted he was in a different frame of mind."

I picked up "different frame of mind" with the question of whether, when you're in "a different frame of mind," you're two people.

Some said no, there was just one person. Others, pointing to the repeated "now's"—"now I can see," "now I'm faced," "right now"—said that in another way there were two people because the "I" now was remembering a "then" and that that was where a legitimate kind of "pretending" came in.

As more and more students took part in taking sides on whether or not there could be said to be two people in the paper, the argument began to mark time, to become the kind of debate that it's better to discard the terms of than to seek to resolve.

"Look," I said, "what is it about the writing of this paper that makes it possible even to raise the question of whether or not it's a cop-out, of whether there are two people here or not?"

"For me it's how he sounds. Even if he *is* dusting things off he's being honest about it. He's not like the writer of the first paper."

"He's not like the writer of the second one either," said somebody else. "He doesn't cop out with a lot of generalities."

"OK. It's the sound of honesty in the paper I find engaging too," I said. "In trying to make a subject out of the specifics of his own frustration as a writer, in trying to talk about his own experience rather than dealing just in generalities, the writer creates the illusion of somebody who isn't hiding anything. He becomes somebody you can at least listen to, because you can imagine having a conversation with him. Because he has a subject, he develops a voice, and vice versa."

"I can see what you mean by the sound of honesty, but how does that connect with the question of whether there are two people in the paper?"

"If you're honest about something you feel frustrated over, are you going to feel just one way about it?"

"I see what you mean. You're going to have different feelings about

96 it, and you could see yourself as different people when you talk about those different feelings."

"That's it. The same way you could give a voice to memory by seeing him as Mr. Memory."

"But he still doesn't do the Assignment, does he?"

"No, he doesn't. As a reader, I wouldn't feel comfortable saying that the paper is *just* a cop-out; but you're right, he doesn't do the Assignment. Can you see any way in which what he does do in his paper suggests a way he *might* approach the Assignment though?"

"Well, he says he's got to keep on looking for some advice that really means something, but I don't see how that's going to get him anywhere."

"I don't either, mainly because it implies that good advice is something you simply find, like a pot of gold at the end of a rainbow. I was referring to what he says about advice in his first paragraph, that advice is something 'that can be twisted in one's mind to mean whatever one wants [it] to.' Look at the remarks he's referring to: ' "Keep off the grass"; "Study hard"; "Stay in school." ' Could you make a remark like ' "Stay in school" ' mean something stupid?"

"Sure. It would depend on the context I made for it."

"Could you make it a piece of good advice?"

"Yes, I could. It would depend on who I said said it, and how, and on how I took it, I suppose."

"How *do* you understand it as advice, or as anything else, without, as this writer puts it, twisting it?"

"You can't. You have to give it a context of some sort."

"So, in other words, there's nothing in the remark itself that makes it either stupid or not, good advice or bad advice? You always have to make it mean something and what it means depends on what you make it mean?"

"I guess so, yes."

"OK. Now, to judge from what's interesting about this paper, the way the writer twisted the Assignment to make it mean something in terms of his own experience, what might he do to find some advice that means something?"

"I get you now, I think. He could show himself making a remark like 'Stay in school' into good advice by dealing with that in terms of his own experience."

"He could use the same technique that makes him interesting in this paper to 'find' some good advice by showing how he made something in his experience into what he calls good advice. And he could do this by showing what one part of him (or one person) said, and how another part of him responded. That way he'd be concerning himself with the process of what he calls a 'rewording of the meaningless,' but in order to make meaning—the only way, perhaps, that *any* meaning is made. For anything. By anybody. Ever."

ASSIGNMENT 10

Self-given good advice
that you did follow

Describe a situation in which you gave yourself what you consider to be very good advice that you did follow.

What was the occasion? What was said and done?

Did you pretend to be two people upon this occasion? Once again, explain your answer.

As with Assignment 9, the problem of Assignment 10 was to find a way of expressing a "you" as well as a "yourself" which violated neither a reader's undramatic sense of the wholeness of a single identity nor his dramatic sense of the ways in which such an identity could be believably divided. It was easy enough for a writer to come up with two voices: Steve Jekyll versus Steve Hyde ("Get off that grass, you fathead." "Good point, I'm on my way"), or to assume the sort of single-mindedness that would render conflict irrelevant ("Noticing that the grass had been newly planted, I decided it would be a good idea to remove myself from the premises"). But to contain multiplicity and oneness within each other, to present conflict through its expression and *at the same time* express conflict through its presentation—this the students did not find easy. Understandably. Before having read the papers addressing it, I would not myself have seen the Assignment in such seemingly impossible terms, let alone taught it that way. It was a student paper that suggested to me both the terms and the fact that they were not impossible.

To set off the achievement of this paper, I began class with one in which a writer attempts, unsuccessfully as I see it, to contain wholeness and division within each other:

This summer Washington D.C. was invaded, but not by Communist sympathizers or a civil rights group. I was one of a hundred boys and about seventy counselors who visited the Nation's capitol as a part of the National Youth Science Camp. Like most summer camps we had sports and games, but we also had classes and lectures by professionals in various fields of science. Also, the two campers who represented each state had been chosen because of their participation in science, such as building science fair projects.

Our little invasion was quite friendly and would have been completely peaceful except that we had been deep in the hills of West Virginia for two weeks and we hadn't even seen any girls in that time. We were reminiscent of a group of drovers just in from a cattle drive who had taken their baths and were ready for a festive time.

Instead of just messing around I decided to take advantage of being in Washington and see the Smithsonian. To some of the fellows who had been in Washington many times before, this would probably have been boring. For me it was a new and exciting experience. For four hours I walked through the three buildings which house the displays in a daze. There was so much to see that four days instead of four hours would have been required to see the things the way I would have liked to. Exploring the natural history section was like taking a course in anthropology and biology. The science and technology section which interested me most started with the most primitive of man's tools and followed their progress up to particle accelerators and electronic computers. To me the Smithsonian was like a giant book in which pictures were used for words and actual full size objects were used instead of pictures.

When I compared the experiences I had had that night with those of the others who had gone to shows and just roamed around I was glad I had made my decision. I had done something that interested the real me, not some made-up person I pretended to be.

I read that last sentence aloud twice and asked the students to locate (in such a way as to distinguish between) "the real me" and the "made-up person" in the paper as a whole. It quickly became clear that The Smithsonian Visitant, wandering happily through those dazed buildings, is just as much of a "made-up person" as The Festive Time

100   Seeker, and that neither has any more feel of reality than a piece of wax fruit ("our little invasion"; "instead of just messing around"). Also, at no point in the paper are these two caricatured states of mind combined into anything like the expression of a single sensibility (the ostensible "change of mind" is buried, rather than contained, in the single word "decided"). Hence the paper is both split and single-minded in equally unconvincing ways. As one student put it, either the writer is too candy-assed ever to have believed himself one of those vulgar "drovers" to begin with (in which case "we" doesn't mean "we"), or his visit to the Smithsonian isn't something he can pass off as *simply* "new and exciting" (in which case the "I" isn't an "I"). One of the Boys doesn't become a prig that way, nor can that kind of a prig become one of the Boys.

It was a nice setup for one of the best papers we'd had to work with so far that term, and one I particularly looked forward to doing with the class, because I saw in it both a way of continuing the line of thought we had started with the paper on the dialogue over the math problem as well as a way of going on with the conversation we had had the period before about seeing the self as a mixture of selves.

It was the fall of the year, but the loudspeaker seemed to have been going all summer:

"Pledging, pledge books, and fraternity or sorority jackets are not permitted in the school. It shouldn't be necessary to go over this again, but every year we run into the same situation; it's childish. This is senior high, and you're not children who have to be slapped on the hand any more. I'm asking you—no, I'm telling you—that there will be no fraternity or sorority activity in this school. I sincerely hope there will not be an occasion for me to have to make this announcement again."

The hoarse voice of Mr. Stark, assistant principal and school disciplinarian, faded out in the static until the power finally clicked off. A week before I had been slipped an envelope as I was going through the halls during the day, but I didn't feel guilty because of today's sermon. I knew some of the boys in my homeroom had received four or five envelopes; many were gloating in the back of the room with the girls, making the most of Big Mike's speech. Others looked scared, although they made efforts to laugh and joke.

I wasn't frightened, and I didn't brag. I had made up my mind not to join a fraternity before school even started. They just weren't me. All those parties and the pledging. I didn't have the time to devote to a fraternity. Why should I cheat them and myself? I wouldn't be one of the guys if I didn't join, but that was OK. I didn't care to be, I told myself.

I had a lot of friends in fraternities, even though I wasn't an athlete and have worn glasses all my life. I liked to be able to associate with them when I wanted, not at every meeting and party. Fraternity members were much better at socializing than doing homework, and college in a way was even more important to me then than it is now. I was full of good advice.

Every Monday I heard the reports of the previous weekend's capers:

"Wait until Paul's parents get back and see what that party did for the house."

"Gerry was really plowed, and hell, he had only three beers. I had six and man, I was riding nice and high."

"What a body that Sue has; she must be about a forty."

I don't need to be in a fraternity; I could repeat the Monday dialogue myself; it's all the same—pretty dull, I told myself.

The paper on the solving of the math problem in the study lounge had made clear that one way of being convincing on the subject of advice was to present both the giving and the taking of it as a process connected with the giving and the taking of identities or selves. The paper above deepens this notion in suggesting that since identity is multiple, shifting, various, a matter of selves rather than a single unchanging self, what is given or taken will also be multiple and various. Advice, therefore, when it is seen with anything like an attempt to approximate someone's full experience with it, will always carry different levels of meaning simultaneously. Hence, the ostensible advice of the paper, "do not join a fraternity," at the same time means "try again today not to mind not joining a fraternity even though, as well as particularly because, you understand the various things that 'join' and 'fraternity' can mean."

As I read the paper, the writer makes this meaning chiefly through his ability to suggest the conflict of desires he experiences in giving himself (and in taking) the advice that he does, a conflict leaving him with a position involving losses as well as gains. Unlike the writer of paper one, who claims to be able to turn his back on his friends' "messing around" in Washington without a second thought; the writer of the second paper is acutely, even painfully, aware of the attractiveness, excitement, and security of what he has renounced—or rather of what, day by week, he has to go on renouncing. Very consciously, he doth protest too much. All of his namings are made in such a way as to suggest that there is another part of him that names another way. His "obedience" to the rasping hokum of Big Mike Stark, his "interest" in his homework, his plan to enter college, his nominal disparagement of those weekend doings, his isolated individuality—not one of these things does the writer feel only one way about, and what I particularly admire the paper for is his ability to suggest how deeply he is involved in all that he does feel about them.

I began by asking what, exactly, the advice of the paper seemed to be. The response was:

"Well, here's another goody-goody. Steve gives up fraternities."

I've experienced that sort of derailment enough in the classroom not to be surprised that it happens, but when it does my initial reaction still is one of fury with the seemingly uncanny knack of the students to turn insensitive only when I am least prepared for it—and only, it seems, when we as a class have the most to lose. In this case, for example, it was the *first* public response made to the paper, a response that has to be handled carefully no matter how stupid it may be. If I'd chirped up with something like Does Anyone Have Another Opinion, they'd have smelled me out immediately, but I couldn't risk an open attack on the shallowness of that first response without making it impossible to have the kind of conversation I wanted to have. So, because I couldn't think of a good way of giving the fellow any more rope than I had to settle for hoping he'd take, I waited.

"There's no conflict here that I can see," he went on. "He says he made up his mind not to join a fraternity before school even started."

I could see Harvey, who'd written the paper, with his head down, his eyes hard on the mimeographed sheet in front of him. When the hell was Dan going to say something? Or Dave? Where was Jerry?

"And," this dismissively, "he thinks he's better than everybody else, too. He's conceited."

"Right," I said, unable to stand it any longer. "He hates beer and parties and girls. A boy's best friend is his ol' slide rule. It's OK with him that he isn't athletic and wears glasses, and that he got only one envelope while the boys in the back row got four or five each. Who'd care about a size forty when he had a set of differential equations warming on the stove back home."

"That's it. He's phoney."

"I thought you said he thought he was better than everybody else?"

"Well, he does. He's phoney because he doesn't want to say that he really does like parties."

"But he hates parties, he says. He says he knows the Monday dialogue by heart. It's all pretty dull."

"Oh, I think he likes parties."

"No sir. Not this guy," I said firmly.

From there on it was no longer just the two of us, and I let the rest of the class bring up the details, one by one: the fact that the writer says he wasn't athletic, that he'd worn glasses all his life, that college then "in a way" was more important than it was now, that he got only one envelope, that it was OK if he weren't in the swim, and so on.

"Gee," I said after a while, "wouldn't it have been wonderful if the writer could have admitted some of this to himself, if only he could have been honest as a writer instead of such a phoney?"

"But he does admit it, he knows damn well he likes parties." That was Dan, God bless his profane eyes.

"Admits it where?"

"All through the paper. There's too many of these remarks. The glasses and the envelopes and especially that 'I told myself.'"

"You mean he's not a phoney?"

"No. I wouldn't say so. He's got to study, sure, but not that hard, not the way he did and I think he knows that. When he says things like 'why should I cheat them and myself,' he's covering up. Or rather he was covering up and he knows now that he was covering up."

"So it's more than just sour grapes?"

"Sure it is. It's sour grapes that he knows are sour grapes. He isn't like the guy in the first paper who was never tempted at all."

"The way repetition in the poem we looked at back in Assignment 6 became something more than just repetition because the writer knew what it was?"

"Yes. It's sort of like that here. The guy knows he kidded himself once, but he's not kidding himself now."

"Is that distinction he makes between the then and the now a distinction that could suggest two different people the way some members of the class said the use of 'now' in the last paper we looked at last time suggested two people there? Is this writer two different people in his paper?"

"At least. Part of him wanted to party even then back in high school. That's one person. Part of him wanted to study; that's another. But he was afraid to party too, that could be another person."

"And afraid not to study maybe, which could be still another. And sorry that he couldn't stop, could that be another? And then of course there's the guy who knows all this, who's writing the paper; there's even another person."

And from there it was a matter of working out how much more was

104 meant than was said in sentences such as: "I wasn't frightened and I didn't brag," in the wryly ambiguous "I was full of good advice," and in the nonsentence "All those parties and the pledging," which one student pointed out could not be made a complete sentence because there was no way of concluding it without destroying the balance of longing and self-contempt expressed in the fragment.

I would have liked to have had a fuller, more immediate recognition of the complexity of the paper, and more of a community effort to earn the right to admire the quiet dignity of the identity the writer makes for himself in it than in fact we had. I would also have liked to use the paper to draw together more of where we'd been as a class than I was able to. On the other hand, I knew that what we'd done that period we could not have done two weeks earlier—not even with a paper that would have given us that chance. They were coming along.

ASSIGNMENT 11

What can you teach?
What can you be taught?

We all love to instruct, though we can teach only what is not worth knowing.

Jane Austen, *Pride and Prejudice*

Where do you stand on this issue?

Do you believe that you "can teach only what is not worth knowing"?

Do you believe that you can be taught "only what is not worth knowing"?

However you address yourself to these propositions, be sure you make clear on what your stand depends.

I devised Assignment 11 as a way of inviting the students to see the problems involved in what it means to give or take advice in terms of the problem of education, what it means to teach and to learn. My hope was that the Assignment would make possible a conversation about the dynamics of this process as involving more than a simple giving and receiving—the teacher as subject or doer, the student as object, as receptacle. And I expected that the way to such a discussion, after all our work with situations, would be through someone's handling the proposition from Jane Austen with a situation that would *show* the complexity that could be involved in a teaching-learning situation. But no one chose to go at it quite this way. There was a lot of puffy general talk about how "the teaching process could not exist without a corresponding learning process" and a great many wrap-ups on the order of: "If, therefore, I am able to learn what is being taught, or if others are able to learn from what I teach, then the teaching process is successful, and that which *is* worth knowing *is* being taught." But no one sought to shape a situation in such a way as to *express* such propositions. I did, however, get one paper the writing of which I thought I could make a case for as a metaphoric enactment of the paper's argument.

I began with a different paper, one that I wanted to use to take care of something else altogether, a kind of creeping slovenliness that I was sick of dealing with in the work of certain students. The writer of what I chose to work with I knew was intelligent, but his work had all the marks of someone whose earlier teachers had let him get away with a lot more a lot longer than they should have. Here is the relevant paragraph:

"... we can teach only what is not worth knowing. What is something "worth knowing?" To me it would be physics or chemistry; to someone else, something entirily different. Yet everyone most consider something worth knowing or he would have no goals whatsoever. If nothing were worth knowing, every student in the world and every one who ever lived, which is a fairly large poplation, are idoits. If some things are worth knowing, there must be someone who can teact them or else we would not know about them in hte first place. Therefore, we can teach something which is worth knowing. By using "all" and "only, Miss Austen invalidates the entire second half of of the sentence. Do "all" want to instruct? A third grader? An insane person? "Only what is not worth knowing?" Possibly in context this phrase had more meaning.

What kind of sloppiness was this, I asked, and what could be inferred from it about the attitude of the writer toward what he was doing?

"There are a lot of typos in the paper. Is that what you mean?"

"Of what?"

"Typos. Typographical errors."

"Why do you call them that? Does a typewriter make mistakes?"

"OK. So a typewriter doesn't make mistakes. What I mean is, these mistakes are silly."

"You mean he knows 'the' isn't spelled 'hte' and that most of the

What can you teach? What can you be taught?

107

time 'must' has a 'u' and not an 'o' for its vowel. OK. You call these 'silly' mistakes. Why 'silly'?"

"Because these aren't mistakes he'd make ordinarily. He knows how to spell 'must' and 'the.' He spells them right in that same paragraph."

I pointed out what else he seemed to know without bothering to make use of. He uses ellipses correctly, but in the same sentence doesn't conclude a quotation with quotation marks. "Everyone" he has taking the singular in one sentence but not in the next. "Silly" mistakes. Not mistakes he'd make "ordinarily." What did "ordinarily" mean then?

"It means when he thinks it really makes a difference, when it really matters."

"And what's that mean that the writing of the paper seems to have meant to the writer?"

"It didn't matter to him."

"Not even enough to bother to read over before he turned it in. It looks like something he knocked out between stops on the Rapid Transit. So what would you write alongside a paragraph like that, 'sp'? 'agr'?"

"No. I'd tell him to cut it out, to quit sounding like a slob."

"Would he understand that? Wouldn't that offend him?"

"We talked about this before. If he's offended, that's his problem."

Indeed. We had talked about it before, and if the writer was offended that was indeed his problem.

We then turned to an example of double-talk, a forensic con-job. Its promising beginning and pseudological terminology had sucked me into reading it two or three times, and I was annoyed that it had taken me that long to conclude that the paper is less an argument than a series of mock-distinctions arranged to look like one:

My stand on the issue of whether or not it is possible to "teach only what is not worth knowing" depends on which connotations of the words "teach" and "worth knowing" I use as a frame of reference. With this in mind, I decided to explore two sides of the argument.

The argument that "we can teach only what is not worth knowing" depends on the use of negative meanings for the crucial words. "Teach"ing in this system means the formal, classroom presentation of knowledge for the sake of the knowledge. The knowledge is provided because it is the job of the teacher, or because the knowledge is that needed for survival or for getting along in a job. This system of teaching attempts to imprint the desired information on the subject, and requires no initiative or

108   curiosity on the part of the student. The words "worth knowing" emphasize the opinion that pragmatic information useful only for the physical aspects of existence is crass, and not worth knowing. Since all concepts can be considered pragmatic, this is a weak point in the argument. Both of these facets of the argument imply that the level of intelligence and/or experience of the student is below that of the teacher.

The opposing side, which maintains that it is possible to teach something worth knowing, describes teaching as a process of guidance rather than of control. Knowledge is presented as an aid to the student in the formation of his own concepts of the material being presented, rather than as dogma. The role of the teacher in this situation is to provoke the student into response, for a student will never think much about a topic or devote much time and energy to it unless that interest is aroused. When this occurs, the teacher can become a student as well as a guide, for the questioning and consideration of the presented knowledge or opinions can produce concepts and views of the material which the teacher himself had not previously recognized. Here, knowledge that is valuable either in a physical or mental plane is "worth knowing." In this argument, all knowledge is considered to be practical and therefore valuable. Here the word practical must include any information that provides a basis for future decisions, that provides enjoyment, or that provides satisfaction.

Using the first set of premises, I agree with the opinion expressed in the quotation; using the second, I do not.

After what I'd been through coming to terms with it (and how long that had taken me), I knew that simply to read the paper aloud and put it up for grabs the way we sometimes did would have produced an unfocusable sprawl of speculation that might easily have swallowed the period, so after reading it aloud I went directly to the subject-verb sequences of the second and third paragraphs with the question of what could be inferred from them about what the writer was imagining a student to be. What in each case did the teacher do? What did the student do?

Well, in the first instance the teacher just laid it out there; this was the "process . . . of control." The students had something called "knowledge" presented to them, just "provided" for them. They were "imprinted" with it, therefore. By an Imprinter. A Very Bad Thing educationally, everyone seemed to agree.

How so, a Very Bad Thing?

"Because the student's just an object that way. He doesn't get a chance to question anything or present his own views."

What can you teach? What can you be taught?

109

"I see. Have you experienced this, this process of control?"

"Sure. Everybody has."

"Where? In what course specifically?"

"Well, I have to go to chemistry lectures with three hundred other people."

"And you're imprinted in there? You're just an object?"

"I don't get a chance to ask questions in the lecture."

"Sure, but why would you, a blank page, the imprintee, want to ask a question? What could you as imprintee possibly ask a question about?"

"Sometimes he goes too fast. Sometimes I don't get all the connections. Lots of times I have questions."

"But not as an imprintee you don't have questions. Does paper question a printing process? Do objects have questions or worry about connections?"

"I'm more than an object, is that what you mean?"

"Don't you think you'd better hope so? And you said that 'in the lecture' you don't get a chance to ask questions. Is there any place you can?"

"I have a recitation section."

"Where you can ask questions. Of whom, by the way? Of a teacher of just your 'level of intelligence and/or experience?' Why not just ask Dan here about Schroedinger's wave equation?"

The boy laughed. "He's as screwed up on that as I am."

We turned then to the ostensible Utopia of "the opposing side" where the student was "provoked," "stung," "aroused" and so forth, like a frog's leg twitching at the shock of an electrical impulse. Was the alternative really an alternative? How exactly did a teacher go about becoming "a student as well as a guide"—which several members of the class scorned as apple-polishing because it fit so badly with what else the writer had said. We could all be all for a student's "formation of his own concepts," but how exactly was this to be brought about? What was the difference between the "presentation of knowledge for the sake of knowledge" and "knowledge presented as an aid . . . rather than as dogma"? "Stinging" didn't seem to be much more viable as a metaphor than "imprinting," because neither metaphor expressed the mutuality of the educational process. Whether the writer is speaking of teaching as a "process of guidance" or as one of "control," his hypothetical student stands in exactly the same relationship to his teacher: as object of the verb teach, not subject of the verb learn.

110   We then turned to the paper I'd been using our conversation to work
toward. It was the only interesting piece of writing to come in on the
Assignment:

"We all love to instruct, though we can teach only what is not worth
knowing."

When I first read that statement, I was inclined to disagree with it.
After all, I hadn't spent twelve years in school being taught things not
worth knowing. I could point to four years of high school math,
physics, chemistry, etc. and say I had been taught many useful things. But
in another sense I would be wrong to say this. Sure, I was taught how
to set up a chemical equation and solve it, or to solve quadratic equations,
but these things alone are not worth knowing. Without the ability to
use these things in situations not laid out in a textbook, these "useful" bits
of knowledge become parlor tricks with no real value but to impress people.

The really valuable things can be learned but not taught. At first, this
doesn't make much sense, but if you think about it, it really isn't as absurd
as it sounds. For instance, take the English class I'm in. If the way to
good writing could be taught, we would have been taught it by now
and our class would have no purpose. The professor could just
come in and say:

"Now, boys, today we are going to be taught how to write good papers.
First we need a subject." And so on. I remember, as a matter of fact,
an exchange I had with our teacher on just this approach way back when.
"Sir," I wrote at the end of the Theme I'd written for Assignment Three,
"Sir: it would help if you could tell us what you wanted." When I got
the paper back, he'd written this in bright red: "Us? I can tell you that
of *you* what I want is what you want for yourself when you're proud
of yourself for having wanted it." I was angry when I read that, but I
think I understand it a little more now than I did then. The trouble with
the "Now, boys" sort of thing is that it's useless. The thing that really
counts is the "how" of the whole process. Anyone can teach me that a
paper should be interesting, clear, and concise, but I have to learn
how to make it that myself.

Similarly, I could teach anyone the parlor tricks of writing; that is,
I could tell them they must have an opening, a body, and a closing
in their papers. They could learn all this easily enough, but continue to
turn out the dullest prose imaginable. I would have no idea how I could
teach them to make their papers something besides what a computer
could turn out. I could teach them the mechanics; they'd have to learn on
their own how to make their papers say something.

In the end, I find myself agreeing with Jane Austen. When this
paper is finished, I am not going to be able to put it away and close it

What can you teach? What can you be taught?

111

out of mind any more than an astronomer packs his astronomy away with his telescope. I'm wondering how much of what I've been taught will remain worthless just because it is in a textbook and I live in a world of human beings.

My way into the paper was through the chance remark about apple-polishing that had been made in reference to the one we'd just finished. Wasn't this an instance of the same thing? Look at that smooth bit of flattery about me, The Perfesser.

"It may be just flattery, but I don't think so. Anyway, it isn't like that last paper with all that debate team stuff."

"I don't see exactly the connection you're making yet."

"I guess what I'm saying is I like the way this guy talks. He sounds like the guy in the paper who couldn't find a piece of meaningful advice, except here the guy doesn't dodge the Assignment. Sure, he mentions the class. He even quotes one of your . . . your little gems. But he uses it. He's doing more than just making points, I'd say."

"Voice. Is that what you're getting at? You respond to the voice of the paper?"

"Partly. Yeah, I guess it is voice. This other writer's like a guy selling Dristan or something, the way he comes on with all that 'pragmatic' jazz. He's just trying to snow me. But the writer here isn't yelling at me. He sounds like he wants to talk."

"Or at least as though he were someone you could talk to. OK. I'd like to go back for a minute to what you meant earlier when you said that he 'uses' the remark I made on his paper. How do you mean 'uses'? 'Uses' as opposed to what?"

Someone else took over by saying that he thought he knew what Jerry had meant.

"The way he uses that quote I don't think he's after points either. It's part of his argument. And it's part of the way he levels too. I mean it's part of why I think he's straight in the paper. He didn't have to say it made him angry, but he does. And he says he understands it only a *little* more. I mean he doesn't say 'now I see the light and what a dope I was' the way a brownie would."

"OK. I follow that. By the way, Sam, it's a 'quotation' he uses, OK? not a 'quote.' 'Quote' is a verb. Does this writer make anything else from class part of his argument?"

"Yes, that thing about the astronomer. I like the way he uses that too."

"How does he use it?"

"Well, all through the paper he's talking about how he has to do something for himself, and there he really does it. He's talking about this course, and he's pulling things from different places in it to show he's doing something for himself. Something for himself here in the course I mean."

"OK," I said. "And the way he connects the remark about the astronomer with textbook and human beings makes it more than just a quotation he's remembering. As a class we talked about the astronomer in terms of amateurism and professionalism. He moves it outside that context so as to extend its meaning, so as to make it mean something in his own terms. It's that process, too, which seems to me to suggest he's honestly doing something for himself."

"And he does that same thing with that remark of yours, doesn't he? I mean, if all he'd wanted to do was show that writing was hard, there were probably a lot of your remarks he could have used. He picked the one he did deliberately."

"That's the illusion the writing creates, anyway. Does what we've said about this paper make it any clearer what the writer might have meant by saying in his first paragraph that 'these things *alone* are not worth knowing'?"

"I think he means that information isn't enough. You've got to know how to use it."

"As in this paper, at least for me, he shows he can. He's doing more than just coming up with an answer. It's *his* answer he's coming up with, an answer for himself, which he expresses by making what he's saying the same thing he's showing and doing."

ASSIGNMENT 12

Define advice

On the basis of what you have written in your last five papers, define advice.

Is there anything you have left out or would care to add? Be sure to explain your answer.

I hadn't read ten papers worth of baby talk addressed to Assignment 12 before realizing that the nominal subject of advice had gone dry for us as a class. To be sure, the Assignment itself is not very imaginatively written. I could have phrased things so as to have made a remark like "on the basis of what you have written" a lot more helpful to the students than I did:

> *Look back over your last five papers. Select some of the phrases and sentences you used to define advice. How would you characterize them? What sort of voice do they create? Are you the subject or object in those sentences? Do you see your status now, grammatically as well as in other ways, in the same way you did when you wrote the sentences?*

But I'm almost certain that such changes would not have made that much difference. The real trouble with most of the papers lay in the spirit with which they were written. The students not only knew better than to attempt to settle for what a lot of them did: they were on the edge of not caring whether they knew better or not. This is the

114 last thing in the world to take up with a class as a subject—or, on the other hand, to acknowledge by making allowances for. But it's also no place to linger. Since I'd already passed out to the students the paragraphs by J. D. Thomas the period before, I knew that all I'd have to worry about was a way of squeezing one more class meeting on the subject of advice before things opened up again. All I had to find was one paper out of fifty that could give us a class. I was lucky.

The best way I could think of dealing with the collective cop-out of the class without involving us in a pointless confrontation was to work only with individual sentences from individual papers. For our first "paper," therefore, I mimeographed seven of them—six lead sentences and one final one (example E). In class I offered to prove, if anyone wanted me to, that each sentence was a fair representation of the style and manner of the paper from which I'd taken it. As another way of showing The Game as a game, I then asked the students to infer what they could from these sentences about the papers which had in each case been written around them.

A

The question asked on this assignment consists of three words, "What is advice?"

B

I believe advice can be interpreted as advice only by the person who is receiving this so-called thing called advice.

C

Advice is the attempt to apply one's past experiences to a present situation in accordance with one's conscience.

D

As a critique for good advice I would propose three standards.

E

Therefore all advice is someone giving consultation or if it is self-advice then it is a hunch.

F

Advice means different things to different people, therefore it cannot be defined.

I really don't know what advice is; it would be rather useless, therefore, to try to define it in terms which have significance for me.

The obvious emerged easily enough. The in-place jogging of sentence A changed the terms of the Assignment (which most of the students had done; no one attempted to create anything out of the context of the sentences he himself had written), and as a consequence left its writer in a perfect position to play any variety he wanted of the game of Anything Goes. The restrictiveness of B had looped its writer into a Gordian knot. C was Voodoo, the mumble of a witch doctor over a pot. And so on. F and G were called set-ups for a cop-out which of course they are, but I had placed the sentences at the end of the list because I wanted to raise more with them than just how they opened the doors to happy anarchy:

"OK. You're right in suggesting about F that the rest of the paper could easily be—in fact it was—no more than a matter of simple mnemonics. Still, isn't it true that 'advice means different things to different people'?"

"I suppose it is."

"Then does this mean that you think the writer of sentence F is right, and that the writer of sentence G is too? I'm speaking now only of whether or not you agree that advice can't be defined, and that it's useless to try."

"Well, in a way advice *can't* be defined, but I think something's getting left out if you put it just that way."

"Can you say what?"

"I'm not sure."

"OK. Here's a paper in which the writer plays with just that proposition. Let's see if it helps."

"I don't know what you mean by 'glory,'" Alice said.

Humpty Dumpty smiled contemptuously. "Of course you don't—till I tell you. I meant 'there's a nice knock-down argument for you!'"

"But 'glory' doesn't mean a 'nice knock-down argument,'" Alice objected.

"When *I* use a word," Humpty Dumpty said, in rather a scornful tone, "it means just what I choose it to mean—neither more nor less."

"The question is," said Alice, "whether you *can* make words mean so many different things."

"The question is," said Humpty Dumpty, "which is to be master—that's all."

116   Substitute "advice" for "glory," and you have both the problem and the results of this assignment and several definitions of advice. Advice can be "Steve" telling you how not to move the ashtray or how to throw a football. Advice can be Karl Marx telling you that the best way to run a political system is socialism. Advice can be a warning from your advisor that you're overloading your schedule. An example is a form of advice. The stereotype of clean living with Tide thrown at you from commercials is advice, but who would take that as advice on an equal basis with Newton's "Principia"—advice on how things will behave in an inertial system? "Advice" in this assignment is to us as "Happiness" is to Charley Brown or Linus in "Peanuts": each person has a different concept of what the word means to him. This was evident in the papers we read in class. Advice is: how to stay 'cool'; why not to buy a car; what to do over the summer.

The trouble with this assignment for me, the reason that I haven't been able to define "advice" thus far, is that I don't have a clear concept of what the word means. To me, advice is information that can be applied to a problem. This may be a suggested code of ethics "advising" me how to live. It may be a remedy from "Merck's Manual" for hives. It may be what a teacher tells me about a method of problem solving when he wants me, not him, to work out a problem. When someone tells me that Concord makes a better tape recorder than Webcor, that's advice too, especially if I'm in the market for a recorder.

There are several things that I have left out, that I would like to have added. These are the things which I don't have the language to discuss. Things like whether accepting advice involves acknowledgment of the superiority of the person giving it; whether advice has to be given— can it be offered and is there a difference; whether (and I believe there's a difference between this and the first question) the person listening to the advice must be inferior to the person providing it; and whether advice has to be explicit or whether it can be implied by the words or actions of another person.

In the use of this word, all of us are like Humpty Dumpty—even you. From the discussion in class it emerged that no one had a concrete idea of what "advice" meant to him, what "advice" really was, and how he would recognize "advice" when it was given to him.

There was a long silence until one student finally ventured: "Well, we are but we aren't too. That's the trouble with this damn subject."

"What do you mean, we are but we aren't?"

"I mean we're all like Humpty Dumpty but we aren't, too. Words *can* mean different things, but there's a limit somewhere. I can see a cure for hives as advice the way this writer says, but I can't see advice meaning little blue rabbits."

"Your shoes aren't Buicks, you mean."

"No, and I don't live in a tree."

"Where Humpty Dumpty is?"

"In a way he is."

"I think you're right, which is why he's out of this world, the talking Easter egg from Wonderland. You mean there's something different about where you live, where you and I live, where one and one make two?"

"We have some things we can agree on, anyway."

"Like one and one making two?" This was Harvey I was talking to, a math major.

"Things like that."

"What about that as an example? Do one and one make two? I mean always?"

He stopped.

"One, the number in a given mathematical system, plus one, the same number in the same given mathematical system equal two, the number in the same mathematical system, yes."

"What system?"

"A decimal-based system."

"How about a nondecimal-based system—what could one and one equal there?"

"Almost anything."

"You say 'one, the number' and 'two, the number'; do you mean 'number'? Do you mean this, for instance?"

I went to the board and wrote:

$$2,\ 1 + 1,\ 3 - 1,\ 4 - 2,\ \frac{6}{3}$$

"Are those numbers?"

He stopped again.

"No, they're numerals representing the number two."

"How do I represent the number two without numerals?"

"You can't."

"How do I think of the number two then?"

"You can't."

"I can't? How do you know?"

Another pause.

"Well, maybe you can think of it, but I can't know what it is you're thinking of. The number two might be a totally different thing for you than it is for me."

"But we can know something, can't we? We don't therefore just

118   throw mathematics out the window. Look at where this writer says that
       'each person has a different concept of what the word means to him.' "
       I went back to the board and made a diagram:

number	numeral	thing	word
"two"	1 + 1, 2, 3 − 1	"happiness"	happiness

"What if we understand the writer as meaning that we all have
different concepts of what words *represent*. On the basis of this analogy, does the fact that my happiness is not your happiness mean any
more than that I'm not you?"

I had intended that question to do no more than return us to the
notion of language as symbol, as representative of a way of seeing or
thinking (and in this sense descriptive of a see-er or thinker) rather
than expressive of the way things in themselves are, but my analogy
of words and mathematical notation opened rapidly into more speculation than I could begin to shape or direct. It was the idea of mathematics as a language, of a mathematician as a language user, that
fascinated the students, of course; but I didn't know enough about
mathematics to be of any help to them. For me, the last fifteen minutes
of that period were a nightmare. The more interesting the students'
speculations became, the less certain I grew not only of how to develop
the analogy I had made, but indeed of whether it had been a responsible analogy to begin with. Was Humpty Dumpty a mathematician?
I remember that's coming up. And who then was Alice? Did a mathematician deal with the term "3 − 1" the way a dictionary did with the
word "happiness," and did this then mean that a language user's position with the English language was only quantitatively different from
the position of a mathematician with mathematics? Or would the analogy work out better if one began by saying that though mathematics
was an abstraction, mathematics applied to the world (in, say, a system
like the Dewey Decimal System for arranging books) was something
else again? What else again? Mathematics was a great deal more than
a matter of numbers, wasn't it? But "more" in just what way, exactly?
I was in the awful position of feeling that with such questions we were
at the heart of something I couldn't quite understand, of being sure
that there was a way of making sense of where we were that I simply
couldn't find. It was a period I was awfully glad to see end.

ASSIGNMENT 13

J. D. Thomas

Here is a statement about writing:

MIDDLE TECHNICAL STYLE

Function. A large group of intelligent and well-educated laymen occupies a position midway between the specialist and the man on the street. (Included in the group are many technical experts in certain fields, who may be only "intelligent and well-educated laymen" in other departments of scientific knowledge.) A substantial part of technical composition is directed to such persons. Reports, for instance, often are prepared by experts for consideration and action by industrial boards or public agencies having group authority, and perhaps wide individual experience, but lacking specific skill in the matter under consideration. A purely technical style might be a mistake in business correspondence concerning a specialized activity, such as a phase of engineering, when the addressee is not a professional colleague; neither may a "popular" manner of expression be warranted unless the addressee is wholly outside the industry. Many books, articles, and public lectures bring the scientific knowledge of experts to mature readers and audiences who have a good general education but little, if any, training in the subject under discussion. Efficient communication then depends upon a "middle" range of technical style.

Characteristics. On the whole, the structures of language in this style are more normal than in the two other basic technical styles. The extreme simplification and the sometimes awkward repetition required in popular treatments of science are not necessary. Reliance is placed less on avoidance of the proper idiom and nomenclature of the subject than upon definition and explanation. Occasional reference to a dictionary may be expected of the reader, but of course the writer does not display rare words by preference. Although such purely technical devices as equations, drawings, and graphs may be indispensable, they are not allowed to push the text altogether aside. Nearly always, a point made symbolically is also expressed in ordinary sentences.

Advantage for the course in technical English. The middle style is particularly advantageous for a course in technical English. It meets the frequent complaint by students of the sciences that their language teachers, being mainly interested in aesthetic literature, slight the subjects of most vital concern to the class. On the other hand, it does not confront an instructor with the task of marking papers that sometimes consist chiefly of symbols rather than of ordinary language. The average student in a professional curriculum receives ample training in purely technical communication, such as the preparation of routine laboratory reports. The purpose of the class in technical English is to reinforce—not to duplicate—that work by concentrating effort upon general principles of logic, sound composition, and correct language in the service of scientific and technological subject matters. Very often, too, sections are not composed exclusively of students enrolled in the same departments of engineering or theoretical science. Through the medium of a middle technical style, members of a mixed group can improve their proficiency in English by writing and speaking, with full intelligibility to one another (and to the instructor), on topics within their respective fields of specialization.

J. D. Thomas, *Composition for Technical Students* (1965)

Describe the voice you hear speaking in the passage above.

What is there about this voice you would call professional?

What is there about it you would call amateur?

Why?

I wrote Assignments 13 through 16, which ask the students to compare the advice of some professional writers on how to write about science, in order to give us a chance to draw together some of our concerns with our two nominal subjects (amateurism and professionalism and advice) in relation to our real one. For a scientist, what constitutes professional advice about how *he* ought to use language? Assignment 17 then asks the students to consider an example of a professional scientist in the act of defining himself through the defining of his subject.

The passage by J. D. Thomas is taken from the introduction to a text called *Composition for Technical Students,* a handbook that has gone through a lot more editions than it should have. Its tone and manner are a perfect example of what can happen to talk about writing when the subject is approached as an abstraction, without reference to a given arrangement of words in a given context. "Middle technical style" is either dead writing, as the aridity of Thomas's mechanically perfect prose would seem to suggest; or a circular definition of any-thing anyone may choose to call "good" writing on a technical subject. Hence the heavy reliance of the passage on platitudes, such as "effi-cient communication . . . depends upon a 'middle' range of techni-cal style," and "occasional reference to a dictionary may be expected of the reader, but of course the writer does not display rare words by preference." Such remarks, particularly when they're qualified to the point of nullity that they are ("may," "might," "perhaps," "often," "nearly always"), are true in the same way it's true that good writing ought to be Clear, Logical, and Coherent. They create the illusion of an explanation which is actually no more than a restatement of what needs to be explained. The result is a lot of high sentence that is more than a bit obtuse. And worse. For in pretending to confront (rather than in really confronting) the issues raised by his subject, I think that Thomas opens himself to criticism on more than intellectual grounds.

There were two major difficulties with the papers the students wrote addressing themselves to Thomas's passage. Those who chose to praise his professionalism and embrace the "advice" of the passage as helpful more often than not ended up sounding very much as he does. They intoned the virtues of Clarity and Precision and spoke admiringly of something they called "Thomas's presentation of the facts" about writ-ing. The Clear and Simple syndrome. Those who were irritated by Thomas, on the other hand (I was glad to see it was a healthy majority of the class), had a tendency to settle for name-calling, spitting and sneering so as to become themselves worse than what they were at-tacking. And in both instances the writers unloaded their rocks or their bouquets as far from Thomas's prose as it was possible for them to get. I wanted to have a class on what the right to judge depends on.

I started with an example of judgment that is unearned, with a paper of minimal response to the Assignment which begins by equating textbooks with dreariness and teachers with boredom, and yet which ends up, even after two weeks of work on the subject of advice, for God's sake, allowing that Thomas is "able to instruct others."

The passage entitled *Middle Technical Style* sounds like it comes right out of a textbook. It states the facts in three dull, colorless paragraphs. The drab voice of the instructor permeates the passage, pointing out the functions, characteristics, and advantages of the style of writing.

He plods through the first two paragraphs in the same tone. However, the third seems to change slightly. Instead of the English teacher methodically expounding a point, it switches to the English teacher explaining the problems he faces in this type of course. The writer's feelings seem to creep into the passage when he mentions the complaints of students and the purpose of the technical English class.

The writer is clearly a professional. He is fully acquainted with the aspects of technical writing and is able to instruct others in this field.

The class had little trouble with the silliness here: the general terms of the paper, the distance between its assertions and Thomas's sentences, the fact that the argument of the paper might as easily apply to any one of a thousand pieces of prose. One of the things that interested me about the paper, however, was the writer's fumbling with the matter of Thomas's "feelings." Did anyone have any idea what the writer might be referring to in the Thomas passage?

"Well, Thomas does change his subject in his third paragraph. I think that's what this guy is pointing out."

"Where exactly do the 'feelings' come into the paragraph though? In which sentence?"

"I think he means they come in where Thomas talks about what teachers are supposed to be interested in."

"Supposed by whom? Look at the way Thomas's sentence is written:

It meets the frequent complaint by students of the sciences that their language teachers, being mainly interested in aesthetic literature, slight the subjects of most vital concern to the class.

Who's doing the supposing there?"

"Isn't this supposed to be what the students think? I mean isn't this Thomas saying what he thinks students think?"

"Well, is it? How about those commas? The phrase is nonrestrictive as Thomas punctuates it. What's the difference in the meaning of the sentence if the commas are left out?"

And then someone said:

"I see what you mean. The way the thing is written it isn't just the students who are bitching. It's Thomas too. He's saying that teachers *are* 'mainly interested in aesthetic literature.' "

"And *do* therefore 'slight the subjects of most vital concern to the class'?"

"I guess so."

"Making Thomas someone who feels deeply the exploitation of students by their teachers? The commas make him concerned with protecting all you Young Boys from Aesthetes like me?"

"Maybe the commas do that, but I don't think he's thinking about students so much, really."

"What do you think he is concerned about, then?"

"I think he's more interested in making sure that teachers do what they're supposed to. The way he talks about purpose a little later on sounds as if he's writing for a teacher, writing to tell him he's supposed to work on 'general principles of logic, sound composition' and things like that."

"And to keep out the greasy literary kid stuff; this is a class on Middle Technical Style. Is there anything wrong with making sure that teachers do what they're supposed to?"

"I guess not, except that Thomas makes it sound like a threat."

"How do you mean, 'threat'?"

"That as a teacher, you damn well better be working on 'sound composition,' if you know what's good for you."

"And if you want to keep your job. I'm right in hearing that that way of talking bothers you?"

"If I were a teacher, I wouldn't like it."

"Wouldn't like being threatened right after being told who you really were, what your 'real interests' actually were. I wouldn't like it either. And don't. Let me ask you also how you, as a student, would like being in the classroom of an English teacher who had to be whipped into position this way? What kind of interest would you have in a class run by someone whose 'real interest' you were convinced was in doing something other than what he was doing?"

"That's it, I think. I think that's what bothers me about Thomas. He makes the whole thing sound like pulling teeth. Everybody's in the classroom just going through the motions because they have to be there. Maybe that's why I don't think he cares about protecting students either. Not really he doesn't."

"OK. Can you do any better than the writer of that paper does, then, when he settles for saying only that 'the writer's feelings seem to creep into the passage'? To judge from what Thomas says, how would you describe what Thomas's feelings seem to be on what you called 'the whole thing,' the teaching-learning process when it comes to the subject of writing?"

"Well, I'm not sure. I think he feels writing's important and all that, but he makes it all so damned grim, somehow."

"It's a difficult thing to lay hold of in the passage. You aren't the only one to have had trouble with it. Let's look at another paper."

This whole paper sounds like it was written in the middle technical style it is describing. It has just the right amount of detail—no more, no less. The structure is perfect; it wouldn't take two minutes to outline. In fact the job is already started, 1. Function, 2. Characteristics, etc. Maybe it was written this way and the letters were simply removed from the subtopics. Except for the use of general words, such as "large," "substantial," "sometimes," and a reference to "the average student," whoever he is, I have no argument with the mechanics of the paper.

All the information on the middle technical style is there, spelled out. The reader is told everything that the author thinks he needs to know, but he isn't allowed to discover a thing for himself. It's not necessary for the reader to think to get the most from this paper. There is nothing for him to decide on the basis of his own experiences and therefore nothing with which to disagree.

When I hear any voice at all it is one of superiority. Mr. Thomas seems to be saying that he is an expert on the middle technical style, but the lack of voice tells me he isn't very interested in telling me about it. The superiority of the voice may come from the fact that Mr. Thomas does know a great deal more about the subject than I. The way in which he exploits his knowledge makes me as uncomfortable as someone who makes up a superior voice.

Mr. Thomas must be a professional at composition; surely he couldn't write such an impersonal thing as this and get any kind of pleasure from it. Because of the lack of a human voice and its outline structure I think that this paper is no better than some we have heard in class. Even if Mr. Thomas is a professional, his attitude toward middle technical style makes him sound like an amateur.

I started our conversation with that paper by noticing the peculiarly similar ways in which paragraphs one and three start out headed for a critical position that in both cases the writer veers away from taking at the very last minute. How was the writer's peculiar conclusion to the first paragraph to be explained: "I have no argument with the mechanics of the paper"? And did anyone see any reason for the double shuffle at the end of the third paragraph in that talk about Thomas's "superiority"?

"I don't know about that 'superiority' business, and I'm not sure I know what this guy means by 'mechanics,' but I'm pretty sure he doesn't like Thomas."

"What makes you say so?"

"The digs he has in here: 'It wouldn't take two minutes to outline,' if 'the letters were simply removed,' ' "the average student," whoever he is'—I don't think he likes Thomas at all."

"Then why doesn't he say so flat out, do you think? Or does he? Do you think he's being ironic when he excepts Thomas's 'use of general words' and his concept of 'the average student'? Is that a way of saying that since that's all the passage consists of, he objects to all of it?"

"I can't see it that way. In the paper I mean. I don't think the guy *is* being ironic. He knows Thomas is being clear and all that, but he doesn't like him being clear in the way he is."

"The way Dan admitted a minute ago that maybe he'd have to grant Thomas's belief in the importance of learning Middle Technical Style, but he didn't like what Thomas seems to be turning the process into. Dan's word was 'grim.' This writer too seems to wonder about Thomas's 'interest' in his subject, says he doesn't see how he could get any 'pleasure' out of writing something so 'impersonal.' Is that what you mean by saying you don't think this writer likes the way Thomas is being clear?"

"Yes. Maybe that's what he means by Thomas's 'superiority,' too, that he doesn't like the *way* he's superior."

"Then why the obscurity? Why doesn't he just say so? Why does he say he has no quarrel with Thomas's 'mechanics' when what he seems to object to is Thomas's mechanical approach to things? And look at that sentence about superiority: 'The way in which he exploits his knowledge makes me as uncomfortable as someone who *makes up* a superior voice.' Does he mean 'makes up' in the sense of contrives? Why the fuzzy comparison between a 'way' and a 'someone'? Why do you imagine he doesn't seem quite able to bring himself to call Thomas's approach mechanical and his voice offensively superior?"

"Maybe he was afraid to. He knows Thomas knows more about the subject than he does."

"Maybe. Maybe he was afraid of Thomas's Authority. Maybe also the writer wasn't very clear about exactly what it was he objected to in Thomas. He doesn't seem to have a way of saying that though mechanics are important, they will only take you so far; of distinguishing between the sound of authority and patronization. Is there anything the writer could have done to have become clearer about what he objected to in Thomas, do you think, to have given himself a chance to find out exactly what it is in Thomas that bothers him?"

This landed us, as I expected, in the nervous system. One would have to think harder, be braver, and so forth, which I let the class

126   flounder with in order to make clear that "advice" to a writer of that sort was not going to be of much more help than telling him he would have to be reborn. I then moved to the last paper with the intention of using it to provide us with another way of talking:

> In "Middle Technical Style" I hear a very professional tone but not what I would call a professional voice. The author, while seeming to make a definite statement about a style of writing that would be of particular value to the technical student, wanders off the subject of definition into the never-never Goldilocks world of neither-too-hot-nor-too-cold.
>
> The professional tone comes from the fact that the author has something important to say and convinces me that it's worth my while to listen. He's obviously thought about the subject and shows it by mentioning such a subtle distinction as technical experts in fields other than the writers'.
>
> The tone fails to graduate into a professional voice when the author begins to hedge the subject. The essay then bogs down in truisms and nonsense sentences: "the writer does not display rare words by preference" is a truism, but coupled with "Occasional reference to a dictionary may be expected of the reader," it becomes, if not a contradiction, at least an uncertain proposition. And in a sentence like "On the whole, the structures of language in this style are more normal than in the other two basic technical styles," the qualifications reduce what is being said to next to nothing. It sounds as though he is trying to lay down the law at the same time he's afraid really to commit himself.
>
> Admittedly, the sentences and the form are all technically correct. But after the first few sentences there is a breakdown between the writer and the reader. The writer fails to win my confidence because of a lack of certainty on his part. At the end of the essay I find myself empty of anything that I can address myself to.

"Does the writer of that paper strike you as somebody who is clear about his objections to Thomas?"

"He sure is."

"What makes *you* clear that he is."

"Well, he really takes Thomas apart; he proves what he says."

"Where, specifically? Go to a sentence, can you?"

"OK. He says in his third paragraph that Thomas 'bogs down in truisms.' But then he shows you what he means by this with a quotation. He makes you see it happening."

"And he doesn't even leave it there. He quotes, as you say. Then he explains what he's heard in what he quotes ('the qualifications reduce what is being said to next to nothing'), then he explains what what he's heard means ('It sounds as though he is trying to lay down the law at the same time he's really afraid to commit himself.'). As you say, this writer makes you see it happening, he makes you see his mind in the act of working, just as when you explained how *you* were clear that he was clear, Tom, I could follow you and your mind working. Does this give you any better way of seeing how the writer of the second paper might have given himself a chance to see what he objects to in Thomas?"

"Yes. He could have gone to Thomas's sentences."

"Which is what the writer of this last paper has going for him that the writers of the first two don't. In both the first two papers the writers suggest that they don't have much confidence in Thomas, but they never face Thomas's prose squarely; they never get a chance to find out where they are with him, because they never give themselves a chance to see where he is or isn't. The writer of this paper, though, doesn't just nail Thomas for wandering or being contradictory or saying obvious things; he places what he's noticed in terms of a fear of commitment and as a lack of certainty, and shows that it's *that* which doesn't win his confidence."

"I like the way he talks about the difference between a professional tone and a professional voice."

"So do I. That's really a nicely controlled opening sentence. What do you like about it particularly?"

"I think it's what had me hung up with Thomas. I didn't like the way he sounded, but I didn't know how to say he was wrong. He does sound like a pro until you look at what he's actually saying—the way this guy does."

"And then compare it with the way he's trying to sound. Right, you are. Not very good advice is it, Thomas's I mean?"

"There's not really any advice here at all."

"Not any, at least to judge from the writer of this last paper, that anyone could use to make mean very much. I know what he means when he suggests that he feels empty because of the way he feels Thomas is."

ASSIGNMENT 14

What is the ideal audience
for J. D. Thomas?

Describe what you would consider to be the ideal audience for Thomas's statement. Are you a member of it? Be sure to explain your answer.

The most interesting papers to come in on Assignment 14 were those in which writers could admit an interest in Thomas's subject at the same time they expressed some sense of dissatisfaction with his treatment of it. Neither total rejection of the passage nor servile acceptance of it seemed to enable anyone to get very far. To claim no interest in what Thomas was talking about was to live in a tree. On the other hand, to claim discipleship simply because one was a student of technology was like imagining that the ideal audience for Billy Graham would be the Vatican Council. It was good to see how many more interesting papers there were than dull ones.

The first paper we worked with is a paradigm of a "misreading" of Thomas which appeared again and again. Thomas's passage does not offer a blueprint for the writing of a paper really, but a great many students read it this way, read Thomas as describing, if not prescribing, a form that a paper ought to take. It was a "mistake" I thought we ought to have a look at some of the implications of.

Thomas's statement is an automatic paper writer. I can use "ordinary sentences" and "ordinary language," press the button, and out it comes.

Since we are lazy, whenever we aren't met with success in something, we usually try to find an easier way of doing it.

Boy Scouts are required to know how to sharpen knives with a whetstone. After practicing this for a couple of hours, they would make an ideal audience for an automatic knife sharpener salesman. They know that they can't use one to pass their requirements, but they can still think that it would be a lot easier if they could. In the same manner, we have had five weeks study trying to become better writers. We haven't met with much more success than the average Boy Scout trying to sharpen his first knife, and we are thinking that there must be an easier way to write papers than the way we have been trying.

I recognize faults in Thomas's writing, but at the same time I want to agree with him. I know that "ordinary sentences" and "ordinary language" are not signs of good writing, but it looks like writing would be much more simple if I could write that way and get away with it.

"Is Thomas's statement an 'automatic paper writer'? Does it tell you *how* to write a paper?"

"Well, no. Not exactly."

"How come so many of you read it that way, then? An awful lot of you did. What I'm asking is whether there's anything in Thomas's passage that could lead someone to say it was an 'automatic paper writer'?"

"I read him that way. I guess because he tends to make writing sound simple, so easy to do."

"Where?"

"All through. It's a pitch. He reminds me of an advertisement."

"Can you find a place to show that?"

He couldn't, but someone else went to the last sentence of the passage.

"This 'medium of middle technical style'—he makes it sound as though nobody would have any trouble getting it."

"Just ask your friendly neighborhood English teacher?"

"Right. Like a box of soap you pick up at the supermarket."

"You mean that though Thomas doesn't offer a formula for writing exactly, it *seems* as though that's what he's doing?"

"Yes. I know he doesn't have all the answers when it comes to writing, and he never says that he does in so many words. But he acts like he does."

"OK. Which is the reason, maybe, that the writer of the second paper we looked at last time seemed to want to condemn Thomas's 'superiority' at the same time he had trouble finding a way to do it. Who do you think the audience for this ad is, by the way, this pitch? The writer here says he wants 'to agree with' Thomas, but he says, a little nervously I think, that that's because he's 'lazy.' Is it lazy people Thomas is writing for?"

"No. I think this guy's in the same bind as the guy who couldn't find a way to talk about Thomas's 'superiority.' "

"How do you mean?"

"He doesn't need to beat himself up this way. It isn't just that he's lazy. I don't think someone's lazy just because he wants to know how to do something, particularly when Thomas is there telling him all it's going to do for him."

"Why doesn't he buy Thomas, then?"

"Because he's been here, in this class. He knows too damn much, like the boy scout who knows he can't use the knife sharpener to pass the test."

"Even though he would still like to have it, or something like it?"

"Would like to have an easier way, anyway. Sure. I would, too. I still would."

"Well then, who *would* buy Thomas? Somebody who thought he could use a knife sharpener?"

"Somebody who didn't know he couldn't."

"Like somebody who wanted to learn about writing, but didn't know enough about it to know he couldn't learn about it this way?"

"Yes. Somebody he could suck in."

Somebody he could suck in indeed—by offering in terms of "is" and "it" a language as hypothetical as perpetual motion and yet which, it is claimed, can be placed like a Xerox copier "in the service of scientific and technological subject matters." Patent medicine. The revivalistic promise. The politician's smile. Youth, it turns out, is not wasted on the very young at all; they need every bit of it that they have.

We turned to the second paper, one which I admire particularly, in spite of the slightly thick phraseology of the last paragraph, for the way in which the writer earns his right to place Thomas's passage as he does.

Problem: how to describe an ideal audience without dragging out a Mickey Mouse characterization. Perhaps I can invert the assignment and describe why I *don't* buy Thomas's statement.

Of course when Thomas makes his offer of a middle technical style I'm intrigued; after all, I'm a technologist who has to communicate with other people. Because I'm involved in this, I want to learn how to communicate my interest and Thomas sounds sure enough of himself to give me some answers. But after reading his passage through a couple of times, I'm no longer sure that he is sure of what he's saying, or that he has any answers for me. For example, the "purely technical style" of the first paragraph, the style I'd use to talk to one of my "professional colleagues," in the third paragraph seems to be the sort of thing I'm to use to prepare "routine laboratory reports." Also, "the popular manner of expression" in paragraph one is renamed in paragraph two as a style of "extreme simplification" and "sometimes awkward repetition." Even middle technical style Thomas says first is to bring "the scientific knowledge of experts to mature readers and audiences," but finally is "particularly advantageous for a course in technical English." When I ask where all this leaves me, I find myself with a lot of double talk on how I should write technically but not too technically. What the paper boils down to is "Do good and avoid evil," which is fine advice but certainly not good advice. I read it once, go over it again and again, and ask "What did he tell me?" The answer is nothing.

If I weren't involved, if I could read through the paper once and say "Yeah, that's nice," and forget about it completely, then it would be a good case of Thomas's being ideal for the audience.

I began with the question of what, for the writer, the ideal audience for Thomas would seem to be.

"Well, he doesn't handle it that way exactly."

"What do you mean?"

"He writes more about how he doesn't buy Thomas than who Thomas is talking to."

"Why does he do that? Does he say?"

"Yes. In the first paragraph. He says he doesn't want to drag out a 'Mickey Mouse characterization.' "

"What's that mean?"

Someone else took over.

"I think he means he doesn't want to make Thomas's audience a bunch of slobs."

"Why not?"

"Because they aren't necessarily, like we said."

"*As* we said. He doesn't characterize Thomas's audience at all then?"

"Wait a minute," Sam broke in, "sure he does. In the last paragraph he says that Thomas's audience would be made up of people who don't give a damn. Maybe they don't know much about writing, but his point seems to be that they don't care whether they do or not."

132　　"People who can say 'yeah, that's nice' and then forget about it?"

"Right."

"The ideal audience *would be* made up of slobs, then?"

"Well, they'd have to be what this guy isn't."

"Which is?"

"Involved, like . . . *as* he says. Involved. Interested."

"Why didn't he just write a paper beating up Thomas's ideal audience then? Couldn't he have done that?"

"Sure he could have, but I think he's more interested in himself, the way Jim said. *As* Jim said."

"He could have if he'd wanted to sound the way Thomas does, maybe; if he'd wanted to talk generally about indifference and the rest. The risk you run in beating up a group of hypothetical slobs is becoming one. Maybe that's why he calls that way into Thomas a 'problem.' What makes you think he's interested in himself, Sam; because he tells you he's 'intrigued,' 'involved,' and the like?"

"He does more than just say it."

"How does he show it then?"

"The way he takes Thomas's prose apart. I don't think he could have found all those contradictions if he hadn't been interested."

"I don't either. And what about his tone? Is he sore at Thomas?"

"He's got every right to be the way he shows he's had to go over him again and again."

"Is he though?"

"Some, I guess. But he's more disappointed, I think. Sorry."

"That he hasn't gotten any advice?"

"That he hasn't gotten any he can use. I think that's why he says that Thomas's advice is 'fine'—he's being sarcastic there a little—but not 'good.' "

And this, of course, is why I too admire the paper. Because the writer's condemnation of Thomas, tinged as it is with something like regret, is what gives what he writes its quality of moral as well as intellectual seriousness.

ASSIGNMENT 15

T. Clifford Allbutt

Here is another statement about writing:

I must not tarry, however, to amuse myself and the reader with the sweet rhythms and tones of literary prose, nor even with the felicity of some medical prose, such as of Celsus, Watson, or Paget; I shall be better employed in this warning—that if we seek merely, or even mainly, for chiming words our message will decline; or, like a painted woman, become odious. When in Pater or Stevenson—not the worst of such sinners by any means—when even in their complexion I see the paint, I am Philistine enough to close the book. Sometimes, even in Virgil or Tennyson, in the lusciousness of form we tremble for the substance. If, as we read, we meditate first not on the bloom on the phrase but on the core of the thought, the art is good; if the phrase is all our charm, the art is decadent. In the sentence, "I will answer him according to the multitude of his idols,"—who, as he takes this message to himself, thinks then of the words of it? Or, to repeat Bright's well-known appeal: "The Angel of Death is abroad through the land; we may almost hear the beating of his wings," who of his hearers thought then of the words? When men began to think "How far away it would have been had the orator said the flapping of his wings," the spell was dissolving. This is literature however, and in letters sweetness is a hardly dispensable element; scientific prose is rarely literature. Literature is not merely the art of expression but also the creation of thought and emotion; a blend of strength of understanding with beauty of sound and cadence. Now and again, some great work even of science appears in a form which men will not forget, but ordinarily scientific language has to be a vehicle of correct thinking rather than a monument of thought; it is the sacrifice of the scientific treatise to discharge its burden into the stream of knowledge and then to be itself consigned to the cockloft.

Nevertheless, if, in saying that scientific prose should run pleasingly as well as forcibly and lucidly, I cannot claim for the first quality the importance of the other two, yet I cannot too often repeat that a harmoniously written paper will make its way when the same argument expressed in ugly phrase, when, as Ascham says, "It doth rather trot and hobble than run smoothly," has no appeal. Bad prose is bad business, even if the badness be nothing worse than discord. Let the ear then have its way as the phrases are conned; rougher rhythms and inharmonious sounds will drag; as we read we resent something wrong, so that we hesitate, and look back to see where was the jar or the limp. E.g. "A more acco*mmo*dating deno*min*ation is *comm*only given to it"; "*Gratitude* for his *rectitude*"; "an organi*sation*al centre of crystal*isation*"; "necessar*ily* tempora*ry*"; "*very* nea*rly* entire*ly*"; "so that it at once commenced"; "the native rulers were as a rule," etc. The cadence of a chief sentence in a recent report ended with "unsolicitedly." And does not this sentence remind us of a looper caterpillar?—"This revelation was the inauguration of a new dispensation, not the termination; also this new dispensation," etc., etc. "Of all I have *known* he could least hold his *own*," is not only an untimely assonance but imparts the alien rhythm of verse. Suppose you have written, "recurrences of this *kind* are *found* to *abound*"—you read it aloud; your ear is set on edge; where was it? You look back, and abate the nuisances. In a passage of otherwise pleasant prose this clause, "one venial *fault* *fr*ustrated the *effect*," displeased my ear though I suspect the jingle was deliberate.

Sir T. Clifford Allbutt, *Notes on the Composition of Scientific Papers* (1923)

Describe the voice you hear speaking in the passage above and its ideal audience.

Do you see yourself as a member of that audience?

The passage by Allbutt is one I knew the students were going to have to rise to. It's not something we could have touched without a substratum of agreement that writing about writing, like writing itself, can be taken seriously. The passage, in other words, is one that I hoped the *activity* of our class would have prepared us to have a conversation about. When art is the subject, it's the only kind of preparation that really means anything—the creation of an atmosphere, a tone, inside of which the possibility of respect and the need to repudiate are reflexes of one another.

Most of the papers were attempts to come to terms with Allbutt as a writer. There were, of course, those who in objecting to his idiom simply gave up on him. Thus Allbutt became a name-dropper, a pedant, unconscionably fancy. He used too many metaphors, too many examples. His sentences were hard to read. I didn't bother to reproduce such a paper, though I did read one out loud to start the class, a very sniffy and disparaging dismissal of Allbutt as "trying to pull a snow job." Without commenting on what I'd read, I went straight to what I'd mimeographed for us to work with, with no more of a lead-in than the question of whether it were possible to read Allbutt another way and of how that way of reading might be defended.

We began with the opening paragraph of a paper that unfortunately never went on to live up to its own promise:

> You have to make friends with this type of writing. When I looked
> at this passage and didn't understand it, I felt that it was my fault
> instead of the fault of the passage. I looked at myself instead of the author.
> Upon closer reading the quotations make more and more sense; they
> become expressive examples of what the author is saying. Instead of
> merely stating what seem to him obvious facts, Allbutt uses the thoughts
> and feelings of the reader to make him convince himself. The reader
> is made a thinking partner in the communication process.

I had no idea of exactly what part of the passage the writer was referring to; he never went on to specify anything in Allbutt which would have enabled him to talk about what he heard. But I was interested in whether the *class* could find a section of Allbutt with which to explore the writer's opening metaphor, whether they could locate anything in the passage which could legitimately be said to lead a reader to impugn his own understanding rather than Allbutt's prose.

"Let's take it first from the 'snow job' point of view. What is it that Allbutt does which looks at first like a snow job tactic?"

"All those quotes . . . I mean quotations, he uses."

"Such as?"

"Well, the one from Ascham, for example: '. . . Yet I cannot too often repeat that a harmoniously written paper will make its way when the same argument expressed in ugly phrase, when, as Ascham says, "It doth rather trot and hobble than run smoothly," has no appeal.' "

"What makes that look like he's trying a snow job?"

"I'd never heard of Ascham, for one thing."

"Did you look him up?"

"In the dictionary, yes. He was one of Queen Elizabeth's teachers. A scholar and a writer, it said."

"A scientist?"

"No, he wasn't. At least the dictionary didn't say he was."

"Was Allbutt?"

"Yes, in a way. He was a doctor."

"Yet he quotes Ascham. Just to be impressive?"

"I don't think so. That's why I don't think Allbutt's just doing a snow job. I mean he could have picked a more famous man if he was just out to dig up impressive quotations. And he could have picked one from a scientist. Besides, the phrase doesn't look like the kind of thing he could have dug up. I have a feeling that he remembered it."

"And even if he did dig it up he must have gone to some trouble to do it. OK. If that isn't a snow job, then what do you call what he's doing?"

"I think he really believes in what he's saying."

"He really believes that 'bad prose *is* bad business'?"

"Right. I think he really means that, if he goes to all the trouble he does to say it."

"And to pull in as many examples of badness as he does, and to talk about an element of writing that he admits is minor, particularly in what he calls 'scientific prose.' What kind of a man would be concerned with the minor aspects of a subject this way, with getting the details right?"

"Somebody who really cared about the subject, I guess."

"An amateur?"

"He looks like a pro to me."

We then went to Allbutt's mention of Celsus, Watson, and Paget in the first sentence, and I asked the students how their responses to his use of names might have been different if the sentence had named the standard literary figures: "I must not tarry, however, to amuse myself and the reader with the sweet rhythms and tones of literary prose such as of Shakespeare, Milton, and Wordsworth, nor even with the felicity of some medical prose; I shall be better employed. . . ." In the light of where we had just been, they could see that obvious references to well-known literary figures might easily have read as no more than name-dropping. Allbutt's use of Celsus, Watson, and Paget, however—the names function as metaphors really—is what helps to produce the illusion of a sensibility that is informed, discriminating, yet unpedantic (no pedant would have buried his pedantry in such a parenthetical aside). The illusion is deepened at the same time it is extended by the way in which Allbutt qualifies his references to Pater and Stevenson in the next sentence (and to Virgil and Tennyson in the sentence following that)—"when . . . not the worst" and "Sometimes, even"—a technique which suggests both the speaker's fair-mindedness and his capacity for respect.

As an example of what the writer of the first selection might have meant by "the reader ['s being] made a thinking partner in the communication process," we turned to a section of another paper:

Allbutt definitely shows, but never shows off, his ear for good prose; and this is crucial in convincing me that he's not talking down to his audience. In fact he is talking directly to me. "Suppose you have written, 'recurrences of this *kind* are *found* to *abound*'—you read it aloud; your ear is set on edge; where was it? You look back, and abate the nuisances." I'm complimented; here I am a literate person doing some "abating," but at the same time not a dilettante because I realize that what I'm abating is merely a "nuisance." A man of less highly refined sensibilities might have written, "Such assonances as these destroy the smooth flow of a sentence and should be eliminated from all good and proper English compositional forms."

"Does the writer here convince you that he's convinced that Allbutt isn't talking down to him?"

"He sure does. I'm not sure what he means by 'dilettante' exactly, but I see what he means by saying he's 'complimented.' At least I think I do."

"What does he mean, do you think?"

"Well, I think he means that Allbutt gives him some credit for hearing what's wrong in the sentence and lets him get rid of it by himself."

"Pays him the compliment of saying that he's already done it in a way, too."

"Yes. It's one pro talking to another, in a way. I'm given credit for knowing what a 'nuisance' is—*and* for knowing how to get rid of it."

The first half of the first full paper we worked with that period creates another writer who convinces me he's hearing what he claims to be hearing:

The voice I hear in Allbutt's statement is one of overwhelming, but not overweening, confidence. The roll of the sentences suggests the prose of John Donne: "We *tremble* for the substance." "Who of his hearers thought *then* of the words?" This is an English voice, rich in past English literature: "I shall be better employed. . . ." It is this fluency, the ease with which Allbutt's words and sentences flow together without hiding their content, that denotes a skill that ~~deserves~~ wins my confidence. "If, as we read, we meditate first not on the bloom of the phrase but on the core of the thought, the art is good; if the phrase is all our charm, the art is decadent." This is not the pedantic voice of Thomas speaking, but

138 it's at least as professional a one which "will make its way when the same argument expressed in ugly phrase has no appeal" and convinces me of its sincerity while I enjoy listening to it. Another sign of the professionalism of the voice is the tongue-in-cheek humor shown in its metaphors. Only a superior and supremely confident writer could afford the wit contained in phrases like "—when even in their complexion I see the paint, I am Philistine enough to close the book."

In Allbutt's writing the humor ("In a passage of otherwise pleasant prose . . .") and palatable presentation of truisms ("it is the sacrifice of the scientific treatise to discharge its burden into the stream of knowledge and then to be itself consigned to the cockloft.") make his superiority seem natural, unassumed, right. The reader comes to the conclusion of the writer's superiority by himself. This is in revealing contrast to what one student pointed out about Thomas, saying "The way in which he exploits his knowledge makes me as uncomfortable as someone who makes up a superior voice."

Pleasing, Clear, and Coherent as it is, Allbutt's writing has its chief value to me in the suggestions and comments it has to offer. While some of these may seem obvious or superfluous, no good technical writer ignores them. In condensed form, these include:

1) Good technical writing never calls the reader's attention from the message to the style or words with which it is written.

2) Scientific writing, unlike literature, is not an art of expression with the creation of thought and emotion as its objective, but is a vehicle of correct thinking rather than a monument of thought.

3) While not more important than the force and lucidity of a paper, its polish and harmony are important, as a concept expressed smoothly is more likely to be accepted than the same one presented roughly.

In addition to merely stating his thoughts on the subject of technical writing, Allbutt uses them effectively in his writing, which lends conviction to his argument and convinces me that I should and would use any suggestions he has to offer.

An ideal audience for this statement would be anyone interested in improving his writing (in any field but literature). Since I am in that category, I am a member of that audience.

I began by asking what kind of an ear the writer seemed to have.

"A really good one. I like the way *he* uses quotations."

"What do you mean, 'the way *he* uses them'? Isn't he just making statements and giving examples?"

"He is, yes, but he's doing a little more than that, just the way Allbutt is. He's weaving Allbutt into his own stuff."

"Weaving?"

"Sure. Look at where he compares Allbutt with Thomas: 'It's at least as professional a one which "will make its way when the same argument expressed in ugly phrase has no appeal." ' That's his thought, but he uses Allbutt to make the point."

"I see what you mean. He's made friends with the writing, become partners with it in a way. He enacts the claim that he enjoys listening to Allbutt, and that he admires him. Does he do this in any other way in that first paragraph?"

" 'Any other way'? I don't follow you."

"I was thinking of the underlined words. They aren't underlined in Allbutt: 'tremble' and 'then.' "

"You mean it's the way he gets the money up for using John Donne?"

"Something like that, I think; for me as a reader, anyway. It also gets the money up for 'this is an English voice, rich in past English literature.' If he'd had those remarks alone, without the quotations, or even if he'd had them alone *with* the quotations but without the underlinings, I wouldn't have been nearly so ready as I am to believe that he's hearing something he's having a hell of a time putting his finger on. I'm not sure I get exactly what he means about Donne and Englishness, but as the writer of the first paper says about his relation to Allbutt, I feel that my not getting *this* writer is my fault. And there's one other thing. You see where he writes 'deserves' but then cuts it and replaces it with 'wins' in his first paragraph? Why do you think he did that?"

"It sounds better the second way."

"Why?"

"It's hard to say exactly, but it does."

" 'Denotes'–'deserves'?"

"I see, the rhyme or something. The alliteration."

"Which might have, as Allbutt says, 'displeased [his] ear' because 'the jingle was[n't] deliberate.' That's a guess, of course, but it's another way I'd use to make a case for the writer's weaving of Allbutt into his own stuff. What about the second half of this paper, which no one has mentioned yet; the 'condensed form' of Allbutt's suggestions? Is there any difference between this writer's condensation and what Allbutt says?"

"These three points sound a lot like Thomas."

"How so?"

"I think they *are* 'obvious,' as he says."

"And 'superfluous'?"

"In a way. You could condense them even further if you wanted to."

"To what?"

"Well, number One says, 'Be Clear'; Two says, 'Be Correct'; Three, 'Be Polished.' "

"OK. Now, what about Allbutt? When you condense his sentence about the bloom on the phrase to a matter of Being Clear, do you change anything?"

One student mentioned the loss of the metaphor, but that was about as far as anyone could go. I referred them back to the section of the statement of the course in which I'd talked about everyone's knowing that "Good Writing should be Clear, Coherent and somehow Pleasing to the reader," and moving down a sentence read off the metaphor I'd used for the construction of a certain kind of paragraph, one put together "as if it were a building made of building blocks." What was the difference between that metaphor and Allbutt's, the metaphor of a plant?

"A plant's alive. A building isn't."

"And what's the most important part of a plant? The flower? The roots? The leaves?"

"They're all important. Equally. You can't talk about how a plant works without mentioning all of those things."

"Then what's Allbutt suggesting about writing when he uses the metaphor of a plant to describe it?"

"OK. That writing is all one, style and message and the rest. But if that *is* what he's getting at, how come he says that no one thought of Bright's words when they first heard them? Isn't he separating words and meaning there?"

"Let's look at the phrasing exactly: 'who of his hearers thought then of the words.' You take that to mean that words and meaning are being separated?"

"OK. I'm probably wrong, but I don't see how yet. I did read the sentence to mean that the words weren't important, yes."

"Come on, Tom, 'wrong.' Look. I want to make a *case* for another way of understanding it, OK? Now, have you ever had a remark made to you, or heard one, that seemed so right, so appropriate to the occasion, that you felt under what Allbutt calls a 'spell'?"

"I remember Kennedy's 'Ask not what your country can do for you; ask rather what you can do for your country.' "

"And yet you remember the words?"

"Yes."

"And exactly?"

"I think so, yes."

"OK. Then maybe there's a chance that the words are important precisely because they produce a sense of their own *unimportance*. It's like an actor who is so good he can make you forget he's acting—which is *really* acting. I don't know for sure of course; there's no place you can look any of this up; but I think that that may be what Allbutt is getting at in saying that with good writing 'we meditate *first* not on the bloom on the phrase but on the core of the thought,' whereas with 'decadent' art 'the phrase is *all* our charm.' In other words, he doesn't, at least for me, say that Bright's words didn't matter, but that they were so damned good that no one who heard them thought *then,* at that moment, of the words as words."

The second complete paper we dealt with that period I didn't have enough time to do justice to. I think the writer of it is wrong about Allbutt, but his ability to hear and the attempt he makes to articulate what he hears is what I wanted to praise:

This seems to be a subtle satire on various mistakes in technical writing. The author ingeniously shows how absurd lofty expressions can sound when used at the wrong time. He condemns a type of expression by using the very language and form which is associated with that which he condemns.

He denounces unnecessary musical effects with "if we seek *merely* or even *mainly* for chiming words. . . ." In telling how to detect a word which is inappropriate he says: "as we read we resent something wrong . . . and look back to see where was the jar or the limp"—I certainly looked back at those words. In denouncing "poetic" prose, he says: "in the lusciousness of the form we tremble for the substance . . . if the phrase is all our charm, the art is decadent." Throughout the article he praises clarity, and yet I was forced to read it several times before I began to understand it.

His complicated use of words which makes them seem archaic and perhaps his knighthood make me imagine him as a contemporary of Rutherford or maybe Maxwell. The audience which seems ideal for him is the same one which would listen to a lecture delivered by one of the latter two, a group of old, bearded, but sharp-witted gentlemen. I would like to include myself among that audience, however, because he certainly amused me with "felicitous prose."

There is no question that Allbutt makes use of a variety of rhetorical devices, sometimes with witty intent—"the jar or the limp," "a looper caterpillar"—but I understand the devices as adjuncts of meaning rather than uncomplicated self-parodies, ends in themselves. I can agree that there is alliteration in a phrase such as "rougher rhythms" or "as we read we resent." But I do not meditate first on the bloom on the phrase. I do not think then of the words that way.

I read the paper through and asked the same question about it I had about the last one: what kind of an ear does the writer seem to have?

"I can see what he means. He underlines the same way the last guy did, and he's got plenty of money up."

"Right you are. Do you think the writer's right about Allbutt, that he's written a 'satire,' a parody of sorts?"

"I don't know. He could be right, I guess."

"How would you make up your mind?"

"I don't know."

"Well, if this is a satire," I said, "is it consistently satiric? Do you think the passage is written to be deliberately obscure, for example?"

"No. I don't think so."

We were opening up again, but from another angle, the question of the fallacy of imitative form, but I knew there wasn't enough time left in the period for me to lead the class into posing and addressing that question for themselves. So I went directly to Allbutt's sentence "Bad prose is bad business, even if the badness is nothing worse than discord" and put my questions about it rhetorically. What about the alliteration there, the repetition? Was the rhetoric of it ironic or not? I then explained how I saw the sentence's working, how the two "bads" in the first clause force a reader into yoking "prose" with "business" by setting up the expectation of a pattern upset by a different second term. The first part of the sentence is fused with the second in the word "badness," picking up both the earlier "bads" and the "ness" ending of the different second term—all of which lends a weight to "discord" at the end of the sentence which the complementary qualification of "nothing worse than" keeps from being exaggerated.

"So when it comes to the question of whether the writer of this paper is right or wrong," I concluded, "I'd say that for me his *terminology* would be wrong. I don't read the rhetoric of that sentence, or of a lot of the other sentences in Allbutt, as ironic. But I wouldn't have read them as well as I think I do now had I not been forced, as this paper forces me, into explaining to myself how I *do* read them. In the face of that, I think I'd be ungrateful to see the rightness or wrongness of this writer's argument as anything other than finally irrelevant."

ASSIGNMENT 16

How helpful are Thomas
and Allbutt to a writer?

*To what extent and in what ways do you find the statements of Thomas
and Allbutt helpful to you as a writer?*

What is there you wish to know about writing that they do not tell you?

How are you going about getting it?

It was not until I had read the papers addressed to Assignment 16
that I saw how bad an assignment it is. The core of the difficulty, I
think, is that I'm of no help to the students in setting up the issue of
the Assignment as a writing problem. I never really framed what I
guess I must simply have vaguely hoped the students would see as its
challenge: that since the Answers to the Assignment's questions can
have validity only to the extent that an individual writer makes them
into answers for himself, the problem for each writer is going to be one
of how to dramatize *his* wanting, *his* getting, in terms of his *own*
writing experience. Ideally then, what I should have had the students
do was find a way of enacting the truisms of a writer's relationship to
his writing that, in consequence of that enactment, a reader could
experience as more than truisms. At least I might have set things up
so as to have given the students a chance to realize how a way of getting what in their writing they were claiming to need and want was to
make that writing the best possible expression of both. Also, in my

144   writing of the Assignment I should have been a great deal more explicit than I was in inviting the students to see a connection between the passages by Thomas and Allbutt and our consideration of good advice as involving the illusion of an identity shared through the sharing of a language. After reading the students' papers I drafted an assignment that I think is closer to the sort of thing I should have given them to begin with:

> *Both Thomas and Allbutt could be said to be offering a kind of advice about writing. Neither of their passages tells you how to write exactly (though this may sometimes be the illusion they create), but both could be said to be talking generally about things that someone wanting to learn to write might well be interested in.*
>
> *Think back over our work with the nominal subject of advice. From such a perspective, is there any way in which you can see the advice of Thomas or Allbutt as helpful to you as a writer? Do you find the advice of one more helpful than that of the other? However you choose to address these questions, make clear what you mean by "helpful."*
>
> *But whatever help Thomas and Allbutt may be said to be, neither passage tells you what you really want to know about writing, does it? What is it that you really want to know? How are you going about getting it?*
>
> *Before you make up your mind just how you want to address these final and very difficult questions, you might consider whether you wish to say only that you want very badly to improve your own writing, and that practice makes better if not perfect. Are you sure you can do justice to this matter with such simple moral language? Do you really want to bother with the clichés? If you can't just say you're working very hard and say very much of anything for yourself, what can you do?*
>
> *Perhaps no easy way of dealing with the problem here occurs to you immediately. What then? Are you satisfied to settle for silence?*

Having to work with the Assignment I'd written and distributed to the class landed me in a double bind. Not only was the Assignment itself useless as a way into what the students had understandably failed to make it mean, but I also found nothing in any of the papers that I could use to create the problem of it as I should have created it in the first place. No one had found a way of talking about "helpful" which rose much above a demand for the hammerishly utilitarian ("Neither Thomas nor Allbutt teaches me to use the semicolon"); no one could make what he really wanted to know about writing into much more than a statement ("What I really want to learn is how to improve my *own* writing"). The Answers everyone had, but because no one had any more than this, no one had much of anything.

For class, on one page I mimeographed a student paper and the Assignment as I had rewritten it above. On a second page I remimeographed Assignment 6 and also that Assignment as I had rewritten it (see pages 60–61). At the beginning of class I passed out only the mimeographed sheet containing the student paper and the rewritten version of Assignment 16. The student paper I chose was the most representative sampling I could find of the general mediocrity:

Thomas's and Allbutt's statements are of little help to me as a writer. Allbutt says not to use excessive flowery language, rhythm, and alliteration. Thomas suggests using the middle technical style which doesn't oversimplify the subject or snow the reader. While both of these ideas are good, I have heard them from almost every English teacher I have ever had.

When it comes down to writing sentences, Thomas and Allbutt have told me nothing that I didn't already know. I have always been able to form opinions on things I understood, but to put them into words is something else. What I need in writing is the ability which we have said cannot be taught. The practice in this course seems to be the only way I have a chance of improving my writing. If I do improve, it will not be from suggestions like those from Thomas and Allbutt.

I began with the implications of the last sentence of the paper, which is not quite the fallout shelter that I think the student imagined it was going to be when he wrote it, at least not in context.

"What suggestions, to judge from the rest of the paper, do you think this writer *would* consider helpful when it comes to improving his writing?"

"I don't think he knows."

"How do you mean?"

"Maybe I'm just talking about myself here, that I'm not sure I know what a helpful suggestion would be, but it's the way this guy goes at things. No, Thomas and Allbutt aren't much help, he says, and what he needs is practice, and that's about it. That's about all he says."

"Not much sweat on the sentences, you mean?"

"None at all really. There's nothing in this paper that *I* didn't already know either. Or that anyone else didn't."

"Including the writer. OK. I follow you. But that's more an argument that the writer didn't care much about writing this particular paper than that he doesn't know what would be helpful advice about writing, isn't it? He does mention the practice of the course."

"Sure he does, but who couldn't? I said the same thing, but that's just the trouble. We probably all said the same thing."

"And sounded pretty much the same way in saying it. Yes, you did."

"OK. But what the hell else *is* there to say? Thomas and Allbutt *don't* tell me how to improve my writing. I *am* trying to get it by practicing. I know what's wrong with saying that, but I don't know what else to say."

"Well, is there any difference between one kind of practice and another?"

"Of course there is. I thought of that, too. I don't need any more practice in writing Thomas's way, if that's what you mean. Neither does this guy. But how do I explain what another kind of practice is? How would I explain what I'm getting out of a course like this, for God's sake? Sometimes I wonder myself."

"How about finding a way of saying that, Kurt, with just that tone?"

"What do you mean?"

As a way of explaining myself, I read the Assignment aloud as I'd rewritten it and asked whether the terms of it seemed to have any bearing on where we were.

"Well, this way at least you admit that the question's a tough one."

"I do that. Score one. I mean, do the terms of the Assignment, written this way, have any specific relevance to the question I put to Kurt about finding a way of saying what he was saying? Look at the last sentence of the next to last paragraph of it: 'If you can't just *say* you're working very hard and say much of anything for yourself, what can you do?'"

"Kurt didn't say he was working very hard."

"Right. He didn't *say* that. He didn't say he was sore either. Was he?"

"He sounded it."

"You mean he said it without saying it. He showed it. And he did a damn sight better than just saying 'I'm angry about this Assignment,' or 'with you' or 'with the course.' He behaved in such a way as to let *me* say it, to let us say it. Did *that* say anything about his working hard?"

"Sure it did," said someone else. "He wouldn't have been angry if he hadn't worked."

"Any other way he showed he'd worked?"

"Yeah. He was one step ahead of you on those questions about practice."

"Score another. On the whole question of practice, including the fact that everybody who opted to talk that way sounded like everybody else."

"So in other words to write about what you wanted with writing, you'd have to show you already *had* what you wanted?"

"Well, maybe to write about getting what you wanted, improvement or whatever, you'd have to write something that would enable someone *else* to say, 'I can see he's practicing, and how he's practicing. I can see that "practice" here means "getting." ' You'd have to make the term 'practice' mean *your* practice, *your* getting, not just anyone's."

"And you'd have to do it indirectly. You couldn't just say it."

"I think so, by means of a metaphor of some sort, an order of words that means more than it says, the way Kurt's being ahead of me back there showed that he'd worked. This is why I find the 'advice' of Allbutt worth so much more than Thomas's. No, Allbutt doesn't teach me how to use the comma, and he doesn't teach me how to write either, not any more than the fellow's helping the guy with the math problem in the study lounge solved the problem for him. But the way Allbutt moves around with language creates the image of someone in there huff-puffing, sweating it out with words in the same way I have to when I write—it's *that* I find helpful, somehow. He doesn't make writing easier, but he makes it easier to work at by showing me how hard he knows it is—if that makes any sense."

"The way Kurt's being angry about this Assignment makes me feel better."

"So long as by 'better' you mean more than satisfied with having talked in generalizations, yes."

"Could I ask you one question?"

"Sure, shoot."

"Why didn't you use this Assignment instead of the one you gave us?"

"Do you think it's a better Assignment than the one I gave you to work with?"

"Obviously. Don't you?"

"Of course I do. My question now is how you know it's better."

"I think it gives me a better idea of how to go about writing a paper for it."

"OK. That's one of the reasons why it's better. My question is still how you see that."

"How? Well, it's because we've talked about it, I suppose."

"You mean things get clearer after we talk about them?"

"Sometimes. Not always. Not for me, anyway. But this time they did."

"They did this time for me too—and by 'this time' I mean when I was reading your papers as well as now. Not easier, maybe. Not any more than Allbutt's advice makes writing easier. But clearer. Which is how I came up with the second version of the Assignment. That version, the one I should have given you to work with, I didn't know enough to be able to write until I'd had a chance to—as you put it—talk about things, until I'd had a chance to use your papers to see where I'd gone wrong. It happened the same way once before."

I then passed out the two versions of Assignment 6 and explained why the original version of that Assignment had also been a bad one.

"And you didn't say anything then about why you thought Assignment 6 was bad, because you didn't think we'd have understood what you were talking about?"

"Not exactly. You'd have understood why the Assignment was bad, I think. But a month ago we didn't have a way of making our seeing that it was bad *mean* as much as we do now. Would you have believed me if I'd simply said to you then, for example, that going over your papers had helped me to see a lot, helped me to get things clearer?"

"I see what you mean. We hadn't had a chance to talk about enough things then."

"And we hadn't had a chance to talk about things enough either. I needed to develop a way of *showing* you I'm learning from what we're doing, and that that learning for me too involves making mistakes, falling on my face sometimes. I needed a way of showing you that even if we're not in the same boat, we've all got the same weather to worry about."

ASSIGNMENT 17

Charles Darwin

Here is a passage written by a scientist:

It is interesting to contemplate a tangled bank, clothed with many plants of many kinds, with birds singing on the bushes, with various insects flitting about, and with worms crawling through the damp earth, and to reflect that these elaborately constructed forms, so different from each other, and dependent upon each other in so complex a manner, have all been produced by laws acting around us. These laws, taken in the largest sense, being Growth and Reproduction; Inheritance, which is almost implied by Reproduction; Variability, from the indirect and direct action of the conditions of life, and from use and disuse: a Ratio of Increase so high as to lead to a Struggle for Life, and as a consequence to Natural Selection, entailing Divergence of Character and the Extinction of less-improved forms. Thus, from the war of nature, from famine and death, the most exalted object which we are capable of conceiving, namely, the production of the higher animals, directly follows. There is grandeur in this view of life, with its several powers, having been originally breathed by the Creator into a few forms, or into one; and that, whilst this planet has gone cycling on according to the fixed law of gravity, from so simple a beginning endless forms most beautiful and most wonderful have been, and are being evolved.

Charles Darwin, On the Origin of Species

Describe the sensibility of the writer of the paragraph above as you construct it from the voice you hear speaking and the audience you imagine for it.

What is Darwin's achievement in this passage? For what do you praise him?

150   The challenge in writing about the selection from Darwin is one of finding terms that will do justice simultaneously to both its multiplicity and its wholeness, for the most remarkable feature of the passage is its fusion of a scientist's seeing, a poet's seeing, a man's seeing, into the illusion of a single identity. It is a gathering limned in the very shape of Darwin's prose, where all separateness moves to unity; what appears diverse and tangled turns out to be interconnected, complexly dependent. Hence one thing "leads to" another, which, in its turn, has "a consequence," which then "entails" something else; a law called "Inheritance" "is almost implied by" another law called "Reproduction"; "from" one phenomenon ("the war of nature") metamorphized into another ("famine and death") a still different phenomenon "directly follows." Similarly, the metaphoric transformation of a "tangled bank" into an ordered world simultaneously links the terrestrial with the cosmic, the beginning of time with infinity, the sensuous with the abstract, variety with oneness, death with life. The cycles loop to embrace each other like Möbius curves; the logical, the metaphorical, the aesthetic, the scientific, the spiritual in becoming one also become poetic vision. The voice of Darwin is in fact the voice of a poet, which, throughout the passage, from the serene humility of "It is interesting" to the liturgical reverence of "from so simple a beginning endless forms most beautiful and most wonderful have been, and are being evolved" speaks with the supreme selflessness of one who contemplates what he has created less as a testament to his powers of creativity than as a tribute to the mystery of the creative process. By finding as he does the ungraven image of God in the vastness of time and space before which he stands in wonder, Darwin elevates what could have been mere self-adulation into praise of himself as a praiser. The voice of the passage is not only the voice of a poet then, but of one who has attained that deep "impersonal center" which, as Eliot says, no poet can reach "without surrendering himself wholly to the work to be done." The emergence of the self through its suppression, victory through surrender—this is Darwin's achievement, and there is grandeur in his view.

Although in the students' papers there was some skittering into irrelevancy ("Not until Charles Darwin's Theory of Evolution did the world of science . . ."), most writers worked hard to come to terms with Darwin's prose. There was, for example, a great deal of talk about something called "literary devices" and Darwin's ability to "combine logic and emotion" in the passage. But the students had difficulty moving their observations beyond the level of statement (Here is a metaphor), and, understandably, trouble gathering their isolated insights into something like a whole response to Darwin's wholeness.

I began class with a section of a paper in which a writer, at a convenient distance from Darwin's language, seems to me to miss the special quality of Evolution's thereness as Darwin's sentences render it:

The sense of Darwin's statement is that the complex order of life has been produced by some scientific law. On the contrary, however, it is the fact that nature is ordered that makes man produce the scientific law. Nature was ordered a long time before Darwin produced the Darwinian Theory.

Darwin compounds this error further down on the page: "Thus, from the war of nature, from famine and death, the most exalted object which we are capable of conceiving, namely, the production of the higher animals, directly follows." Darwin seems to be saying that *because* of his theory we're able to contemplate these exalted objects. If Darwin said that his theories helped us to conceive of the mechanism which produced the higher animals, then I could buy that statement.

Was it true, I asked, that men produced scientific laws as a result of nature's being ordered; that nature had been ordered, in the way that the writer of these paragraphs seems to assume it was, a long time before Darwin produced the Darwinian theory?

"No, it isn't true, not this way, not if, as we've said, you could imagine the earth going around the sun or the sun going around the earth and get a rocket to the moon either way. It seems to me that scientific laws are what produce the order."

"Did Darwin order nature, then?"

"In effect he did, yes."

"Can you show this process of ordering taking place in the passage anywhere?"

"Yes, in the sentence where he talks about Growth and Reproduction and Inheritance and the rest. He's ordering there."

"How?"

"Well, in the way he strings them together, for one thing."

"OK. In the linkings, this thing's leading to that thing's entailing something else and so on. What about the terms themselves, though? What it is that's getting linked with what? What's the difference, for example, between seeing the world of nature as something expressing

152   the laws of Growth and Inheritance and Variability as opposed to seeing it as an expression of famine and death, or as a war?"

"Well, if nature is a scene only of famine and death and war, it's
pretty damned depressing."

"And purposeless and mindless and chaotic, right you are. So it's in
Darwin's terms themselves that I'd see ordering, as well as in the way
he links them together. He seems almost dismissive of such Themetalk
as war of nature and famine and death, particularly in the way he
concludes the sentence."

"I see what you mean, I think. It's as though he were saying: 'Look,
this whole thing was once terrible, I mean seen as terrible, but if you
look at the terribleness another way you can see that it isn't terrible at
all. Without it, man wouldn't even be here.' "

"Would that mean, then, that Darwin was saying that it's *because*
of his theory [that] we're able to contemplate' the production of the
higher animals the way the writer of this paper says he is?"

"You know, it's funny. That's true. I mean it *is* because of Darwin's
theory that we can look on nature as we do. But Darwin doesn't say
that exactly."

"You mean as Darwin writes the passage it's the laws which do the
producing, not the man?"

"Right, but the man discovered the laws, so in another way it *is*
because of his theory that we can see what we do."

"And in still another way what we 'see' is what this writer calls 'the
mechanism which produced the higher animals.' So the theory isn't
as important as the mechanism."

"Yeah, but without the theory there wouldn't be a mechanism."

"And around and around endlessly, which is why, maybe, you speak
of Darwin's 'discovering' the laws. It's an appropriate term. If I ask
myself whether Darwin discovered the laws or whether he invented
them, I'd have to say that he invented them. But as a reader of this
passage I see him describing himself, offering himself, more as a dis-
coverer than an inventor, and as someone serving something larger
than he is, one who 'contemplates' as much as he 'reflects' and 'takes.'
No, Darwin doesn't say that his theory ordered nature, exactly. He
does better than that. He talks in such a way as to make me say it—the
way Kurt last time talked in such a way as to make us say he was
working."

From this conversation it was an easy step to papers two and three,
both of which, although in different ways, create impressive images of

their writers through the ways they seek to come to terms with Darwin's image of a consecrated life.

The voice I hear in Darwin's *Origin of Species* is one of knowledge and respect. I call it knowledge because Darwin has organized all his observations on a difficult subject to explain. I call it respect because Darwin knows he is trying to discuss the power of Nature with human terms. The language he uses expresses his sense of his own inadequacy as an interpreter.

His first sentence, in which he tells the reader "it is interesting to contemplate a tangled bank, clothed with many plants of many kinds, with birds singing on the bushes, etc." has nothing outstanding about it. It might even be considered childish. But there is something about that sentence that I accept and like. He is using "tangled . . . singing . . . flitting . . . and crawling" to illustrate the delicacy of the simpler forms of life; and yet he shows his admiration for it by finishing the sentence with references to "elaborately constructed forms . . . dependent in so complex a manner. . . ."

In the second sentence Darwin intensifies his respect by speaking of the laws of Nature with capital letters. In the third and fourth he speaks of the "most exalted object we are capable of conceiving, . . . grandeur in this view of life . . . originally breathed by the Creator." Nature is treated like something kingly or, better yet, the work of God. And in the last sentence Darwin admits the inadequacy of the laws of science to explain totally the evolution of forms. "Most beautiful and most wonderful" I don't question because, considering the style above, any other phrase would fail to maintain the voice.

Darwin is speaking to an audience which is going to be hard to convince. For years, only the religious interpretation of evolution existed. Darwin had the task of spanning the gap between religious explanation and scientific explanation. To do so he used a style which would give the impression of the divine relationship of evolution to science. Darwin achieves this connection without sacrificing his scientific theory. Furthermore, unlike Thomas who didn't recognize that you couldn't explain the unexplainable, Darwin sees the futility of total explanation of evolution and places his method of explanation, science, rightly in second place. I praise him for his awareness in handling the topic.

I began with what for me is the core of the paper, the writer's conception of Darwin as respectful in admitting "the inadequacy of the laws of science to explain totally the evolution of forms." What exactly did the writer mean by saying that Darwin's language "expresses his sense of his own inadequacy as an interpreter"? Where, specifically, in the last sentence of the passage was the admission of "the inadequacy of the laws of science"?

"I think I see what he means about Darwin's last sentence."

"Go ahead."

" 'Endless.' 'Endless forms.' There's no limit, particularly since it's all still going on and always will be. No limit in number, in quality, or anything. That's something science is inadequate in the face of."

"OK. And what about 'into a few forms, *or* into one'? It's that 'or,' the force of it, that this paper made me feel the function of in Darwin's prose. Maybe it was just one life form from which everything started, maybe it was several. There's no way for science, at least according to Darwin, to know for sure."

"What about 'whilst this planet has gone cycling on according to the fixed law of gravity'?" said someone else.

"I'm not sure I see what you mean," I said. "How are you reading that?"

"Well, doesn't Darwin mean something like even though the world has been spinning on predictably since the beginning of things, inside the law that keeps it going on and on there's all kinds of changing and developing that science can't fully explain?"

"Dan's notion of 'endless forms.' I see what you mean. Maybe so. Maybe that's why the writer of the paper feels the rightness of 'most beautiful and most wonderful' in the sentence too. They're not very scientific terms, but they seem to be terms that have to take over when science doesn't provide any. Also, maybe 'with its several powers' is another reference to your point about all kinds of change and development, Sam. Maybe life has powers that haven't been worked out yet. Or that can't be. All life forms are connected, as the writer shows in his second paragraph where he points out that Darwin makes the simple and the complex dependent upon each other, but the connection itself, in spite of the laws that determine it, is mysterious. So it's not only *Darwin* as an interpreter who is inadequate, it's 'his method of explanation, science,' science itself, that's inadequate."

Paper three is a different sort of tribute to Darwin, an emulation of his method which fuses the writer's understanding of Darwin with his admiration for Darwin's achievement as an artist:

Rather than exhibiting a single sensitivity, the conclusion of *Origin of Species* develops three levels of perception: the scientist, philosopher, and writer are interwoven in a manner which characterizes

Darwin the man. It is interesting to contemplate (without disrespect) this tangled paragraph, clothed with ideas of many different kinds, with the sensibilities of three people flitting through it, and to reflect that these elaborately constructed sentences and concepts, so different from each other, and dependent upon each other in so complex a manner, have all been produced by the same mind. The observation of nature, the jump to the assumptions of cause-effect relationships, the inspection and description of the laws governing these relationships (. . . Growth . . . Reproduction . . . Inheritance . . . Variability . . . Ratio of Increase . . . Struggle for Life . . . Natural Selection . . . Divergence of Character . . . and Extinction), the surge of inspiration that prompted the linking of the cycle of life and death in the lower animals to the evolution of the higher animals (including man) as ". . . the most exalted object which we are capable of conceiving. . . ," and the humility of the genius who recognizes that life, for all its grandeur and complexity, is a small and simple product of a superior Creator; the flow of the paragraph itself depicts Darwin as a unique amalgam. This presentation of the progression from the writer to the scientist to the philosopher is the achievement for which I praise Darwin as a writer. It is his accomplishment as a scientist.

What was the effect, I asked, of the writer's imitation of Darwin's language.

"Well, for one thing, he didn't have to put in that 'without disrespect.'"

"You mean that he doesn't need the remark, that the effect of the imitation itself is to suggest that he respects Darwin?"

"It does for me. The way he weaves his own ideas into Darwin's writing is like saying that Darwin said it all, said it the best way it could be said. He makes Darwin's writing for him into what all creation seems to be for Darwin."

"And without ever trying to take Darwin over, any more than Darwin in his writing tries to take over God."

"And it's great the way he does it the same way Darwin does. Darwin orders nature but then praises that order as made by God; this guy orders Darwin's writing but then praises that as Darwin's accomplishment."

"Which is why I praise him. He's achieved with Darwin what Darwin has achieved with nature. That's *his* accomplishment as a writer."

ASSIGNMENT 18

What have you been doing in this course so far?

Take stock for a minute so far as your experience in this course is concerned. You have written seventeen (or more) papers yourself. There are the assignments, the sample papers, the class discussions. You might also have had conversations about the course outside the class.

Write a paper in which you try to explain what it is you think you have been doing in your humanities course this semester. Write this paper as though it were a letter to a friend who is planning to enter Case next year. Be as clear as you can in explaining to him just what it is you think you've been up to. Try to be helpful in preparing him for what you think he ought to know about writing when he gets here as a student. Give him the best advice you have to offer.

As with Assignment 16 (or rather, with what Assignment 16 should have been), the problem of Assignment 18 was one of creating an order of words which would say metaphorically what could not be simply asserted ("you must learn to avoid generalizations") or claimed ("I have learned to avoid generalizations") and amount to very much. I prescribed the audience for the paper that I did ("a letter to a friend") as a way of trying to move us past the dangers of incestuous speculation about the intent or purpose of the course ("You are trying to make us see that . . ."). And I recalled the subject of advice in order to revive the notion of good advice as involving the acknowledgment of otherness. I wanted to suggest to the students that a writer's responsibility to someone else could come only through his seeing that his first responsibility was to create himself for himself.

I don't think that to have been more explicit on this point in the wording of the Assignment would have helped those who had trouble with it: "Please bear in mind that 'friend' in this situation means friend and not slave, or boob, or backboard." When things went wrong in a paper, the difficulty could generally be traced to the writer's misconception of his audience, but the real source of such trouble generally lay deeper—in the shakiness of the writer's relationship to himself as a writer. This uncertainty, faced for what it was, would have made (and in one case did) a marvelous subject for a paper, but very few students seemed able to imagine they could afford to face it. Instead, they buried their nervousness in patronization, smugly suggesting to Art and Harry and Jim, who were all still wallowing around back there in the protozoic slime of high school English, that they'd just have to wait and boy oh boy the pain, man, the *pain!* Not many of the students' letters would have needed a return address.

My way into this was to invite the class to open and read a letter:

Dear Mark,
   The English class I am in has got to be completely different from any that is taught at Canfield. In fact, if I majored in English at Ohio State, I would probably not run into a class of this type. The first few days that I attended class I wasn't sure what I was doing; I'm still not too sure. We write three papers a week and, in class, read through selected papers and slice them apart. We don't butcher for the fun of butchering, though; we try to make our criticisms constructive. Every now and then we try to cut up a paper only to find that we can't slice certain sentences or paragraphs. *Now,* when I write a paper, I try to express ideas in a way that I mold my ideas and arguments, not that my "ideas" mold me. If this sounds easy to you, I'd like to see you do it; so would my teacher. We just don't achieve these results too often. You'll see.
   There are no rules for writing, as such, that will write the paper for me, and there is nothing that Prof. Coles actually is able to teach the class; we learn through practice—and that gets to be a very hairy problem. I mean, it's about the most frustrating class I am taking. Our teacher will not discuss grades, so I have no idea what will be on the midterm "report card."
   We have been writing on amateurism, professionalism, and advice as a basis for discussion. These seemingly simple topics, I discovered, are not so simple when I try to write about them. I never knew that I

could become so confused over things like these! I often feel like muttering, "the hell with it," but I don't believe I would really want to quit this class. It does help me to write better. I don't really know how it goes about helping me, but if it didn't enable me to improve my writing, what would be the use of having the class?

If you happen to choose Case, don't expect to have English classes such as those you have been taking at Canfield High; not that high school English classes are no good, but college sure is different! Institutes are different also. I can't tell you to make any special preparation for a Case Tech frosh English class, because I can't imagine what a student of Prof. Coles last year could have told me to prepare for. It's frustrating.

"Now, what I'd like you to do," I said after reading the paper through, "is to imagine yourselves as Mark. You've just received this letter. What's your response to it?"

"I'm not sure what I'd think. I think I'd be a little mad, though."

"Mad at what?"

"I'd wonder who he thought he was talking to. 'I'd like to see you do it' and 'you'll see.' He sounds like he can't wait to see me gutted."

"OK. Smugness. Bullying. Does he take that tone all the way through?"

"Well, it's that pushiness in the letter I don't like."

"I know. But you began by saying that you weren't sure what you'd think about the letter, that you'd wonder who the writer here thought he was talking to. My question is what there is in the letter that makes your response tentative. Is there anything *other* than bullying or pushiness in it?"

"He isn't being pushy when he talks about the class. He says he's still not too sure that he knows what he's doing, but that *now* when he writes a paper he seems to know what to do, how to mold his ideas and arguments. Whatever he means by that."

"How does he sound there?"

"Well, he isn't being pushy. I'm not sure I know what he's being."

"Or that he does. Or that Mark would—would know how to put the smug certainty of the letter together with its Nervous Nelly-ism any better than we can."

And for other readers there were analogous difficulties. What was Mark supposed to have made of the question at the end of the next to the last paragraph: if the course "didn't enable me to improve my writing, what would be the use of having the class?" How was he to have handled the seeming coyness of the writer's saying that there's little he can think of to help his friend, because he "can't imagine" what help anyone could have been to him? College is "different." So are "institutes." But where would such observations leave Mark? There were plenty of tones to the letter, but no one could meld them into anything anyone could imagine Mark would know what to do with.

I then moved to a moment in another paper, to a paragraph which is such a nice expression of frustration that it was too bad the writer hadn't gone on to develop the implications of it.

All you're required to do is turn in a piece of writing on a particular subject every time the class meets—three times a week—which often seems like three times too many. You'll find yourself up until three in the morning staring at a blank piece of paper; you'll find yourself jotting down ideas in the cafeteria; you'll put it all off till tomorrow; you'll let physics go to get it done today; you'll dust it off in calculus just before class; you'll waste paper; you'll break pencils; you'll swear; you'll quit—but when you walk into class, you'll put that paper in the pile with all the others.

My opening question was what could be inferred from the sentences about the writer's relationship to the course.

"He doesn't like it, obviously."

"All those broken pencils and lonely nights. OK. What keeps him up so late though? What makes him jot down ideas in the cafeteria?"

"I don't know. The fear of failing, I guess."

"Failing in what sense—the fear that he's going to get a bad grade?"

"Yes. I think he is concerned about his grade."

"Wait a minute," said someone else. "Sure he's concerned about the grade. Who isn't? But I don't think that's what keeps him up nights, not the way he puts it. In the first place he's got no way of knowing about the grade. Also, he sweats things too much."

"You mean he wouldn't do all this for a grade?"

"Not over and over again the way he says he does, no."

"Does he say he does the same thing over and over again?"

"I think so. Well, in a way he does and in a way he doesn't. I mean he's talking about more than the way he wrote just one paper. Sometimes he writes them right away; sometimes he puts them off. Sometimes he stays up till three in the morning; other times he dusts them off. But he's always sweating it. I don't think a guy working for just a grade would work this way."

160   "Or talk this way, at any rate. Getting it all into one sentence so that the suggestion seems to be that it's some sort of process he's immersed in, a process that seems to have produced a state of mind. What do you call that state of mind, by the way? What keeps him up some of those nights, if it's not just worry about a grade?"

"I'm not sure. He doesn't really say."

"What do you think Mark would guess?"

"He probably wouldn't know either. But he'd be interested, I think. I don't think he'd be angry the way he'd be if he got the first letter."

"Why not? Why don't you think he'd be angry?"

"Because the guy hasn't talked down to him."

"Doesn't he tell him he's going to have to sweat it?"

"Well yes, but not just that way. It's himself he's talking about. All he says the guy is going to *have* to do is turn in three papers a week. From then on it's like he's predicting."

"Which suggests less that Mark is in for it than that the writer believes he's the kind of guy who has the stuff to be affected in the same way. 'Here's the way you'll respond, too,' the writer seems to be saying, 'because you're the kind of person who is capable of' . . . well, 'caring' would be my word for it, for what keeps this writer going. keeps him sweating it, as Jim said. In other words, this letter, at least this paragraph of it, is like an invitation. 'You' and 'I' and 'us' as pronouns begin to slide into each other so that what I'm doing becomes what we're doing, becomes what you'll be doing. I think Mark would be interested, too. Puzzled, sure, but interested, because what the writer has offered as advice here is himself."

And then we turned to the last paper.

I can understand your asking me whether I can be a little more specific about the requirements for my humanities course and what I'm learning in it. You're not the only one. My roommate, Hal, who has a different teacher and a different section, which really means that he has a different course, is always asking me the same thing. Not really though, because at this point he only pretends to. The other night I was at my desk writing. He was sitting on the edge of his bed in his pajamas winding his damned alarm clock. I'm sure I told you that Hal-baby wears pajamas. "How's the goddam course, Rick," he says with that idiot grin of his. It's the line he always uses when he gets to sack in before I do. He and his pajamas. Hal sometimes thinks he is a very funny boy. In Hal's course they're reading *Moby Dick*. Since the beginning of the term they've been reading *Moby Dick*. So far Hal has written two papers. So far I've written nineteen papers: seventeen assignments and two rewrites. "The goddam course," as you know, was my line first.

I've already told you how many papers we have to write and what sort of assignments we have to work with, but I know you want to know whether it's worth the time and effort and what it is you can get out of it. Well, a couple of days ago it seemed worth it. Hal was at it again and I picked up the last page of the most recent paper he was writing on *Moby Dick*. He ended the thing this way: "Thus we can see that the shining whiteness of the whale functions symbolically in a variety of many different contexts at once."

"That's a sentence?" I asked him. "Who are you *really* kidding Hal-baby? Who do you think you are anyway, the Jolly Green Giant? Who's 'we'? You and the other giants?" When he told me to jam it I paused at the door long enough to say: "The question is, Hal-baby, who are *you* when you tell *me* to jam it." I felt pretty good about the course then.

But I got a letter from Gwen a couple of weeks ago in which she said "cause I love you loads" and it annoyed me. And then I got annoyed that I got annoyed. So the course works both ways. There are a lot of things you see differently from the way you did.

What sort of advice, I began by asking, could you call this.

"I think this is really neat. I don't know about advice, but he's sure got a great soft sell."

"What's he selling?"

"Well, that's not the right word, really. He isn't selling anything, exactly. I mean he doesn't put down the guy he's writing the letter to. And he doesn't try to snow him either. And he's great on that room-mate. 'Hal-baby' and his pajamas. I love that."

"Does he put down the roommate, then?"

"Sure."

"He's a bully, then, the writer of the letter? Smug?"

"No. Hal-baby deserves it. Two papers for God's sake. And those pajamas."

"And that little dig at bedtime, and the alarm clock, and that phoney prose he writes. You mean Rick isn't acting superior, then?"

"Right. It's Hal-baby who's smug. My roommate tries to pull that sometimes. He doesn't have to write that many papers for his course either. He calls me Shakespeare. 'You and the other giants.' I'll have to remember that."

"What do you think the Mark who got this letter would think,

162 though? Wouldn't he see the course as no more than a way to be one up?"

"I think he'd see a little more than that. I think he'd see that Rick had learned something."

"Does he say he has?"

"No, but as you'd say, he does better than that. He shows it the way he quotes all that jazz about the shining whiteness of the whale. He couldn't have picked that out unless he'd learned something."

"He shows it, to use Kurt again, just the way Kurt did last week in here when he got angry, when his language, the way he behaved, let all of *us* say 'he's angry, and he's angry because he's feeling frustrated even though he's worked hard.' What this writer comes up with is a metaphor for the process of learning. He *shows* he's learned, as you say, Bill, through his use of that quotation. He also shows it for me in the way he places his roommate, as Ron was saying. And how about the comment on Gwen's letter? Does he show anything to Mark about his learning with that?"

"Maybe that's a warning that it's not all a downhill ride. Fun, fun, fun."

A warning and perhaps a realization as well.

At any rate, the last person to have blamelessly pretended that a liberal education is a riskless experience was Eve. And she was under the influence of a seducer, not a teacher.

ASSIGNMENT 19

J. D. Salinger

[For this assignment I gave the students a passage from *The Catcher in the Rye* by J. D. Salinger. The passage, a paragraph that begins with "The book" and ends with "Eustacia Vye," may be found on pages 24–25 of the original edition published by Little, Brown and Company and on pages 18–19 of the Bantam paperback edition. Permission to reprint this paragraph has been denied by Mr. Salinger.]

Describe the voice you hear speaking in this passage [from *The Catcher in the Rye,* identified above] *and its ideal audience. What is it you call professional here? What do you call amateur?*

In order to suggest to the students something of the resources of language available to a writer as a definer—resources that can be used as well as abused—I followed the Assignments on Darwin with two assignments designed to illustrate how words can come together in unconventional ways to make meaning. So far as evaluating those meanings was concerned, I figured with both Assignments to have an argument on my hands, that the students would be ready to admire what I didn't and vice versa. Sacco's letter as it turned out was not the problem I thought it was going to be. Salinger I figured, rightly of course, they were going to be suckers for.

Holden Caulfield is no more dated in his appeal for college freshmen than the Cinderella story is for children. In fact, by his admirers

164   he is thought of less as a character than as a person, less as a person than as a myth—an effect that is as carefully calculated as it is insidious. For the appeal of Salinger's ingeniously extended sentimentalization of the already sentimental tradition of the Noble Savage is based on an attempt to seduce the young into believing that Holden Caulfield is who they are. Holden Caulfield is *not* who young people are, of course, any more than they sound the way he does, but in being made to sound the way young people would like to *believe* they sound, and to behave as they would like to believe they behave—with a touching fumble-tongued awkwardness that is but the rough side of an absolutely unerring instinct for the true, the good, and the beautiful—Salinger's character, or rather the effect of Salinger's character, is to confirm the young in the lie they wish most to believe about themselves as young people: that they already know what in fact no one can know without learning; that they already are what in fact no one can be without trying to become. More than a fiction, Holden Caulfield is an impossibility. *The Catcher in the Rye,* for this reason, is a lie about life. Its ideal audience is adolescents of whatever age who wish to remain adolescents at the same time they have the need to pretend they are all grown up. The novel may traffic in the myth of the Noble Savage, but in its workings it enacts the myth of Frankenstein.

The passage I picked from the novel for the students to work with is a good example of both Salinger's ability as a writer, the source of his popularity; and what I would call the betrayal of that ability, the fraudulence of his appeal. The amateurish sounding voice of the passage, for example, is actually a very slick professional achievement; there is no question of Salinger's skill to manipulate dead language in order to produce the illusion of a sensitive and knowing creature. This effect he creates mainly through the yoking of certain kinds of contrasts.

"I'm quite illiterate, but I read a lot," immediately following the explanation of how Holden has come to read Isak Dinesen, connects a sterile, teacherish conception of education ("illiterate") with a phrase that not only explodes it, but in so doing suggests that the speaker (even though he does not realize it) actually reads with more insight and appreciation than does the reader who is conventionally "literate." The word "killed" is played with in an analogous way. When "this girl gets killed," the word signifies death—a meaning that carries into and deepens the more slangy connotations of the same word in the following sentence. The montage-like juxtaposition of these two meanings is what creates the image of Holden's hypersensitivity, particularly in that he is responding to an artistic rendering of an optionless situation (developed by the repetition of "married"). "Funny" is first used in its ordinary sense, but is jiggled in meaning almost immediately by "crazy" and so takes on the overtones of "queer" or "odd." The two meanings coalesce in the second use of "funny" to suggest that the speaker "likes" literature that makes use of the sort of pattern he describes in the Lardner story, and possibly that he needs the humorous to alleviate the pain of his hypersensitive response to what "just about" kills him.

The fraud of the passage, however, is a matter of its being based on a lie that is made to seem like something other than a lie. Holden Caulfield cannot be what he is said to be and know what he is said to know without also knowing that he knows what he does. But since such an admission would expose the myth of the Natural Sophisticate as a fiction, Salinger must arrange things in the passage to suggest that it *is* possible for someone to possess an awareness he can neither display nor act on, that the capacity for appreciation and the ability to discriminate *can* exist in total independence of the understanding, that in fact one *may* live on a level other than the languages he knows. He must, that is, arrange Holden's values and preferences *for* him—without getting caught at it.

I wanted to catch him at it, particularly after reading a set of papers that showed the students, almost to a man, solidly hooked by Salinger. But even in their praise, a number of writers had had trouble finding language to describe the speaker of the passage, so I began class with an excerpt from a paper the last sentence of which seemed a good way into this as a problem:

To use proper English would have restricted him even further, to the point where understanding would become virtually impossible. As it is, he is trying to express concepts he doesn't understand in a medium he hasn't mastered. These are not the neat, logical sentences of a professional writer; instead it is the painfully wrought prose of a boy who is unable to express himself, but does so with a beautiful, illuminating clarity.

"How is it that someone can express 'concepts he doesn't understand in a medium he hasn't mastered' and yet do this with what this writer calls 'a beautiful, illuminating clarity'? Who *is* speaking in Salinger's passage, anyway?"

"Well, it's a young boy, I think—I mean to judge from the language he's using."

"You mean Salinger wrote this when he was about fifteen?"

"No. I mean he's imitating a young boy. He's talking the way he thinks a young boy would talk."

"So it isn't just a young boy's talking?"

"No. It's Salinger too. He's pretending to be a young boy."

When we stalled on the question of how one knew it was Salinger's pretending to be a young boy, I turned to an excerpt from another paper:

> So the voice of the speaker is what is amateur in this picture. It does
> not know the correct English to use, but that doesn't mean that
> the voice is not interesting. It merely means that I wouldn't identify
> the speaker with any person who is a professional.
> What is professional in this passage is J. D. Salinger's ability to make
> me actually visualize the speaker talking to me. He makes simple talk
> seem appealing in this passage. Such things as "My favorite author is
> my brother D.B." make me take an interest in the speaker and in what
> he feels. It takes talent to create a subject like the one talking in this
> passage. This talent is what I would link with professionalism.

"Is this the sort of thing you meant, Rick, that Salinger has the ability to make you 'visualize' the speaker?"

"Yes, I think he does."

"How does 'my favorite author is my brother D.B.' make you 'visualize' the speaker? Do you know anything about him from a remark like that?"

"I know his brother means a lot to him. He doesn't seem jealous of him or anything."

"OK. You know that he has strong affections and that there's nothing mean about them. There's a kind of openness to him, a kind of honesty and decency. In other words, your response is a lot more specific than just 'taking an interest in the speaker'—talk that won't get you much farther than the dust-jacket rhetoric of 'beautiful, illuminating clarity.' It's a certain *kind* of interest you have, and it's a lot more than visual. In some mysterious way you move from an order of words to a sense of character, from language to what that language is symbolic of. Anybody, for example, could have said 'I'm quite illiterate.' Anybody could have said 'I read a lot.' But when you put them together the way Salinger does you don't get just anybody."

"You get a guy who's smarter than he thinks he is."

"You get that as an image I think, yes, along with the pathos of the fact that he doesn't know it and maybe never will. Where do you think Holden Caulfield got the term 'illiterate'?"

"From a teacher, I suppose."

"From a teacher, a parent, some so-called authority figure anyway. And the term embodies a concept which the boy seems to accept at the same time the context of his talk suggests how ridiculous it is for such a concept to be connected with him. He not only reads a lot; he reads good stuff."

"So the passage has to be translated, then?"

"Does translate, I think, as all language does. Let's look at an example of this translating process at work in another paper:"

This character is trying awfully hard to act big and be noticed, but at the same time he wants to learn. His use of slang points toward his desire to be a member of the in group; as does the way he talked about the girl being killed. He didn't really think it was funny. He was just expecting a storybook ending, and he was shocked by the way she was treated by Lardner. It was different; and he didn't quite know what words to use to describe it; but instead of seeming to be at a loss for words, he uses "funny." As soon as he says it he is kind of scared by the way it sounds and to avoid going into it further, he changes the subject to "classical books." He is hungry for knowledge, not the kind you get from a classroom, but rather learning about life. He reads books and especially likes those that seem real to him. Wars and mysteries are something he can't quite comprehend (or doesn't want to), so he doesn't like them too well. He likes Lardner because Lardner seems to paint a picture of life that he could accept; and he likes his brother's writing, I suppose, because he can easily recognize life as depicted by him, having lived with him. Also, that sentence about calling up an author of a book that he liked particularly well shows his hunger for knowledge. He isn't satisfied with a good book; it only whets his appetite. Although he tries very hard, as I have said, to be big and noticeable, I don't think he is really that way. When he says that he is "quite illiterate," it is his way of shamefacedly, maybe humbly, admitting that he doesn't read as well as he should.

He also does a lot of daydreaming. When he gets the wrong book from the library, he doesn't even notice it until he gets home. Most people, if they didn't pick it out themselves, would at least make sure that they were getting the right book. When he does get home and finds the mistake, instead of taking the book back he reads it (even though at first he thought it was going to stink).

So what is this a voice of? The voice of someone growing up—fast; in a way wanting to slow down and yet wanting to go faster.

"I see. I can follow what he means when he says that the character uses slang to be a member of the 'in group.'"

"And the way he translates 'that story just about killed me' into someone capable of being 'shocked,' or the remark about 'war books and mysteries' into someone who 'doesn't want to' comprehend war and mystery. The translation going on here is a matter of the writer's moving the way words fall on a page into the human terms for which they're the symbolic equivalents. There was another paper I admired for the same thing:"

The strange part about the voice in this piece of writing is what lies beneath the voice, namely the person. The "flowered shirt" critic, the guy picking his teeth in front of the "hills like white elephants," is the type of man who might pick up *Out of Africa* by mistake, instead of *Day of the Guns* by Mickey Spillane, but he is not the type of man who would read it instead of taking it back. I don't know whether or not it might be a touch of professionalism, but here is a person who doesn't read what someone else has suggested, or what he started out to, but who rather takes advantage of discovering a book he didn't plan on. While the average slob might have picked up *Origin of Species* or *Mein Kampf* by mistake and immediately have taken it back, this person sounds like the type of person who would keep it, read it, and possibly profit by it.

Here is a person who prefers the classics to the usual drugstore selection of war stories and mysteries, and yet who cannot explain why he prefers the classics. He reads a lot, yet he is illiterate; he rationalizes his feelings at the end of a book by his desire to meet the author, yet he reads Lardner unaware that Lardner is dead. *The Catcher in the Rye* is indeed a strange mixture of outward ignorance with an inner knowledge.

As with the last paper, what I praised here was a critical reading become a creative act. I mentioned particularly liking the way that the paradoxes of the writer's final paragraph seem to correspond to the paradox of Salinger's achievement in the passage as a whole, in his having been able to evolve a living voice from dead terminology.

"Does either of these two papers, by the way, give anyone an idea of how to address the question we bogged down with earlier, the question of whether this is a young boy's speaking or whether it's someone's making a young boy speak? 'Pretending to be a young boy' was Bob's phrase."

"I think it's definitely Salinger talking."

"Why?"

"Because I don't think a fifteen-year-old could show all this. I don't think he could mean what we've said the passage means."

"You mean he wouldn't talk bad English this well, this artfully?"

"That's part of it. No, I don't think he would."

"OK. Now, is Salinger believably rendering the consciousness of a fifteen-year-old, do you think, or is he simply making his mouth move, using him for his own purposes?"

"I don't understand what you mean."

I then turned to the last paper:

Just as it is difficult to separate what is said in a paper from the way it is said, it is difficult here to separate the voice of the writer and what his character is saying from the voice of the character and what the author is saying. Just what *is* being said here? On a superficial level, the voice of the character, someone with poor grammar, explains that while he doesn't read too well, he reads a lot of books that are funny at least once in a while and that he wishes he knew the authors of the ones he likes. Does the character actually mean this, or may Salinger be saying that the best literature gives the reader (even one who calls himself an illiterate) a picture of the author that carries his personality vividly enough to make the reader wish he were his friend? What makes *The Return of the Native* or *Out of Africa* seem better than *Of Human Bondage* in this respect and in this or any instance? Could this be one of the reasons that writing is an art instead of a science—the fact that what makes outstanding literature better than good literature for a given reader is something called style or tone, something a writer must develop for himself, something that cannot be taught, an intangible characteristic of the writing that strikes each reader differently?

Another characteristic of the voice of this paragraph is contradiction, such as "I'm quite illiterate, but I read a lot." Contradictions are here too in another less obvious sense coupled with the question of who is really speaking. The character's grammar and vocabulary aren't the best, but he has the discernment to give *Return* the title of classic in the sense of worth rather than of age (does he really know what he's saying?). In what appears to be a deliberate refutation of his apparent ignorance of good English, Salinger's character proceeds to sit in judgment on Maugham. "He just isn't the kind of guy I'd want to call up, that's all." What kind of illiterate reads Dinesen, Lardner, Maugham, and Hardy—and has the audacity to evaluate them, even on his own terms? Isn't the term "illiterate" a contradiction, whether by the character or by Salinger?

The first level of writing in this paragraph presents an amateur in the field of English and literature, but read on and listen to what the character has to say; isn't there a professional hidden in the bushes? Perhaps a professional amateur? The question of where one begins and

170   the other leaves off must, within the context of this paragraph, remain unanswered, as does the question of whether such a point exists. The voice is that of a professional presenting an amateur who is a professional.

The voice of this paragraph has as its ideal audience anyone interested in paradoxes—which here include the writer, the character, the voices of both, and the style of writing. It also includes me. I've been persuaded that I should read the book.

"Now, one of the things that interests me most about that paper is the writer's talk of the passage as 'a strange mixture.' He talks first of the 'contradiction' of the paragraph, but then concludes by saying that the ideal audience for it would be those who are interested in 'paradoxes.' I'd like to raise the question of which is the better term by looking at the passage from Salinger in a slightly different way. Let me read it through with no more than some changes of proper nouns."

I picked up with Salinger's reference to *The Return of the Native*, but for that title substituted *Gone with the Wind*. For "Isak Dinesen" I read "Margaret Mitchell"; for "Ring Lardner," "the writer of Dick Tracy." And instead of Maugham I had Holden not wanting to call up the author of *Crime and Punishment*. He'd rather have called up old Margaret Mitchell. He liked that Scarlett O'Hara.

"OK," I said. "Now what's happened to the voice we've been talking about?"

"The kid's turned into a jerk."

"Do you think it's possible then that the writer of this last paper had a real question in asking 'What kind of illiterate reads Dinesen, Lardner, Maugham, and Hardy—and has the audacity to evaluate them'?"

"You mean he wouldn't be smart enough to evaluate them?"

"I mean would he have the knowledge to evaluate them when the whole structure of his talk, the syntax of it, suggests that what we have here is a mind at best naïve, at worst slobby. How many of you in here have read *Of Human Bondage*?"

A couple of students had.

"Do you know why it's a cheap book?"

"No. I kind of liked it."

"So did I when I read it. I was seventeen. All that stuff about the meaning of life, or rather why life has no meaning. I thought it was real art, and it took me a while, and the help of a teacher, to be able to see how it wasn't. But Holden knows that it's a cheap book right away. That is, he's said to, in the same way that he's said to like Hardy and not be too knocked out by mysteries and war books and all. He doesn't know why, of course, but he knows. You just take Salinger's word for it. Do you see now, Bob, what I meant by asking whether Salinger is making Holden's mouth move?"

"You mean he makes him a great guy by having him like the right things?"

"Exactly. And not the other way around. Using the same technique, and maintaining Holden as the same sort of character, how would you take him to an art museum? What would you have him knocked out by and not knocked out by?"

"Well, I'd have him hate the billboards on the way there, but go nuts over Rembrandt."

"Or you'd have him really flattened by the Impressionists but not so turned on by Claude or some of the more conventional landscape artists. He'd like passion and sincerity and force but nothing stylized. And so on. And what would you have *him* give as his reasons for his preferences? What's all you'd *have* to have him say about them?"

"I know what I like."

"Right on. You'd never have to give a reason. All you'd have to have your character say is, 'I just like it, that's all. I don't know. Those Impressionists just turn me on. That Monet is the kinda guy I'd like to have pizza with, except I hear he's like dead.' And you could work the same trick with Holden on music or politics or life-styles or on any damned thing you wanted."

"Just so he liked the right things and didn't like the wrong ones."

"And just so you were careful to set it all to these rhythms—and all."

"I know what you mean there. When I finished the book I even talked that way."

"Sure. It's the key to Salinger's style—a set of attitudes marching like a parade of circus elephants, tail in trunk, trunk around tail. Only it's hypnotic, that style. I don't know. You just can't get it out of your head, that's all. What I like is a style you can at least get out of your head once in a while. Let me try one more change with the passage:

> The potato chips I was eating were these potato chips I took out of the supermarket by mistake. They gave me the wrong potato chips, and I didn't notice it till I got back to my room. They gave me Stateline Potato Chips. I thought they were going to stink, but they didn't. They were very good potato chips, etc., etc.

"What do you say about Holden on the basis of that change?"

"He's crazy."

"Meaning what, exactly?"

"That I don't understand him. He's either awfully dumb or a mental case."

"Why didn't you say that about him when the subject had to do with getting a book out of the library? That's just as much of an everyday thing as buying potato chips, isn't it?"

"Not for me. I don't take books out of the library that much."

Which, of course, is just the sort of thing that Salinger's stuff depends on. We concluded with my saying that so far as I was concerned, there is indeed, as the writer of the last paper suggests, "a professional hidden in the bushes" here. The metaphor, however, I think is appropriate in more than one sense.

ASSIGNMENT 20

Nicola Sacco

Here is a passage from a letter:

Well, my dear boy, after your mother had talked to me so much and I had dreamed of you day and night, how joyful it was to see you at last. To have talked with you like we used to in the days—in those days. Much I told you on that visit and more I wanted to say, but I saw that you will remain the same affectionate boy, faithful to your mother who loves you so much, and I did not want to hurt your sensibilities any longer, because I am sure that you will continue to be the same boy and remember what I have told you. I knew that and what here I am going to tell you will touch your sensibilities, but don't cry, Dante, because many tears have been wasted, as your mother's have been wasted for seven years, and never did any good. So, Son, instead of crying, be strong, so as to be able to comfort your mother, and when you want to distract your mother from the discouraging soulness, I will tell you what I used to do. To take her for a long walk in the quiet country, gathering wild flowers here and there, resting under the shade of trees, between the harmony of the vivid stream and the gentle tranquility of the mothernature, and I am sure that she will enjoy this very much, as you surely would be happy for it. But remember always, Dante, in the play of happiness, don't you use all for yourself only, but down yourself just one step, at your side and help the weak ones that cry for help, help the prosecuted and the victim, because that are your better friends; they are the comrades that fight and fall as your father Bartolo fought and fell yesterday for the conquest of the joy of freedom for all and the poor workers. In this struggle of life you will find more love and you will be loved.

Much I thought of you when I was lying in the death house—the singing, the kind tender voices of the children from the playground, where there was all the life and the joy of liberty—just one step from the wall which contains the buried agony of three buried souls. It would remind me so often of you and your sister Ines, and I wish I could see you every moment. But I feel better that you did not come to the death-house so that you could not see the horrible picture of three lying in agony waiting to be electrocuted, because I do not know what effect it would have on your young age. But then, in another way if you were not so sensitive it would be very useful to you tomorrow when you could use this horrible memory to hold up to the world the shame of the country in this cruel persecution and unjust death. Yes, Dante, they can crucify our bodies today as they are doing, but they cannot destroy our ideas, that will remain for the youth of the future to come.

> From a letter written by Nicola Sacco to his son Dante from the Charlestown State Prison in Massachusetts on August 18, 1927
>
> Bartolo is Bartolomeo Vanzetti. The third man referred to is Celestino Madeiros. All three men were executed for murder on the morning of August 23, 1927.

Again, describe the voice you hear speaking in the passage above and what you imagine as its ideal audience.

What is it you call professional about this piece of writing? What is it you call amateur?

The papers addressing Assignment 20 didn't have the quality of those the students had written on the Salinger passage. The difficulty most writers seemed to have was not one of responding to Sacco's letter, of hearing the passage; it was finding a way of describing how they heard what they did that gave the trouble, finding a way of moving from language to its effect. I decided to work entirely with sections of papers in order to spend as much time as possible with the Sacco passage itself.

As a way of seeing the most general form of the problem of Sacco's letter for a reader, I worked first with the way one student had begun his paper:

> There is a lot I would like to say about why I believe Sacco is innocent, but most of what I feel about him I can't back up with words or phrases from the paper. He does not write well, but . . .

"Where do you suppose," I asked, "he gets the idea that Sacco is innocent?"

"He says he believes it."

"I know. I mean what's the basis for his belief?"

"It's hard to tell from just this. Maybe he looked the case up. I did. Maybe he went on in the paper to give evidence for it?"

"He didn't, didn't go on in his paper to talk about the case as a case, that is. And that's a subject I'd like to leave out of what we talk about today as much as possible. Let's try to confine ourselves to looking at this letter as a piece of writing, and to the speaker in it as a speaker. With that as our frame, is there anything in the letter just as a piece of writing that that writer may be said to have been responding to? What, for example, made you look the case up, Kurt?"

"I looked it up because I didn't believe the guy was guilty. I know it sounds silly, but I figured nobody could write this way and be a murderer. I think that's what the kid who wrote the paper means too."

"But he says Sacco doesn't write well."

"He says he doesn't write well, 'but.'"

"Implying what, just on the basis of how much of the sentence you have?"

"I guess that he doesn't write conventional English, but that what he writes communicates."

" 'What he writes communicates.' So this writer's belief in Sacco's innocence is really a metaphoric way of responding to Sacco's words and phrases, to the tone and feel of them?"

"Sure. Isn't this what we did with Holden Caulfield, the way some people said that Holden's mentioning his brother the way he did gave them the feeling that he wasn't jealous of him?"

"OK. Now what interests me about the Sacco passage is what words and phrases do that sort of thing here and how they add up, if not to a belief in Sacco's innocence, at least to a sense of something about him that would seem at odds with murderousness. Maybe a section of another paper can help:"

Sacco constantly wanted to see his son, but thought first of the effect a visit to the death house would have on the boy. He allowed Dante to visit him only out of concern for his wife. Sacco implies that much of what he told Dante on his visit concerned the boy's responsibility toward caring for his mother. This is repeated several times in the first paragraph: "I saw that you will remain the same affectionate boy, faithful to your mother. . . "; "Because I am sure that you will continue to be the same boy and remember what I have told you"; "be strong, so as to comfort your mother."

"I can see how he means he knew that Sacco cared for his wife."

"Because of the way this writer groups the words and phrases he takes from Sacco's letter, I can see it too. And his quotations made me aware of something else. Notice the way the writer says that Sacco allowed his son to 'visit him *only* out of concern for his wife' and that a lot of what he told him 'concerned the boy's responsibility toward caring for his *mother*.' I wonder if it isn't more than that too. Suppose you had to talk about your son's responsibility toward caring for your wife. What sorts of things would you say?"

"I'd explain that he was the man of the family now, that he had to grow up in a hurry; things like that."

"I think I might go at it that way too. But look what Sacco says: 'You will *remain* the same'; 'you will *continue* to be.' Is there any difference in the way he goes at things?"

"I think I see what you mean. Sacco isn't giving his son a lot of bad advice. He isn't telling him to *become* anything brand new so much as he's saying he knows that the son already *is* responsible."

"Something like that, yes. He seems to be expressing his faith in what Dante's going to be by telling him he believes in what he is. And that's what enables me to see that final quotation the writer makes use of as more than what you call bad advice, Dan. 'Be strong in your *own* right,' he seems to be saying; 'then you'll be *able* to comfort your mother.'"

"Which means Sacco is as much concerned with his son as he is with his wife."

"Exactly. And more than 'concerned with,' it's 'concerned for,' isn't it? He seems concerned for one through his concern for the other in such a way as to make it impossible to tell who comes first. He's a father as well as a husband, and he's more than that as well. Look at the next to last sentence of his first paragraph, the one beginning 'but remember always'; who is he concerned with or for there?"

"Other people. Workers. Comrades."

"As well as for Bartolo, and for Dante, and for Dante's 'better friends,' who are fighters for 'the joy of freedom,' who are as you say workers and comrades. His concern for his family seems to move to concern for humanity in general and back again. He does the same thing in the next paragraph where the voices of children take him to the 'agony of three buried souls,' which in turn serves to 'remind' Sacco of his son again and of the son's 'sister' (not his daughter), Ines. Simultaneously, he sees himself as a husband, father, cause, and martyr without becoming any of them to the exclusion of the others, and without obliterating his identity as a someone, a person who *can* see himself in those ways.

From this we moved to a paragraph by another student.

This is a very emotional situation and a very emotional paper. I cannot completely describe these feelings here, but I do hear them. An indication of Sacco's thoughts comes to me in "To have talked with you like we used to in the days—in *those* days." Those days must have been more to him than a period of time. If he had said anything like "the days when" and had gone on to specify what happened in them, they would have been just time. He did not go on. In fact something very funny happens to time in this paper, but I'm not sure just what it is.

It was the writer's feeling his way to that never-quite-articulated statement about what happens to time in the Sacco passage that interested me. I came at it by asking whether it were possible to speculate on why Sacco "did not go on" from "in those days."

"Maybe he didn't know how."

"In what sense?"

"I mean maybe he didn't know how to talk about specific things in a way that wouldn't be painful for Dante."

"And for himself," said someone else. "Maybe *he* just couldn't have stood it."

"Which helps me," I said, "to understand what the writer means by saying that 'those days must have been more to him than a period of time,' that they had a value for him that time wasn't going to touch. He didn't go on, the illusion is, because he couldn't bear to. I'm still not altogether sure, though, what the writer means by saying that 'something very funny happens to time.' Anyone have any idea?"

"Maybe he's talking about the tenses."

"How do you mean?"

"Well, there was one place in the first paragraph I had to read over a couple of times. It's where he's talking about what he used to do with his wife. But it isn't just what he used to do. He's telling Dante to do it."

"I see what you mean," I said. " 'What I used to do,' the past, becomes the present 'to take for a long walk,' which is the future too, 'I am sure she will enjoy this very much.' It's like the way he makes son and comrades and workers and fighters and a cause all part of the same thing. It's nice also the way the closeness of the relationship he had with his wife is made to *include* that of father and son, which in turn includes and is included by the closeness of son and mother."

"But was Sacco conscious of this, do you think? I mean he doesn't seem to know English well enough to have planned all this out this way, does he?"

"I guess I'd say that it's because I have the sense that he *didn't* plan it, any of it, that I find the letter so moving. From one point of view the letter is just a hodge-podge. There's that revolutionary terminology—'prosecuted,' 'victim,' 'comrades,' 'poor workers'; the highfalutin—'affectionate,' 'sensibilities,' 'tranquility'; there are clichés—'dreamed of you day and night,' 'cruel persecution,' 'the youth of the future'; and above all there's that inadequacy with idiom—'the conquest of the joy of freedom,' 'the mothernature,' 'down yourself just one step.' But there's something about the way it all comes together that suggests somebody who's not going to let what he doesn't know get in the way of what he wants to say."

"He's going to use English no matter how well he knows it."

"Right. He's going to use everything he's got, what he's heard or read, what he's only half-learned. And he's going to hammer it, twist it, wring it until what isn't familiar becomes familiar, does what he wants it to. It's that effort, that struggle, which for me seems to justify the way he's using English, purges it of the mistakes somehow—that effort and his attitude, the tone he takes toward what's happening to him."

And with that we turned to the last selection:

The style used in this passage is the broken English spoken by immigrants to the United States, so I might conclude that this is the "amateur" in the paper. But behind this façade lies the idea of giving of yourself to others. The voice of Sacco is one of sorrow, not one of spite. At no point does Sacco sound as though he wants revenge on those who have condemned him; in this respect, he displays Christ-like virtues and for this I admire him.

"What is it in the passage that enables this writer to speak of the voice of Sacco as 'one of sorrow, not one of spite'?"

"Well, he doesn't seem to want Dante to pay anyone back for him or anything like that."

"Doesn't he tell Dante to take up the same fight, and to use what's happened as something to fight with: 'use this horrible memory to hold up to the world the shame of the country'?"

"Yes, but he's not after revenge exactly. He wants Dante to do this for himself, as we've said."

" 'In this struggle of life you will find more love and you will be loved'?"

"That's it. He seems to be saying that in a way, no matter what happens to him, it's all been worth it."

"Which is how he can advise Dante to get himself into things. What he believes in has brought him so much that in spite of what has been done to him, he can still offer it as a way of life to his son. That's scarcely the stance of a bitter man, someone's seeing himself as just a victim. His victimization he sees in plural terms ('our'), and also possessively, as though it were in some way his portion. It's not that he's glad to die; it's more that he seems ready to if he has to, ready to die for the worthwhile because he has lived by it in such a way as to have been given a life in the process. Where does 'sorrow' come in though? Suppose instead of speaking of the 'shame of the country' he'd said, 'the evil of the country'?"

"When he says 'shame' it sounds like he *is* sorry. If he'd said 'evil,' he'd have been saying the United States was no good."

"I think so. The way Sacco puts it, the United States has standards and ideals that, so far as he's concerned, in this instance aren't being lived up to. It's almost as though he wants what is being done to him used as a means of recalling the worthiness of the United States to itself."

"I know we're not supposed to get on to the case, but this guy just had to be innocent."

"It's hard to believe, anyway, that prose like that could have been written by someone who didn't believe that he was. For me it blows Salinger right off the page. What I hear in Salinger is a professional's presenting an amateur who is really a professional amateur. In Sacco's letter I hear someone who's an amateur in one way, a professional in another. From this point of view I'd question the accuracy of the last writer's metaphor 'behind the façade.' I know what he's pushing for, but for me there's no 'façade' here, not any more than Sacco is 'behind' anything. That language of his, so far as I'm concerned, he's in. He's it. And it's him."

ASSIGNMENT 21

"I Saw a Peacock"

Here is a poem:

I SAW A PEACOCK

    I saw a peacock with a fiery tail
    I saw a blazing comet drop down hail
    I saw a cloud with ivy circled round
    I saw a sturdy oak creep on the ground
    I saw a pismire swallow up a whale
    I saw a raging sea brim full of ale
    I saw a Venice glass sixteen foot deep
    I saw a well full of men's tears that weep
    I saw their eyes all in a flame of fire
    I saw a house as big as the moon and higher
    I saw the sun even in the midst of night
    I saw the Man that saw this wondrous sight.

Anonymous

Begin your paper with a brief statement of what you understand this poem to be about and what kind of a poem you imagine it to be. Describe its ideal audience as you imagine it.

Do you call anything professional about this piece of writing? Do you call anything amateur?

Assignments 19 and 20, concerned as they were with some unconventional ways of making meaning with language, I designed to take the students to a sense of the resources of language available to them as language users. The assignments on nonsense (21 through 24), I wrote as a way of inviting the students to see the *importance* of their becoming aware of such resources, the importance of knowing as much about as many ways of putting symbols together as one can learn. For if, as seems to be the case, each of us with the languages or symbol systems he knows creates the worlds that make him who he is, then the more consciousness one has of himself as a creator with language and of the various ways in which language can make meaning, the more ready he will be to become the master of language rather than its slave, the better equipped to create worlds reflecting what he most wishes to be. Nonsense is a good way into the implications of this proposition (and it is only in its implications, and as an individual works them out for himself, that the proposition is important), because no one can read nonsense or write it without in some way understanding it as a world that is created through the use of language which in turn creates its creator.

Read as a poem, for example, "I Saw a Peacock" is a poem about itself, and in this sense a poem about the virtuosity of its contriver. It is a kind of verbal illusion, a literary joke, the point of which is that its pattern is made up of a number of never quite realizable patterns arranged so as to frustrate any attempt to order them into a coherent whole. The poem never, in conventional terms, "makes sense," but it never quite degenerates into meaninglessness either, never releases a reader long enough to enable him to decide that what he is reading is gibberish. The illusion of control is too prevalent for that, the suggestion of meaning too strong. Thus the poem is a kind of trap. So long as one stays in the poem there is no way out of it. The only way for a reader to solve his dilemma as a reader is to see the trap as a trap, to come to view the performance of the poem as a performance from some point outside the circle of its attainment.

I say "read as a poem" because there is another way of reading "I Saw a Peacock" which seems at first to conflict with a reading of it as nonsense. When the last part of each line, that which follows the subject-object sequence of its opening, is understood to begin a new sentence and is read on into the first part of the line following it, the poem becomes a puzzle and in this way may be said to "make sense." "With a fiery tail I saw a blazing comet. Drop down hail I saw a cloud." And so on. But the conflict between these two ways of reading "I Saw a Peacock" is apparent only. Like Humpty Dumpty's explana-

182   tion of *Jabberwocky*, the reading of the lines which "makes sense" is a complement to the poem read as nonsense in that it *too* is nonsense. In being quite literally a "message" or "hidden meaning," the poem read as a puzzle is actually a confirmation of the terms by which the poem is conceived as nonsense; the message or meaning turns out to be simply another version of the poem hiding it. Nonsense is nonsense is nonsense—at least in the hands of a pro.

The students' attempts to square the circle of "I Saw a Peacock" led to some fantastic displays of ingenuity. Speculations about the meaning of the poem ran from vexatious assertions of its meaninglessness ("this poem doesn't mean anything, because I can make it mean anything I want to"), to solemn considerations of it as Vision ("the blazing comet is retribution: the flaming eyes are the wrath of God"). But both the meanings that were asserted and the assertion of meaninglessness the students made at a convenient distance from the text. Whether the students generalized or selected on the principle of Procrustes, getting out of the trap of the poem for too many writers too often meant getting away from the poem altogether.

I began with a rug woven from the stuff that dreams are made of, the sort of carpet on which W. C. Fields would have loved to fly:

I have seen the distant planets, the many stars, the many clusters in our galaxy and many of the galaxies in our vast universe. It amazes me how small I am in relation to this planet which revolves around our sun, which revolves around the center of the galaxy—our galaxy, which is hurling through space at fantastic speeds. As I see myself as a speck on a large globe hurling through space, the man in "I Saw a Peacock" sees himself in relation to his society. The man in the poem is describing scenes in the world metaphorically. He describes higher education as a cloud with ivy circled round, symbolizing knowledge with the cloud. He also describes an old man walking with a cane as a sturdy oak that creeps on the ground. He continues on with his descriptions until the last two scenes. "I saw the sun even in the midst of night and I saw the Man that saw this wondrous sight." The sun symbolizes hope in the blackness of the sorrow and hate which he has described previously as the "well full of men's tears that weep" and "the eyes all in a flame of fire." The Man, he sees, is himself.

The ideal audience for this poem is a group of people who read poetry and have some insight into the use of terms like peacock, blazing comet, raging sea, sun, etc., when they are used in a particular context.

The writer is a professional in his choice of words for his descriptions, but he is also an amateur. "A raging sea brim full of ale" is a good description of a revolt. I can imagine a crowd rioting because they are "drunk" with an idea. But the author is also an amateur because his main idea is not a continuous build up of one scene, but involves many random scenes. The poem leaves me with a feeling of doubt because I wonder if I have interpreted it correctly.

"I don't think it's hope the sun symbolizes," someone began. "Isn't it God? God's vengeance? I mean at the end the sun is destroying everything, isn't it?"

"No," said someone else, "it *is* hope that's represented by the sun, because even when everything seems dark there's still light."

"How about the sun as inner peace," I said, "or the cloud not as higher education but as the aristocracy? How about the sun as higher education?"

"It's possible."

"Is it? Look at the writer's last sentence. Why do you think he wonders if he's interpreted the poem correctly?"

"Because anything in here could stand for anything."

"And there's no way to decide one way or another, no way the meaning is in any way controlled? There's no pattern to the items of the poem, for example?"

"Well, all the things in here are impossible."

"There's no way you can imagine a peacock as having a firey tail, no way an oak can be said to creep on the ground?"

"OK," said someone else. "Figuratively those things *could* be possible. But don't we sort of move from earth to heaven in the poem? Isn't that a kind of pattern?"

"Then shouldn't the clouds and comet come after the oak and pismire? Or if it's the other way round that the poem moves, from heaven to earth, why are the sun and the moon last?"

"How about the possibility that each one of these things is a kind of a joke?" said another student.

"How do you mean?"

"Humorous. Ants swallowing whales, clouds covered with ivy."

"How about 'I saw their eyes all in a flame of fire'?"

"OK. That one doesn't work. But the pismire swallowing up the whale can't be serious, so you can't make everything in here tragic either."

"Right. And I run into the same trouble if I try to make the poem move from the literal to the metaphoric or from metaphor to some

184   kind of literal statement. I'm not sure whether I have contradictions
here or paradoxes. I don't know whether these images are bizarre or
devotional or just sniggerish. With any pattern I set up I have to
ignore something or warp something or explain away something that
doesn't fit."

"So there isn't any pattern here. The damned thing *is* meaningless."

"Which is to say you could substitute other words for those here,
or change the order of the lines without losing anything?"

"If the poem's meaningless, I don't see why you couldn't."

I went to the board and wrote out "I saw a woman swallow up a
whale," and then asked whether with such a substitution anything in
the poem had changed.

"You don't have Jim's point about the humor any more."

"Why not?"

"Well, the contrast is gone."

"You mean between the conventionally tiny ant and the conventionally enormous whale. OK. Now let's see if we can rearrange the
lines in the poem without losing anything. Of course we'll have to
rearrange two of them because of the rhyme. Does it make any difference if the 'whale-ale' couplet comes after the 'deep-weep' one?"

"In a way it does, but I don't know why exactly."

"What do you drink ale out of?"

"You mean ale seems to lead to glass?"

" 'Seems' is right. And pismire 'seems' to follow from 'creep on the
ground.' In other words it isn't quite so simple as saying there's no
pattern here at all. What we need is a language to describe the pattern
that is here, or at any rate what we have here. Let's go to another
paper."

The first eleven lines of this poem create a series of unusual
impressions for me: "a peacock with a fiery tail," reminds me of a
peacock's particularly brilliant plumage; "a sturdy oak creep on the
ground," somehow makes me think of ivy; "a Venice glass sixteen foot
deep . . . a well full of men's tears that weep," these words remind me
of some hideous illustrations I once found in a book by Bosch: they were
fairy-tale like, containing monsters and such, but they were drawn in
such detail and with such seriousness that I didn't know quite what
to make of them. However, the first eleven lines also seem to be a series
of meaningless contradictions. I would expect them to be the fragments
of the dreams of a drunkard, or something out of the wildest Edgar
Allan Poe story.

When the author says "I saw the Man that saw this wondrous sight," then he seems to suggest that he knows a Man who believes ("saw") in a thousand contradictory things; this Man is made up of many contradictory emotions and feelings. He seems to be commenting that human nature is not simple and easily analyzed. People do not always behave rationally, because there is a part to them that is more or less than rational.

Everyone else's interpretation of this poem will probably differ widely from mine. Some difference in interpretations is to be expected in all writing, but this poem makes the differences acute. The interpretations of it will vary as widely as its audience, since what each person sees in this poem is a reflection of himself. The real meaning of this poem is in the reader, who, in effect, "writes his own paper." In this sense it reminds me of "The Lady or the Tiger." Both seem to be professional in the same sense: they are elegant literary tricks, ingenious and entertaining to look at, but devices which compel introspection on the part of the audience and allow the reader almost free reign with his imagination.

"Isn't he just weaving a rug in that second paragraph?" someone asked.

"Playing the game we did with the sun and higher education you mean? I suppose in a way he is. But what interests me is what he notices about the poem in the first paragraph that leads him to try to resolve things in the way that he does in the second. How is the poem for this writer more than a matter of simple contradictions?"

"Isn't that what he calls the poem though, 'a series of meaningless contradictions'?"

"He says 'also' and 'however.' Doesn't that seem to imply that for this writer there's something else in the poem too?"

"He sees the way the lines seem to go together when he says that the oak made him think of ivy."

"Just the way we did with the ale-glass thing. Anything else the writer says that seems to suggest the poem is more than just contradictory for him?"

"Yes. The way he talks about those drawings he saw. I think what he's trying to do there is explain how the poem doesn't make sense but does make sense."

"It's 'fairy-tale like' but it's serious too, just the way Bosch's paintings of 'monsters and such' are kid stuff in one sense, but 'hideous' somehow. Maybe he's feeling for the same kind of thing with the references to 'the fragments of the dreams of a drunkard' and Poe. That is, the poem, even when it's seen as being made up of contradictions, still isn't quite *simply* drunken. And it's not *a* Poe story that the poem reminds him of; it's like 'something *out of* the wildest Edgar Allan Poe story.' It seems to be the *quality* of the poem he's trying to come to terms with, its peculiar combination, as you say, Jim, of meaning and meaninglessness. Maybe this is why in that second paragraph he tries to find an image in which contradiction and unity will exist simultaneously. So he comes up with the notion of a man who is made up of contradictions. He's got a marvelous ear."

"OK. But do you think the guy's right then when he says that the poem is like 'The Lady or the Tiger,' that it's a kind of trick?"

As a way of addressing this I turned to the final paper:

This poem has all the vividness and simultaneous confusion of a dream. It sounds as though the speaker is recounting a dream while it is still fresh in his mind and real to him. I have to really reach to find any unifying theme. Even after reading through it again and again I am tempted to write it off as nonsense. Besides the uniformity of structure, I could find little to put together and make sense out of.

Some parts of the poem seem to be describing the end of the world. The "fiery tail" of the peacock, and the "blazing comet" and later "a flame of fire" make me think of this. The reference to "a house as big as the moon and higher" with a "sun even in the midst of night" could refer to Heaven. The Man in the last sentence would be God. I can really push my imagination and come up with this interpretation but wouldn't want to try to defend it. I'm not sure it's worth defending.

Finally, I begin to wonder if the structure is as simple as it seems. The end of one sentence makes more sense when read with the beginning of the next sentence. For example, this changes what is walking from a "sturdy oak" to a "pismire." Although I can still get little more of the whole meaning of the poem, each statement makes more sense this way. This clarification of the paper by simply changing the way it is read shows the complexity of expressing ideas. The meaning of a series of thoughts may be changed or destroyed by the way they are put together. When I read the statement one way it means nothing to me. By doing nothing but changing the punctuation the poem becomes sensible, even if I can't discover any deeper meaning to it. Maybe this is a warning to me as a writer, not only to watch my words, but how they are put together.

There were groans of realization as I read through the last paragraph.
"My God, of course. Why didn't I see that?"
"What's to see?"
"Reading half of each line with half of the next: 'Swallow up a

whale I saw a raging sea.' I never got it though. I missed it completely."

"But when you have that 'it' that you missed, what is it that you have? What do you think the writer means here when he says that even though he 'gets' the poem, he still gets little more of the whole meaning of it? He's solved the puzzle. Why isn't he satisfied?"

"I think he means that even then the poem still doesn't make much sense, even if he does say it's 'sensible.' "

"I think you're right. When we solve the poem as a puzzle what do we have? We've got a poem with a speaker who says he sees a glass of beer, a well, a group of men crying, a house burning down, and so on. How do you put all that together?"

"You can't."

"At all?"

"Not any more than you could put the damn thing together to begin with."

"And in the same way. You can't put it together but you can't stop trying to."

"So the poem is a trick then, a kind of Lady or Tiger thing?"

"Except that with 'The Lady or the Tiger' you're at least clear what the options are. Here I'm not sure. I'm not even sure I've got options. I don't know whether I can make up my own meaning. This writer's metaphor of a dream that is simultaneously confused and vivid seems to me a very good one. It's like the last writer's metaphor of Bosch."

"Do you think the poem is a warning about putting words together, then?"

"That hadn't struck me as a possibility until I read this paper. I feel two ways about it. What do you think?"

"Well, it is a way of putting the poem together."

"Right. At the same time he avoids the trap of it. He gets outside the maze, as it were, to see the maze as a maze. I admire his ability to do that. What about the warning idea? Do you buy that?"

"It seems a little far out."

"What do you mean?"

"The poem doesn't seem that serious. It seems more like a joke."

There wasn't time that period to raise the question of the ways in which such a joke might be said to be an achievement, or of how the terms amateur and professional might be involved in what we'd been talking about. But The Willowdale Handcar, coming up next, and on which we'd have two periods, would give us more than world enough and time.

ASSIGNMENT 22

The Willowdale Handcar
or
The Imprudent Excursion

One summer afternoon in Willowdale, Edna, Harry and Sam wandered down to the railroad station to see if anything was doing.

There was nothing on the platform but some empty crates. "Look!" said Harry, pointing to a handcar on the siding. "Let's take it and go for a ride."

Soon they were flying along the tracks at a great rate. Little Grace Sprocket, playing in a homemade mud puddle, watched them go by with longing.

At Bogus Corners, the next town down the line, they stopped to buy soda pop and gingersnaps at Mr. Queevil's store. "How are things over in Willowdale?" he asked. "Dull," they said.

A few minutes after starting on their way again, they saw a house burning down in a field. "Whooee!" said Sam. "The engines will never be in time to save it."

The next morning they wrote postcards to everybody, telling them what they were doing and adding that they didn't know exactly when they would be back.

At 10:17 the Turnip Valley Express rushed past. A frantic face was pressed against a window of the parlor car.

"Gracious!" said Edna. "I believe that was Nellie Flim. We were chums at Miss Underfoot's Seminary. I wonder what can have been the matter."

In Chutney Falls they hunted up the cemetery and peered at the tombstones of Harry's mother's family.

Later they ran into Nellie's beau, Dick Hammerclaw, the local telegraph operator. He asked if they'd seen her. He seemed upset.

Near Gristleburg they saw a mansion on a bluff. "That's O Altitudo," said
Edna, "the home of Titus W. Blotter, the financier. Come to think of it,
Nellie is his upstairs maid."

Several days later a touring car drew up alongside them. The driver called
out something unintelligible concerning Dick before he shot away out of
sight.

From an undated fragment of the "Willowdale Triangle" which they found
caught in a tie, they learned that Wobbling Rock had finally fallen on a
family having a picnic.

In Dogear Junction they paid a call on Edna's cousins, the Zeph Claggs.
He showed them a few of the prizes from his collection of over 7,000 glass
telephone pole insulators.

The following week Mount Smith came into view in the distance; dark
clouds were piling up behind it.

During the thunderstorm that ensued, a flash of lightning revealed a figure
creeping up the embankment. "Who do you suppose it is?" said Sam.

Some months went by, and still they had not returned to Willowdale.

They visited the ruins of the Crampton vinegar works, which had been
destroyed by a mysterious explosion the preceding fall.

At Wunksieville they rescued an infant who was hanging from a hook
intended for mailbags.

"How much she resembles Nellie!" said Edna. They turned her over to the
matron of the orphanage in Stovepipe City.

From the trestle over Peevish Gorge they spied the wreck of a familiar
touring car at the bottom. "I don't see Dick's friend anywhere," said Harry.

In Violet Springs they learned that Mrs. Regera Dowdy was not receiving
visitors, but through a window they were able to see the desk on which she
wrote her poems.

As they were going along the edge of the Sogmush River, they passed a
man in a canoe. "If I'm not mistaken," said Edna, "he was lurking inside the
vinegar works."

Between West Elbow and Penetralia they almost ran over someone who
was tied to the track. It proved to be Nellie.

Despite their entreaties, she insisted on being left at the first grade cross-
ing, where she got on a bicycle and rode away.

That evening they attended a baked-bean supper at the Halfbath Methodist
Church. "They're all right," said Sam, "but they're not a patch on Mrs.
Umlaut's back home."

A week later they noticed someone who might have been Nellie walking
in the grounds of the Weedhaven Laughing Academy.

On Sunday afternoon they saw Titus W. Blotter in his shirtsleeves fleeing
into the Great Trackless Swamp.

In Hiccupboro they counted the cannon balls in the pyramids on the
courthouse lawn.

At sunset they entered a tunnel in the Iron Hills and did not come out
the other end.

The End

Edward Gorey

190   *Ideally, this story ought to be presented to you in its original form, but unfortunately the book seems to have gone out of print. Each paragraph is accompanied by an illustration drawn by the author and the whole arranged in a format reminiscent of a child's picture book. However, your concern on this assignment is with the words alone.*

Begin by making clear to a reader your understanding of this story. What is the relationship between the various characters in it? What do you make of such details as the Crampton vinegar works, those glass telephone pole insulators? What "happens" in the story exactly? What is the story about?

You may express your understanding in any way you wish: by means of equations, through the construction of a diagram (using color if you find it convenient), with a chart or graph, or by retelling the story in your own words.

(Keep a copy of this paper)

The Willowdale Handcar is like "I Saw a Peacock" in that its point is the offering of a performance with which to celebrate the self-control to be inferred from the kind of artistic control that has made the performance possible. By deliberately intermingling (in order to undercut) the conventions of plot and character with which we ordinarily find our ways through a story, by alternately fulfilling and upsetting our expectations of relationship and direction, and by manipulating, through his ability to mimic, the manners and rhetorics of a variety of story patterns, Gorey calls attention to the contrivance of what he has written in such a way as to focus a reader on his presence as its contriver, one whose ability to make something more than clichés out of the clichés it is playing with suggests in turn the illusion of an identity that is more than what it has built. For, no matter what order a reader makes of people or events in The Willowdale Handcar, with whatever "because" he seeks to replace the story's "and then," he will find his order made at the expense of something in the original context, his "meaning" mocked by a suggestion of a meaning more inclusive than it is. Any attempt to bring a conventional unity or coherence to The Willowdale Handcar will therefore coarsen what it is that Gorey achieves only by playing off such possibilities against each other. The story makes one an amateur in such a way as to bring him to an awareness of Gorey's professionalism, a process one must become in some sense professionalized in order to see.

Again, there were those students who handled Gorey either by spelling messages out of Sibyl's leaves or by writing off the narrative as meaningless. My comments on such papers I phrased so as to recall the conversation we had had on "I Saw a Peacock":

So Ivy + Cloud = Education, then?

Allegory of the Soul? How about the Peacock as symbolic of Evolution?

"Senseless" simply? Gorey's incompetent, then? Or crazy? Any other possibilities?

The majority of students, however, saw *The Willowdale Handcar* as a melodrama at the same time they were extremely uncomfortable in seeing it that way. It was this notion of the story, together with the tone of dissatisfaction accompanying it, with which I started class:

I don't know what *happens* exactly. Some things can be deduced from the events that are given us, but others seem entirely illogical. Maybe this assignment can be attacked in the same way as the Sacco letter, that is, by taking the sentences and trying to understand the significances of certain words; why he used one word when another could have been used, and by understanding what he is *saying* in each sentence.

The place to start is with Nellie. Everything revolves around Nellie. The action seems to wander, but it always comes back to Nellie.

But where do I go from here? Am I supposed to assume that each event or, more correctly, most of the events have some relevance to one another? How much can I deduce from what's given? Am I allowed to read in at all? It seems that I will have to in order to make any sense out of the story. Maybe the story was written just for the hell of it. Maybe it was written just to confuse me. But I keep coming back to those subtle hints that almost make it *start* to appear logical. I can't say for sure.

I wish I had never read this story. I'll never get it off my mind. Last night at supper I asked a guy in my class what he thought of Edna, Harry, and Sam. Another guy there suddenly asked, "You don't mean that one about the handcar with the guys on it where they ride into the tunnel and never come out, do you?"

"Yes, how did you know?"

"I read it in *Holiday* magazine a couple of years ago. Man, that was a cool story."

"Why was it cool?"

"I don't know. It was just cool."

"Did you understand it at all?"

"No."

"Then why was it so cool if you couldn't even understand it?"

192   "Don't ask me. I don't know."

As we've heard, that did not exactly clear things up.

The story *is* cool, as long as you don't have to think about it. But I do have to think about it. I've got to make some sense out of it. But I can't yet. And I bloody well realize that I'm avoiding the subject completely so I won't have to explain it.

One nearly logical way of explaining it would be the following: Harry, Edna, and Sam are me. I see the action through them. Nellie has become pregnant because of Titus Blotter and runs away. Dick, her beau, is worried because she is missing. Months pass and Nellie has the baby. Dick finds out about Titus Blotter and tries to track him down. Titus, meanwhile, finds Nellie and ties her to the track to save his reputation. Nellie ends up in a nut house, and Titus Blotter is trying to escape from Dick. We'll just have to ignore the other parts.

What I really believe is that Harry, Edna, and Sam represent me and at the end they end up in the "Iron Hills," the nut house. And the way I feel now I will too if I try to explain or understand this.

"The writer here prefaces his explanation of the story in his next to last paragraph by saying it's 'one nearly logical way' of talking about what happens in it. Why 'nearly logical,' do you suppose? Why 'one'?"

"Because he's not sure he does know what happens. There are lots of ways the story could be interpreted, just like that damned Peacock thing."

"You mean you could run a different order through the events that seem to have to do with Nellie?"

"Sure. This guy Hammerclaw could just as easily have been the father of Nellie's baby."

"Then who's Blotter fleeing from?" someone asked him. "What's he doing in the story?"

"He could have been fleeing from anybody, that woman who writes the poems, Dick's friend, anybody."

"But they aren't mentioned in connection with Nellie," said someone else. "Titus is. And she's been his upstairs maid."

"What's that prove? That doesn't mean Titus was the father."

"Of Nellie's baby?" I asked him.

"Right."

"How do you know Nellie had a baby? All the story says is that Edna says the baby they take off the mail hook 'resembles' Nellie."

"Well, who else's could it be?"

"By the same logic you've been using, it could be anybody's couldn't it? The question is, how many of us made it belong to anybody else?"

No one had. The same went for the assumption of the baby's illegitimacy and the fact that Nellie had gone insane. No one had assumed anything else. Nor had anyone in his paper seen Titus as being pursued by anyone except Dick; in each case the motive was revenge; and for everyone the revenge was for something Dick believed Titus had done to Nellie. In spite of the assertion that there was no absolute connection between the events of the story, or on the other hand that an infinite number of connections were possible, everyone who had read the story *had* made connections and certain connections everyone had made the same way. Why?

"Well, unless you make up some kind of story here you can't make sense of any of this stuff."

"I know, but how is it we all come up with the same sort of pattern? Why does everybody jump on Jim when he says Hammerclaw could just as easily be the father of the baby?"

"It doesn't fit as well that way. As Ed says, Titus has to be fleeing from somebody. The most reasonable person would be Dick."

"You say 'most reasonable,' and you talk about things' not fitting or fitting. Not fitting or fitting what?"

"The story."

"Whose?"

"What do you mean 'whose'? Gorey's story, of course."

"You mean this fragment of the 'Willowdale Triangle' we've just been talking about, the story of Nellie, Titus, and Dick the way the writer of the paper works it out? That's Gorey's story?"

"Well, we just saw that most of us made the same connections the same way."

"That's true. We all did. But is there anything familiar about the story we all came up with? Have you seen anything like it before anywhere? Wealthy Public Figure gets Young Girl in Trouble. Angry Young Suitor seeks to Avenge her Ruination, and so forth?"

"Sure. It's a soap opera cliché."

"Look at the rest of this writer's paper. How does he seem to feel about the soap opera cliché he's written out?"

"He's pretty edgy."

"How so?"

"Well, he doesn't seem to know whether he's right or not."

"Exactly. He calls his explanation only 'nearly logical.' He says he's going to 'have to ignore' a lot. At the end of the paper he seems to suggest that there's farther to go but that he can't go any farther.

Everything he writes seems to move both to and from that conversation he has at dinner, that fine metaphoric account of his frustration with the story. So what's bothering him? If he comes up with pretty much the same thing everybody else did, why is he still frustrated? Hasn't he gotten the point, the message of the story, the hidden meaning?"

"But there's more *to* the story than that, just the way when we screwed around with the lines of the Peacock thing that didn't solve everything either."

"What do you mean 'more'? What's unaccounted for?"

"Dick's friend for one thing, and the wrecked touring car. *Was* the guy Dick's friend? Only Harry says that and nobody understood anything that the guy yelled earlier except that it had to *do* with Dick. And you've got the wrecked vinegar works along with the wrecked car. I don't know whether there's a connection there or not. And then there's all this other stuff like the telephone pole insulators and cannon balls and the baked bean dinner."

"Why didn't you just leave them out?"

"I did. I had to just the way the guy in this paper did, but I know what he means when he says he doesn't know whether he should."

"You mean because the Nellie story seems to involve things like the touring car and maybe the vinegar works—and how about Wobbling Rock—you're not quite sure what's relevant here to what?"

"That's it. I'm not even sure that the Nellie story is the most important one. Maybe it's about these three people on the handcar. In a way, everything revolves around them. But when I made the story about them I did the same thing we did with the Peacock poem when we tried to see it as a vision."

"You mean you still couldn't get all the details to fit?"

"Right. I thought first it might be a story that symbolized growing up or maybe apathy. Then I figured maybe it was all a joke, that Gorey was just screwing around. Then I wasn't sure again. I'm still not."

"I know what you mean. I wouldn't know how to work Mrs. Regera Dowdy or Grace Sprocket or what Harry, Sam, and Edna do with the infant they find hanging from a mailhook into a story about apathy any more than I'd know what to do with the Crampton vinegar works in a story about growing up. I could invent of course, weave a rug, but that's what I'd be doing. I'd be leaving the story. I'd be generalizing the specificity of it into misty abstraction by making 7,000 glass telephone pole insulators a symbol of communication, for example. Or I'd forget about qualifications such as Edna's saying that she *believes* it was Nellie she saw on the train; maybe it wasn't. Later she places the man in the canoe as having been 'lurking inside the Vinegar Works'—that is, if she's 'not mistaken.' Dick is somebody who '*seemed* upset.' The woman in the asylum (if that's what the Weedhaven Laughing Academy is) 'might have been Nellie' and so on. The story's full of that sort of thing. Above all, to make it either completely a joke or completely serious, I'd have to completely ignore tone. Because the problem isn't just one of whether Wobbling Rock is part of Dick's plan for revenge or Titus' trying to shut up Nellie; it's whether a family's being squashed by something called Wobbling Rock is an event I'm supposed to laugh at or feel pity for. A house burns down in a field. ' "Whooee!" said Sam. "The engines will never be in time to save it." ' Is that the image of tragedy, of irresponsibility, or, as you say Mark, is Gorey just screwing around? The three travelers enter a tunnel in the Iron Hills at sunset and don't come out the other side. Is that intended to be grim, in some allegorically significant way, or is it a parody of allegorical significances, simply a joke? The everyday is constantly merging with the bizarre; my sense of what seems relevant is constantly being upset by what I'm not sure isn't."

"It even goes on with these damned names."

"The Halfbath Methodist Church, you mean? Dogear Junction? Chutney Falls?"

"Those yes. But I was thinking of the names of the characters too. They seem to fit the character's characters, at least most of the time. I don't know about Zeph Clagg, but Hammerclaw really pounds that telegraph. He's got claws for hands. He's violent. Blotter's a financier with a great big desk and blotter in front of him maybe."

"Also he lives way up there above the common people in O Altitudo. But it's a mansion built on a bluff. Titus or Tight-assed Blotter is a phoney. He uses his position to seduce or soak up upstairs maids (upstairs where the bedrooms are), young girls like Nellie Flim, of unformed or flimsy character, whose reputations he blots or besmirches. Would you find all this, incidentally, in a soap opera? Would you find someone named Nellie Flim on *As The World Turns*?"

"No. Soap operas are serious."

"How about a young maiden tied to the railroad tracks? Where would you find an event like that?"

"In an old-time movie."

"And the baby hanging from a mailhook?"

"Well, you wouldn't find that in the same kind of old-time movie. Or in a soap opera. It's a parody, sort of."

"Then has Gorey written out no more than a soap opera cliché?"

"No, I guess you'd have to say he was parodying it."

"Parodying it, or parodying something else?"

To make clear what I meant by that question I turned to the next writing sample, a section of a much longer paper:

One aspect of this story which I considered strange, other than the characters, was the way it was put together. I felt a strange series of feelings: being yanked up, leveled off, yanked up again, and so on. I have described this pattern on the following chart:

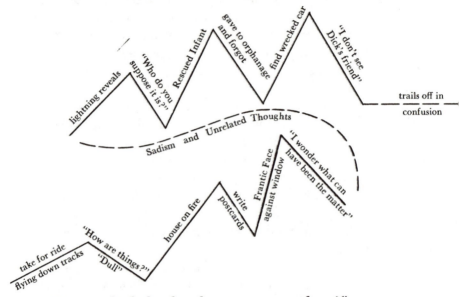

"Do you think the chart here is a very good one?"

"I'm not sure I understand it. I know what he means when he talks about being yanked up and down, of course, but I don't see where he gets sadism, and he only does about half the story."

"Maybe he's not talking about sadism in the story," said someone else. "Maybe he's trying to chart *his* feelings, how *his* interest goes up and down, or how he thinks he understands something and then doesn't. I mean that dotted line could represent how he gets to places where he's wondering how to put things together."

"What do you think the steadily climbing graph as a whole represents then?"

"I'm not sure. A way of talking about his interest maybe, an index of frustration?"

"I'm not sure either exactly, mainly because I'm not sure what feelings the specific dips and rises refer to. But let's go back for a minute into the idea of this being a chart of his feelings. Doesn't that mean he's ducked the Assignment? Wasn't the chart supposed to be one of what happens in the story?"

"Yes. I mean no and yes. My feelings are connected with what happens in the story. I think maybe that's what this guy's trying to say."

"You mean that the writer here seems to be feeling for a way of saying that what happens in Gorey is a matter of what happens to a reader reading it?"

"Yes. I know that's the way it is with me. Every time I'm ready to say this thing is stupid or silly or meaningless, Gorey throws in something that pushes me another way."

"In other words, he doesn't give you a soap opera or an allegory but just enough to get you moving in one of those directions. . . ."

"Before he pulls the rug out from under me."

"OK. Before I see that what I've done is to read into Gorey a pattern that isn't there. Does *The Willowdale Handcar* just make fun of soap operas then, just parody allegories?"

"I think what he's making fun of is me."

"Unless, of course, you're in on the joke."

The professionalism of Gorey's reading of a reader was the next thing to move into.

ASSIGNMENT 23

The Willowdale Handcar:
Edward Gorey as a
professional

Look over what you did with the Gorey story. In a paragraph or two, try explaining how you arrived at the understanding you expressed there.

On the basis of a comparison between your retelling of the Gorey story and the original, which would you say is the more professional performance? Make clear what you mean by professional.

The most interesting papers addressed to Assignment 23 were those in which the students began to feel for some way of moving their "understanding" of *The Willowdale Handcar* as an "it" to an understanding of that "it" as a "he" or an "I." To stick with their original renditions of Gorey's story as an "it" which "is" or "was," which had a "message" or "hidden meaning" that had to be "found" or "extracted" or "dug out," was to have no way of coming to terms with Gorey as a performer or themselves as audience for the performance, no way of making the term professional mean much more than what is involved in the maneuverings of a game of hide and seek. I set up the class with two papers that I hoped would take us to a fuller meaning for the term.

My "understanding" of the Gorey story was in part an attempt to create order from what looked like deliberate chaos and in part an attempt to explain the strange things that happened to time and sequence of events as the story progressed. The discontinuity of the story reminds me of a science fiction story about "homo superioribus," men who had such highly developed powers of reasoning and deduction and such enormous memories that conversation between them consisted entirely of one or two-word sentences. Given the tone of the speaker, his memories, and his own associations with words, the listener could construct entire paragraphs from one or two words. In much the same way, I was able to develop a construct that satisfied my demand for a semi-reasonable explanation of what was going on. It is entirely possible that in doing this I have done the same injustice to "The Imprudent Excursion" that I did to "I Saw a Peacock," which was that I assumed that there was a meaning behind an intellectual trap. Gorey could quite possibly have written the story to frustrate people like me who want order (which is not to be interpreted as stagnation) and dislike inexplicable *non sequiturs.* The professionalism in this type of writing is cleverness in misleading the reader to find "a" meaning or no meaning in nonsense, to create the illusion of reality which would appeal to the snobbery of the reader who believes he gets something out of a story that no one else does.

On the other hand this story *could* have been written to *allow* the reader to "write his own paper" (as I stubbornly maintain, in the face of all opposition, that "I Saw a Peacock" was). In this case the professionalism involved would be of a different sort—the ingenuity to create the skeleton of a story which, while allowing *each* reader to supply his own images, compels *every* reader to come up with the same plot and similar action. Thus I'd be willing to bet that every one of the twenty-odd students in this class has written approximately the same paper on "understanding" the tale. A brand of trickery is involved in this story, whichever way the reader is intended to interpret it. Either the writer wants the reader to change what has been presented in order to create "sense" for himself, or the reader is to supplement what he reads—again to create his own "sense." It can be pointed out, of course, that building another story is the easiest way to "dust off" the assignment of trying to understand the original. However, I still think that if it was an easy assignment, it was because we were intended to hear and react to it the way we did and to have fun doing so.

In trying to compare the relative professionalism of the original story and my "revised" version of it that I presented as my "understanding," I think it is important to realize that I am trying to accomplish something different from Gorey. While he presents a story, I am interpreting it according to the associations that I have for the events in the story. In this respect I think Gorey's effort is better than mine for the simple reason that he is attempting to implicitly rather than explicitly tell a tale, and I am free to say exactly what I think.

I began our conversation about the paper by asking the class to make what distinctions they could between the writer's two ways of understanding the professionalism of Gorey's performance. Was it possible, I wanted to know, to see one as more applicable than the other. It was a while before anyone said anything.

"I guess I'm not sure exactly what his second point is," one boy said finally. "He wins his bet; I can see that from the class we had last time. But I don't get what he means when he tries to tie that in with saying that the 'story *could* have been written to *allow* the reader to "write his own paper." ' "

"You mean you don't agree with the writer, you don't think you can make Gorey's story mean anything you want it to?"

"Not without leaving things out or feeling silly, no. You can't do that with the poem either, no matter what this writer maintains."

"Not finally, anyway. I can defend a lot of interpretations of both the poem and the story, but I can't prove just one. That is, I'm OK with *an* interpretation of either the poem or the story, until someone starts asking me questions (or until I start asking them of myself) about how some of the details fit or whether they couldn't be used in a different way. In other words, there's something about the story and about 'I Saw a Peacock' too, that pushes you past saying 'I can make this mean anything I want it to'?"

"Yes. I can see that the story and the poem too, are written so as to allow me to *think* I can make them mean anything I want them to. For a while."

"But then that possibility becomes just another possibility in a whole mess of possibilities. Do you think this writer is right then in locating the professionalism of Gorey's story where he does first? He suggests first that the story is written to frustrate the desire to make order out of chaos, to mislead a reader into finding ' "a" meaning or no meaning in nonsense.' "

"I think so, yes. If I try to make Gorey mean just one thing, I'm screwed. If I try to make him mean nothing, I'm screwed again."

"Unless you've got a way of saying what you just said. You're not screwed now, are you?"

"What do you mean?"

"I mean if you can see an intellectual trap as an intellectual trap the way you just did, the way the writer of the paper does when he uses that phrase, then you're not caught in that damned-if-you-do-damned-if-you-don't situation any more, are you?"

"Are you saying this thing is a trick the way the writer of the paper says, something you have to catch onto?"

"Well, let's look at exactly what he says. It's at the opening of his next to last paragraph: 'A brand of trickery is involved in this story, whichever way the reader is intended to interpret it. Either the writer wants the reader to change what has been presented in order to create "sense" for himself, or the reader is to supplement what he reads—again to create his own "sense."' Now, in the language of the assignment, how did you arrive at the understanding of *The Willowdale Handcar* you expressed in your last paper?"

"I did pretty much what this writer says. I built paragraphs out of hints. I filled in gaps. I developed a construct."

"And to do that you changed and supplemented?"

"Sure. I had to."

"We all did. We all do. But when we compare what we do in order to read Gorey that way with what Gorey does in his reading of us, though it's important to realize, as this writer points out, that we are doing different things, maybe the phrase 'brand of trickery' can be understood in more than one way. Let's look at a final paper."

"The Great Trackless Swamp," "Titus W. Blotter," "West Elbow," "Penetralia," "Zeph Clagg," all of these are names from the imagination of children. Only the very young can "fly along the tracks at a great rate," and then "stop to buy soda pop and gingersnaps at Mr. Queevil's store," while remaining in their own back yard. The matter-of-fact way in which these strange names and stranger happenings are told is reminiscent of the way in which a child describes the unbelievable. This real-but-it's-not-real tone to the story was partly the reason why I interpreted it as the creation of a child's imagination. And when I did so I convinced myself I was right.

However, there are certain aspects of the story which remind me of the poem which we discussed in class. It seems as though any proposed all-inclusive "explanation" of the story will fail at some point or other, and I must add that mine appears painfully contrived when it tries to account for the incidents at Violet Springs and Sogmush River. This story is like a Cheshire cat, propounding all sorts of riddles, each of which has a thousand meanings and interpretations, and then grinning at the reader as he tries to fit every possible meaning into one grand plan; it is like a huge kaleidoscope in which each little portion may have a meaning by itself but in the whole picture becomes part of a larger design. I think Gorey's is the more professional work because he can fit adulthood with its touring cars, mountain scenery, and cemeteries and childhood with its mud puddles and soda pop all into one story, while I at best have created an approximation of only one part of the picture.

"How would you compare this writer's attitude toward what Gorey has done and toward what he has done with Gorey with the first writer's attitude toward the same things?"

"I think, as you're always saying, that they could talk to each other. They seem to have different attitudes, but I think they'd understand each other. Both writers see that they had to change what Gorey wrote to get it to make sense. The first one says he had to add things, the second says he got only part of the picture. In a way, it's the same difference."

"They're talking about the same qualities in Gorey, yes, but when you say their attitudes are different, you suggest that they're naming those qualities differently, that they're taking a different position in relation to Gorey. How would you describe *that* difference?"

"Well, the writer of the second paper doesn't seem to feel tricked by Gorey the way the writer of the first one does. The first writer seems to think that Gorey deliberately misled him."

"You mean the writer of the first paper doesn't really mean that he was 'allowed' to ' "write his own paper" ' at all, but feels that he was pushed into it, pushed into adding things to the story to get it to make sense?"

"It seems that way to me. He says 'I think we were intended to hear and react to it the way we did and to have fun doing so.' But I think he still resents it a little bit."

"What does he resent?"

"The false trails that Gorey sends him on, the way you can't work anything out in the story for sure."

"Why do you think the writer of the second paper *doesn't* seem to resent Gorey? He says that he too had to contrive things to get the story to make sense, things that he suggests wouldn't work out unless he did contrive them."

"Maybe," said someone else, "because he realizes that Gorey didn't weave the rugs; he did."

"What do you mean, Sam?"

"I mean maybe this guy sees that Gorey didn't send him down false trails just that way. There are plenty of false leads, sure, but we saw last time that there is always some way you can tell that you can't be sure whether you're right or not. The cliché story of Nellie, for instance. Gorey didn't write that out; we did. So maybe this writer doesn't resent Gorey because he realizes that it was his own fault for trying to make those false trails, or one of them, the right one."

"Where do you find all that in the paper?"

"Well, he never comes right out and says so, but when he says that he tried to convince himself that his first interpretation was right, and then talks about the story's being 'like a Cheshire cat, propounding all sorts of riddles, each of which has a thousand meanings and interpretations, and then grinning at the reader as he tries to fit every possible meaning into one grand plan,' I think he's saying that the whole point of Gorey was to lead him to see that he couldn't work the story out as having just one meaning the way he first thought he could."

" 'Lead him to see.' Do you mean that you think he believes Gorey intended him to see that this 'intellectual trap' was an 'intellectual trap'?"

"Yes, I think he did. I mean I think that's what this guy thinks and what Gorey intended both. The first writer feels Gorey is a pro in the way he makes a sucker out of a snob. I think the second writer would agree and would say that he was one of the snobs."

"Which he doesn't seem to resent Gorey for?"

"No, because what Gorey wrote helped him see it by making him look again. I think he admires Gorey. I think he's grateful to him."

"OK. You mean he admires Gorey, or, in the terms he uses, sees Gorey as giving a more professional performance than he first thought he was giving, because the rug he wove of *The Willowdale Handcar* he now sees Gorey as having already woven into something larger, a 'larger design,' as he calls it. Any interpretation of *The Willowdale Handcar* that settles for less than this 'whole picture,' that is made without reference to the kaleidoscope of the whole, will be made at the expense of the whole. There's no question that there's what this writer sees as a childlike wonder at work in the story, but it's fused with what he calls 'adulthood' in much the same way that we saw the clichés about Nellie fused with a parody of them. You can't pry them apart. . . ."

"Any more than you can get them together."

"At least not without reference to the fact that someone is shaping them in such a way as to make it impossible for me to do either. In other words, to continue with the terminology suggested by the writer of this second paper, Gorey sets up his story to force me, or, as Sam

204   has it, so that I force myself, into acting like an amateur, which in this instance means that he forces me to come up with one explanation for a phenomenon that can't be explained with just one explanation. So I'm in a bind, one that the only way out of is to recognize the professionalism of the performance that has put me in it."

"So Gorey makes you an amateur in order to see that he's a pro?"

"In part I think, but it doesn't stop even there if I follow Sam's line with this second paper and ask myself what I've had to become in order to see that I've acted like an amateur."

"You have to become more than an amateur, that's for sure."

"OK. In coming to know what Gorey knows then, I have to become in some sense professionalized."

"You mean when you see you can't beat Gorey, you join him."

"But not *until* you see that. It's a freedom you have to work to, a right you have to earn. And depending on how you feel about what you've come from, and how, and on where it is you finally find yourself, you can see the process in a number of ways. The whole thing can be seen as a trick, as a joke you have to catch onto, or maybe even as a demonstration of the power of language."

ASSIGNMENT 24

What is the sense of nonsense?

In the last three Assignments you have been at work on the subject of nonsense. Like so much else in our lives, nonsense is easy to experience, but a difficult subject to come to terms with.

What do you see as the sense of nonsense?

Is this a sense that you as a writer can make use of?

Assignment 24 is another of those I look back on with a wince, knowing that if I had it to do over again I'd set it up differently, knowing that I could make it better. I'd get rid of the coy patronization of "like so much else in our lives." I'd turn the second question, which as it stands is only nominally a question, and a ragged one at that, into a real question and phrase it so as to try to make it of some help to the students in their formulating an approach to their papers. In other words, since nonsense is identifiable as a phenomenon only as the result of a reader's discovering that what is written has a writer, a writer with whom he has had to establish a relationship, then in the Assignment I'd try to provide the students with a context for "sense of nonsense" which would make clear the crucial importance of this reader-writer relationship to the phrase, whatever else anyone might choose to make it mean. Finally, I would conclude the Assignment by asking the students how understanding what is involved in the writing and reading of nonsense can help to clarify what is involved in the activities of writing and reading in general, what one does to compose a page or to compose one's self to read one. The Assignment would have been better written this way:

> *For the last three Assignments we have been grappling with the paradox of the sense of nonsense. As we have seen from the two texts we have looked at, from the sample papers addressed to them, and from the conversations we have had about both, nonsense seems to occupy a kind of borderland between meaning and meaninglessness, a sort of no-man's land the only way out of which is through a recognition of the nonsense writer as a nonsense writer.*
>
> *As a writer yourself, you may never wish to create anything like "I Saw a Peacock" or* The Willowdale Handcar, *but perhaps the writers who did demonstrated something in their writing that you would like to be able to demonstrate in yours. Whether you envy such writers or not, describe as clearly as you can what abilities they seem to have. Your problem here, of course, will be to make such terms as "competence" and "skill" mean something.*
>
> *What does what you have seen as the ability of a writer of nonsense reveal to you about the activity of writing, specifically your own struggles with your own writing?*
>
> *What does your experience as a reader of nonsense reveal to you about the activity of reading, your own struggles with your own reading?*

The students were a lot better with the Assignment they had to work with than either it or I deserved. The first paper I mimeographed to go over in class, for example, was one in which the writer attempts to find a point for the "pointlessness" of nonsense in his own conception of just the sort of reader-writer relationship I have tried to describe above, that strange meeting through language which creates at the same time a meeting in more than language:

> The way of seeing implied by the Gorey story and the poem seems to be a sort of "give and take" session between the author and the reader. Both the author and the reader give each other credit for intelligence. They are both "in on" what the author has written. Instead of the author's trying to convey a message to the reader by means of a piece of writing, the author and the reader look at the writing together.
>
> This is why I had so much trouble understanding both the poem and the Gorey story. I kept looking for the message that they were trying to get across. I listed the events in chronological order, the introduction of all the characters, the relationship between each character, etc. Finally

I began to see that this was ridiculous. Yet I didn't want to say that the assignment was a joke, either, because the assignment was to tell what happened exactly. But I couldn't and I didn't. Then after the last Humanities class I saw that there was no point to the story in the way that I'd been looking for one, and that *that* was the point. Now I'm at the point of trying to determine the point of the pointlessness.

Gorey, instead of asking "Do you get the point in this story?," says "Get whatever you want out of this story. It's what you make of it. If you want it to be only a joke, it's a joke. If you want to get a deep meaning out of it, go ahead. But whatever you get, it's me you're going to have to contend with, because I wrote it." Once I was "in on" the Gorey story, once I saw what he was doing, I began to hear what he was saying. Then, instead of hating the story, I began to enjoy it. This is the sense of nonsense.

Now I see why I enjoy the comic strips *B.C.* and *The Wizard of Id.* In *B.C.* once, Thor was walking across the desert and saw a sign that said "Duck." He did and a stone went flying over his head and smashed the sign. I didn't get the point of it then, even though I enjoyed it. Now I see why I enjoyed it. I wasn't supposed to get a point out of it that way any more than I was out of Gorey's tale. As with all writing, I was supposed to enjoy the author.

"To judge from the rest of the paper," I began, "what do you think the writer here means at the end of his first paragraph by saying that a writer of nonsense is trying to do something other than 'convey a message' to a reader? What else is there in writing?"

"I think what he's getting at is that with nonsense, at least nonsense that's caught on to, the writer and the reader share something. I think that's what he means when he says that 'both the author and the reader give each other credit for intelligence.'"

"They're both in on the know? They share a joke? Well, how is that different from 'conveying a message'?"

"It's more personal, for one thing. I think that's why he imagines that Gorey is talking to him, why he has Gorey say 'whatever you get, it's me you're going to have to contend with, because I wrote it.'"

"Can you make your term 'personal' anything more than a magic word? Can you make it mean something specific here?"

"What I mean is I think this guy is saying that nonsense forces a reader to deal with the writer of it."

"Forces him, that is, to go through the frustration that the writer describes in his second paragraph. But in order to make him see that he's being manipulated by someone? Is that what you mean?"

"Yes, it forces him to see that there's somebody behind the whole thing, that the story's a put up job, in a way."

"And that's different from 'conveying a message'?"

"Sure, the message here is the guy behind it. It's Gorey."

"He uses *The Willowdale Handcar* to communicate himself then? That's what you mean by 'personal'?"

"I guess it is. I don't know what kind of person he is exactly, but I feel him here."

"And as something more than just what Nellie and Titus and the Sogmush River add up to. I know what you mean. Just as I know what this writer means. Some presence I call 'Gorey' seems to be *in* the way things are arranged, the way they move, in the same way that if I were to say I know you, Dan, I'd mean that I thought I knew how you looked at things, how you put things together. I suppose that's what I mean when I look at *The Willowdale Handcar* and say I have the illusion that I'm looking at Gorey. I'm looking at a very individual kind of putting together, a putting together of things that won't go together and yet somehow do and yet don't, and so on. Forever. A recognition and acknowledgement of Gorey's mind, the 'I' who wrote all this, seems to be the only way out of things."

"And if you don't deal with Gorey's mind you don't *get* out of things."

"Which is why the writer's imagining Gorey's saying he was going to 'have to contend' with him is such a fine way of putting it. Does any of this suggest why the writer likes *B.C.*, by the way?"

"He says he sees now that he thinks he enjoys the author, Johnny Hart; the guy who draws it."

"The reason, maybe, he speaks of the strip in general, of more than the one example of it he gives, and why he connects it with another strip, *The Wizard of Id,* which he implies he responds to the same way. What he likes, what he seems to enjoy is style—the way the doing of a thing creates the image of a doer. This is why to experience a good joke I don't go to one of the collections of Bennett Cerf; I'd rather go to someone I know can tell one. I'd like to ask one more thing about this paper, using the language that Sam used about the last paper we looked at last time. Would you say that *this* writer seems in any way grateful to Gorey?"

"I think he is. I like the way he says that he couldn't hear what Gorey was saying until he saw what he was doing. I think he's suggesting that Gorey was jerking him around to help him to hear."

"It's a nice sentence, that one. The suggestion of it, implicitly anyway, seems to be that to deal with Gorey's art is to have to become artful."

"He also seems to think he sees something about why he enjoys the comic strips that he didn't see before," said someone else. "But at the very end I'm not sure what he means when he says 'as with all writing.' Is he talking about something more than comic strips, or what?"

"That's what I was wondering," I said. "It may be just a tag, an end of the paper flourish. Or it may be that he's trying to suggest that his study of nonsense did something for his conception of reading in general. There's not enough here to be able to tell. But it wasn't the only paper that touched on the idea. Let's look at another one."

Reading these compositions is like trying to read a story rapidly in the dark while a strobe light flashes on and off: you see bits and fragments of prose without really getting the connections between them. In these compositions, there is no final connection to get, although they are cleverly constructed to make the reader look for "the point." But the entire point to both works is that there is no point. Not that way.

There is a similar aspect of unconnectedness about the type of riddle which tells you the brakeman's name, the number of passengers on the train, the color of the fireman's sox, and then demands to know where the engineer lives. It seems obvious, on first inspection, that the problem is unsolvable, yet a certain glimmer of sense or a faint possibility of some connection continually plagues the would-be solver.

The Willowdale Handcar and "I Saw a Peacock" are carefully planned traps for the deep-meaning seekers, those who demand a definite and profound "point" from everything they read, and who therefore miss everything else along the way. This course, for example, is a kind of *Willowdale Handcar,* which is why I think I had so much trouble a few assignments back trying to explain the "point" of it to someone else. I don't mean that I think the course is pointless, not any more than I believe Gorey is. But I couldn't talk about what I'm learning in it by saying that the "point" of it all is to get me to write a perfect paper.

One other way that I as a would-be writer can make use of the poem and the story is to see them as barbs aimed at those who insist on defining the professional as a demigod, amateurs as villains, and advice as something which is purchased over the counter. I have been convinced that the refusal to define life, and ultimately one's self, in grossly oversimplified, black and white terms is necessary for anyone who doesn't want to view himself as a comic-strip character or perhaps as a mere "point" on a line.

"What is it that this writer suggests that the study of nonsense did for his understanding of the activities of reading and writing?"

"Boy. The connections he makes I didn't. I didn't think to."

"I didn't think to either, not in the way that he makes them. Which ones struck you particularly?"

"Well, his point about 'point' for one thing. He realizes that looking for the 'point' of the story and the poem isn't going to get him any-where, the same way the writer of the other paper did, but I like the way he says that the point of that is to trap the 'deep-meaning seekers.' "

"The way the writer of the first paper we looked at last time did, the one who talked about snobbery?"

"Yes, except that this guy carries it farther the way he connects it with the course and what we've been doing. That's what I didn't see before."

"You mean where he suggests that the course isn't pointless, but that he can't talk about it in terms of 'points' and get very far?"

"Yes. If he tries to be a 'deep-meaning seeker' with this course in the way he means—'The point of this class was how you write an in-troductory paragraph'—he's going to miss all of it."

" 'Everything else along the way'?"

"Yes."

"Such as what? What else is there? What more is there to writing than 'conveying a message'? You can flatter me if you want to, Ken."

"Well, there is something else. I know that and I know you do. But I can't say what. I flopped on the same Assignment this guy says he did. And for the same reason."

"If you could say what the 'something else' was so as to make sense to just anybody, then maybe you wouldn't need to be here. Isn't the problem one of how to find language for a process that stands at one and the same time both for itself and the people doing it? That riddle, for example, that this writer refers to. It isn't a riddle at all really, yet I'd enjoy hearing it depending on how well someone told it. The 'point' there would be the performance of the telling—and the fact that I'd been able to participate in it. The guy who could say that the 'point' of someone's going to the last Superbowl game was to relieve tension, I'd know was not in my world. How I'd get him into my world is another thing again. I'd have a problem talking to someone who thought that the 'point' of love-making was to have children, too."

"Wouldn't that be the same as what this guy says is wrong with de-fining advice as something you purchase over the counter?"

"Right. It would be to define what I 'see' in such a way as to define myself as what this writer calls a comic-strip character. That way, with 'point' talk—isn't that a nice pun he has in his final sentence?—*I* become a point, a point on a line, just as he says."

"You remember Ken said that he hadn't made any of these connections?"

"Yes."

"Then you said that you hadn't, either? Is that really true?"

"I said that they hadn't occurred to me in the way that the writer made them."

"But there was a way in which we were supposed to connect the story and the poem with how this damned course is put together?"

That one, I told him, with my best Walter Mitty faint, fleeting smile, was a question I thought we'd just let ride.

ASSIGNMENT 25

Explaining a scientific law
to a nonscientist

Here is a statement from a well-known essay:

A good many times I have been present at gatherings of people who, by the standards of the traditional culture, are thought highly educated and who have with considerable gusto been expressing their incredulity at the illiteracy of scientists. Once or twice I have been provoked, and have asked the company how many of them could describe the Second Law of Thermodynamics. The response was cold; it was also negative. Yet I was asking something which is about the scientific equivalent of: Have you read a work of Shakespeare's?

C. P. Snow, *The Two Cultures*

Perhaps you do not feel as Snow does about the Second Law of Thermodynamics, but, presumably, you feel something about the importance of some scientific law or principle. What law or principle? Explain it so as to make it understandable to a nonscientist, and explain also why you believe it to be important.

Do you think a nonscientist should know about it? Know what, exactly? And why?

I devised the Assignments on nonsense primarily to focus the students on language-using as a self-creating activity. Assignments 25 through 29 I wrote to invite the students to examine some of the implications of that proposition in terms of the nominal subject with which we'd started the course. In this last grouping of Assignments for the term, then, I ask the students, all of whom as freshmen at Case Institute of Technology had chosen to become professional scientists, to make what they can of the implications of seeing different disciplines as different language systems and of the implications of seeing a professional as someone able to use the language of his system to grow as a person.

In addressing Assignment 25, the students had no difficulty in speaking as technicians. Inside the system of, say, Newtonian physics they had little difficulty in relating one symbol to another. What they did not seem able to make into a subject was the recognition that it was symbol systems they were working with, and that the connection of them to other symbol systems, let alone to the world of phenomena, is an incredibly complex if not a finally mysterious business. That there is a relationship between $E = mc^2$ and Hiroshima we can more than take for granted. But it is no more possible to combine the universe of one of these terms with that of the other than it would be to explain the mechanics of motion with Ohm's law. To say that a scientist can "make understandable" to a nonscientist the meaning of $F = ma$ is to speak contradictorily. Either nothing like communication will have gone on, or the nonscientist, as a result of the explanation, will have become a scientist. What looks to be a problem of simple translation in Assignment 25 then, is in fact a problem of identity.

I do not think, however, that Assignment 25 is Assignment 6 all over again (*Try to imagine a world in which everyone was either an amateur or a professional.*). At this point in the course, for a student to have recognized the impossibility of dealing with the problem of Assignment 25 in one way (which no one did), should have been to see the possibility of another way of talking. In confronting the paradox of the importance of "some scientific law or principle" *because* of its meaninglessness outside the system to which it has relevance, there is the opportunity for a scientist to come to terms with himself as a scientist, to discover through his description of the incommunicable nature of something scientific to the nonscientist, the indispensable significance of it to himself. From this point of view, what a nonscientist should know about ("Know what, exactly?") is not "some scientific law or principle," but the importance of a *scientist's* knowing about such a law or principle. The nonscientist who could best under-

214   stand this, the ideal audience for such a description, would, of course, be another professional in another field.

The shift in nominal subject (perhaps it looked also like a move to Familiar Territory), I was discouraged to see, brought with it a kind of reversion in a lot of the students' papers—enough of it for us to have to deal with. The three sentences I reproduced as our first writing sample (all of which represent ways of talking which can come to very little) I drew from the first paragraphs of three separate papers. In each case the tone and manner of the sentence was representative of the drift of the rest of the paper. What, to judge from each sentence, was the rest of that paper like? It was a procedure I expected everyone to realize we'd been through before:

Every well-rounded person ought to know something of the Law of . . .

Without Ohm's Law, your television set, your refrigerator, the lights in your house—none of these would work. This is why we . . .

We can understand the equation more easily if we "translate" it. F stands for force, and for a scientist this means a push or a pull. m stands for . . .

"You mean how do I think each guy went on?"

"If you want to come at it that way. How did he go on? How would you feel about going on as a reader of the paper? They're representative sentences. In tone. Of the intellectual weather of the papers generally."

"Well the first one sounds like the opening of a paper."

"Uh huh. And?"

"It's pretty general."

"Get the money up, man."

"OK. Isn't 'something' a kind of magic word here? At least it could be. How much is 'something'?"

"How round is 'well-rounded'? It's a pretty safe opener, wouldn't you say?"

"Yeah, I guess so."

"Safe how?"

"Well, he's bullet-proofed himself. His explanation doesn't have to be all that good when it's only 'something' you ought to know."

"Who ought? I mean what sort of individual would this 'well-rounded person' be, to judge from the tone there? What's 'well-rounded' mean in that context?"

"I guess he'd have to be a kind of slob. At least I don't see the guy writing this thinking very much of him. 'I'll give you what you need to know, sonny, and it's for your own good.' That's about what I hear."

"What's the writer here really think of the law he's so convinced of the importance of, so far as you're concerned?"

"He doesn't convince me he thinks it's important at all, if that's what you mean. You don't even know what law he's going to talk about. Isn't that why you left it out, to show that it could be any law? That it doesn't matter?"

"Any law or any subject. Shakespeare. English history. Thermodynamics. As you say, it doesn't seem to matter much. If it did he wouldn't pussyfoot around with this 'something' and 'well-rounded' stuff. He'd come on a lot stronger than that. And, in caring whether he explained it, he'd care also whom he imagined he was talking to— a way of saying I guess that you can't care what you're talking about if you don't care whom you're talking to and *vice versa*. Not at least as a writer. What about the other two sentences?"

"That second one is worse. It makes me think I'm back in a sixth grade science unit. 'Now kiddies, you better pay attention. Your TV might not work some night if you don't know about Mr. Ohm and his Law.' "

"And the 'we' in what follows, does it mean 'we'?"

"Hell no. It means I'm up here and you're down there."

"Is it only the tone that makes you think of sixth grade, Dan? What sort of scientific validity does the sentence have?"

"Well, Ohm's Law doesn't make a refrigerator run, for God's sake."

"Not any more than the laws of motion cause people to die in automobile accidents. How about the third sentence?"

"That's second grade. A is for apple. B is for bear. Like I'm a ninny."

We turned then to a slightly more complicated example of the problem of the Assignment. Again, it was only a section of a paper we worked with:

Another example is a falling body. If you were to jump off the top of a tall building, you could look at the windows going past on the way down. At first they would be going relatively slowly. But they would begin to pass faster and faster until you hit. This is acceleration under the force of gravity. This force is constant. You cannot control it like the gas pedal to a car, and your mass remains constant. So you undergo constant acceleration. The longer you fall (neglecting air resistance) the faster you will be going when you hit the ground. This you probably know from experience.

"What is this, anyway?" someone asked me.

"I told you," I said. "It's a paragraph out of a paper. But you weren't really asking a question, were you? What are you saying?"

"I just can't believe the guy's serious, but I'm not sure."

He stopped. Then he looked up. I waited. They were maybe a bit out of shape after those swinging classes we'd had on nonsense.

"You want me to explain," he said.

That wasn't a question either, as I knew he knew both of us knew. I just went on waiting.

"OK. At first this thing looks like one of those three sentences: 'Hey, you down there' the way Dan said. But I don't know whether this writer uses 'you' the same way exactly. Maybe it's that example he uses. I mean you wouldn't use this kind of example with a bunch of sixth graders, telling them to notice the windows as they fell past. It's too ridiculous."

"Maybe he means it that way," said someone else. "Maybe he's making a joke?"

"Out of the Assignment?" I asked. "Saying it's all too silly for words?"

"No. It's like he's making a joke *for* somebody, as though he *expects* him to see it's a joke."

"Who? That seems to be the key question here, doesn't it? Who *is* he talking to? What's his audience?"

"Well, maybe it *is* a group of students, of high school students, say. It's almost as though he's making fun of the 'A is for apple, B is for bear' approach to things."

"Would that kind of parody be successful as a way of teaching?"

"In high school it could be. I couldn't see my physics teacher here coming on this way, but in high school I could see it as very successful. It's not a bad start for explaining acceleration either."

"Why couldn't you see your physics teacher here using it? Why wouldn't it be a good teaching technique in college?"

"It doesn't go far enough. It can't go deep enough."

"In other words, the audience for this kind of thing would be made up of those who were not professionally interested in the subject?"

"And who didn't know very much about it. It's a good attention getter, a good start maybe, but that's about as far as it can go."

"That is, it's limited. I'd praise the writer here for at least trying to find a way of talking rather than settling for trying to find a way to avoid talking. His paper doesn't postulate an audience of ten-year olds or of ninnies the way the first three sentences do. On the other hand, if in those first three sentences the attention to subject swallows the attention to audience which then gobbles up the effectiveness of the writing—here, the attention to audience, as you suggest, Sam, has a tendency to swallow the subject. And it isn't just that the writer can't move that kind of talk into equations; it's that he can't use it to make a nonscientist above the level of a high school student feel the importance to a scientist of what he's talking about, not in the *way* that it's important to a scientist. He can talk, that is, about something you could call 'acceleration.' But he can't talk about *his* acceleration."

"Could anybody? Is it possible?"

"Let's look at the last paper."

I understand why Snow asked people about the Second Law of Thermodynamics. If he had used instead the theory of relativity or the quantum theory, his victims could have squirmed away by mumbling about Einstein and atomic bombs. They could have picked that up from science fiction movies. But to be acquainted with the Second Law of Thermodynamics they would have had to go to roughly the scientific equivalent of a work of Shakespeare's.

Although this Second Law is not widely understood, it is one of the most important statements of physics. Many laymen think they can boil the Law down to a statement that "heat flows from hot bodies to cooler ones"—a statement which turns out to be only the simplest example of a law that is a lot more complicated and far-reaching.

Basically, the Second Law concerns the idea of entropy or the state of organization of heat energy. Heat is said to be more highly organized when the same amount of it is concentrated into smaller quantities of matter. This concentration is really the concept of temperature. Saying that heat flows only from warmer to cooler subjects is then the equivalent of the more general statement that heat moves only from a state of high organization to a state of lower organization. Practically, this means that we can't apply heat to a light bulb and expect to get electricity or heat an automobile engine and get gasoline in return. In each case, according to the Second Law, the heat cannot be put to use because it cannot become more highly organized. This is to say that there are processes in nature that are not reversible.

There are more far-reaching if less practical implications of the Second Law which very few people realize. Our universe is a system made up of hotter and colder bodies. According to the Second Law, heat is constantly flowing from hot to cold ones, but never in reverse. For this reason the differences in temperature are becoming less and less.

218   Mr. Snow would say that the system is becoming more homogeneous. Our concept of the flow of time is tied up with this increasing disorganization. An event is said to occur later when it is associated with greater disorganization than another event which is said to occur before. In effect we tell the past from the future by differences in disorganization. This means that our universe must finally run down. In this state of complete homogeneity there will be no difference in past, present, and future.

The Second Law has to do not only with the laboratory concept of heat transfer, but also with such universally important things as temperature, time, and the ultimate fate of the universe. For this reason it is relevant to nonscientists as well as scientists. I think the layman should be aware of this Second Law, but like many scientific principles it is not necessary that he understand it as a scientist must. This would require as much effort as a scientist would expend in becoming completely familiar with Shakespeare, if that is possible. The layman should realize, however, that he may seem as illiterate to the scientist as the scientist may seem to him. There should be mutual respect for each other's type of literacy and mutual understanding of the gap that exists between them.

"Whew," said the first student who spoke. "*He's* sure not talking to an audience of ten-year-olds or to high school students."

"What about the electric light bulb bit, and the 'we': 'we can't apply heat to a light bulb and expect to get electricity'?"

"But he's not talking down to anybody there. That's not a simple-minded example either. I appreciate it at that point. I need it."

"So do I. I need as much of that kind of thing as I can get in this paper. Does he give you what you 'need' as a reader at any other point in the paper?"

"He does it a lot. When he talks about that light bulb, for instance, he says '*practically,* this means. . . .' He's trying to put theory into practical terms for me."

"As well as showing that the theoretical has practical consequences. Where else does he do it?"

"Well, he finishes that paragraph by saying 'this is to say that there are processes in nature that are not reversible.'"

"There he's turning the specific back into the general. Any place else?"

"Yes. 'Mr. Snow would say that the system is becoming more homogeneous.' And 'this means that our universe must finally run down.' And in the last paragraph he connects the Second Law with temperature, time, and the fate of the universe."

"OK. All of these could be said to be explanations for a reader, ways of showing him the importance of the Second Law of Thermodynamics by showing its extending from what the writer calls 'the laboratory concept of heat transfer' into all sorts of other areas. My question about *that* is, what do these explanations explain to a reader about the writer? What does the fact that they're in the paper in the way that they are tell you about him?"

"You know, it's funny. I'm not sure I understand all the connections he's making, but I know damned well he thinks the Second Law of Thermodynamics is important."

"You mean what those explanations could be said to explain is the writer's belief in the importance of what he's talking about?"

"Right."

"But you also said that you didn't think you understood all the connections he made—which I don't either by the way, particularly in that incredible next to last paragraph where temperature moves into time which moves into the obliteration of time. Does this mean he's talking above his audience?"

"Well, he's talking above me, at least with what I know right now."

"How do you know he's talking sense then? What makes you so sure that this isn't just nonsense all over again?"

"I just don't believe it is. If this were just a snow job, I don't think he'd work as hard trying to explain things. And I know he's right about what I do understand. I checked him out on the entropy stuff."

"Also, if it were just a con job on the part of the writer, I don't think he'd end up talking the way he does about 'mutual respect for each other's type of literacy.'"

"Right, or about how he as a scientist has got to understand the Second Law in a way he wouldn't expect a nonscientist to."

"And which a nonscientist couldn't, not without first knowing all that he knows—in the same way that to understand one Shakespeare play the way a Shakespeare specialist does you have to become, as he says, 'completely familiar with Shakespeare.'"

"So in a way he hasn't explained the Second Law. It is impossible."

"'In a way.' I think you're right. But in another way hasn't he done better than make the Second Law of Thermodynamics understandable to me, a nonscientist? Through his constant attempts to show the importance of that Second Law, which is also an attempt to try to bring down to my level what I see *can't* be brought down to that level for all of his trying, he's made me aware at one and the same

220   time that I can't know about the Second Law without knowing more than I do, without knowing in fact what I believe he knows, and also that it's important for him to know what he's made me believe he does. Maybe that's as far as we can go with one another? And as more than members of different disciplines? We'll have to see."

ASSIGNMENT 26

A comparison made
by C. P. Snow

In the paragraph from The Two Cultures *you were given with the last Assignment, you will notice that C. P. Snow sets up a comparison between the Second Law of Thermodynamics and "a work of Shakespeare's."*

What are the assumptions that lie behind this comparison? Do you share them?

"He doesn't know what he means," says F. R. Leavis on C. P. Snow as the author of *The Two Cultures,* "and he doesn't know he doesn't know." The accusation is a good deal more charitable than mine would be. Though I am no longer as certain of Snow's deviousness as I was, it still seems to me incredible that a writer of his experience and (at least) mechanical accomplishment could have been as completely unaware of what he was saying in his essay as he seems to be. There's a kind of informed viciousness about the piece—a quality which is particularly apparent in the passage I gave the students to work with—that suggests Snow knew very well what he meant and also knew enough to realize that he was going to have to hide it. In the passage I used for the Assignment, for example, Snow seems, on the surface, interested primarily in making a case for science as a respectable way of knowing the world and for scientists as knowers. But the assumptions that underlie his comparison between the Second Law of Thermodynamics and a work of Shakespeare's suggest that Snow is only pretending to do what he seems to be doing in order that he may really do something else. As I read the passage, Snow is not really interested in making a case for science as a discipline; nor is he being critical only of frivolity, prejudice, and narrow-minded complacency in those who will not admit its importance as a discipline. The real purpose of his remark, indeed of his essay as a whole, is to attack traditional culture itself, traditional culture and the traditionally cultured. But in order to do this, Snow deals neither with traditional culture nor the traditionally cultured; he deals instead with a superficial snobbery that he can *call* "the traditional culture" in order to seem to have destroyed the real thing.

I was gratified to see that the students were in general very sharp on the problem of the Assignment, the comparing of incomparables, and inclined also to be sharp with Snow himself. Our class, therefore, I set up a little bit differently from what was usual to us. Instead of dealing one at a time with the three papers I'd chosen to talk about, I decided that I'd begin class by reading aloud all three papers seriatim and have the students as I did so put checks alongside anything in the papers that interested them—anything they particularly agreed with, or didn't, or wanted to question, or didn't understand. I then broke the class up into four groups of four or five members each to talk among themselves for ten minutes or so about what they'd checked. I told them that one of the things I wanted them to consider specifically in their conversations was what the three papers seemed to have in common in their attitudes toward Snow.

Here again is the paragraph from Snow's essay:

> A good many times I have been present at gatherings of people who, by the standards of the traditional culture, are thought highly educated and who have with considerable gusto been expressing their incredulity at the illiteracy of scientists. Once or twice I have been provoked, and have asked the company how many of them could describe the Second Law of Thermodynamics. The response was cold; it was also negative. Yet I was asking something which is about the scientific equivalent of: Have you read a work of Shakespeare's?

And here are the three papers addressing that paragraph that I chose to work with:

1

In assuming that the Second Law of Thermodynamics is comparable to "a work of Shakespeare's," Snow says that both have common elements.

He assumes that both are of the same complexity. More specifically, Snow maintains that their vocabulary, style, and interest levels are similar. He assumes that the Second Law of Thermodynamics should be known by everyone.

I'm quickly running out of assumptions. And those I've given are contrived. I don't know whether this resulted from my lack of understanding or a weakness in Snow's argument. Since I can't write intelligently about Snow's assumptions without understanding them, I will try to come at the problem in another way—by attributing my confusion to the weaknesses of Snow's statement.

The faults in Snow's assumptions begin to show up in the first sentence. There, Snow admits he asked his question of a group who could answer only "by the standards of the traditional culture." Apparently their culture is one which leads them to nonscientific ends. The culture does not compel them to be up on scientific theory. Their culture demands more attention toward the humanities. Consequently, without much exposure to scientific theory, only few of the cultured would be able to "describe the Second Law of Thermodynamics."

It is the tendency of an unscientifically-minded culture to be disinterested in scientific laws. People of that culture do not understand the foreign-looking vocabulary of the scientific language. Their way of thinking does not follow scientific lines. No doubt they could handle scientific theory, but there is no necessity in their culture for them to do so.

Further on in his statement Snow asks, "Have you read a work of Shakespeare's?" A doubt arises here as to what Snow means by "read" when compared to the "describe" two sentences above in the essay. I know a lot of people who have "read" Shakespeare and who could answer "Yes" to Snow's "equivalent" question. But many of those same people could not go on to interpret or explain the work of Shakespeare. All they could do is regurgitate the tale, tell the action of the story. In the same way, many people could describe the Second Law of Thermodynamics by writing you a formula or expression similar to: work output of a system $<$ work input. If that's all Snow intended by "describe," then his question is satisfied. But if "describe" means to explain the formula, the answer leaves much to be desired. Explaining the Second Law of Thermodynamics, then, entails an extensive background of molecules, electrons, atoms, heat, efficiency, work, energy, etc. How's a nonscientific person going to be able to answer?

I believe Snow lets emotion obscure his thinking as a scientist. A group of people said they couldn't believe how illiterate scientists were. Naturally, being a scientist, Snow resented this. And I do too. The group's statement was a stereotyped image of the mad scientist who sits up weeks on end, queerly staring at equations and fiddling with test tubes. The Einsteins, the Schweitzers, and the Da Vincis are ignored.

224 But still, while Snow was trying to save face and protect his stand, he should have realized that any scientific principle he asked to have described could be countered by an equally irrelevant question from the literary side. The scientist and the nonscientist would be trapped in a futile psychological battle: "You're illiterate"; "Describe the Second Law of Thermodynamics"; "Let's hear you explain why Lord Jim *had* to kill himself"; "Explain quantum mechanics"; "Explain the significance of the wheat in *The Octopus*"; etc. Where does this leave Snow? Where does it leave anybody?

It was startling to me to read Snow's statement about the Second Law of Thermodynamics and to realize that I didn't know what the Law was. I felt embarrassed that after getting all the way to Case Institute of Technology I had to look on page 430 of my physics book to find out what the Second Law of Thermodynamics was all about. Surprisingly, none of my suitemates knew, and I would be willing to say that 90% of the freshman class doesn't know either. As for the works of Shakespeare, if it hadn't been for my experience in high school English classes, I probably would never have read any Shakespeare. I'd say Snow used a bad example in trying to prove his point. Whatever the case, I feel that being embarrassed by my ignorance about the Second Law caused me to take a hostile attitude toward Snow's position from the beginning.

2

What is C. P. Snow's comparison between Newton's laws and Shakespeare's plays? From the paragraph presented I would be hard put to push the comparison beyond a simple exposé of the hypocrisy of certain people who criticize the scientist as a literary boor.

Nothing in the prose seems to justify any other interpretation. Snow carefully sets up his victim: "standards of the traditional culture"; "people who . . . are thought highly educated." Points out the vast numbers of the foe: "A good many times"; "gatherings of people." Pats himself on the back: "A good many times I have been present at gatherings"; "once or twice I have been provoked"; "I was asking." And then identifies the foe so that all may know him: "who have with considerable gusto been expressing their incredulity at the illiteracy of scientists." (Doesn't that paint a picture? "When I asked him what he thought of Joyce Kilmer the only thing he could say was 'Who's she?'") Then Snow quickly exposes the hypocrisy of these people by asking them to display a very rudimentary form of scientific literacy. He then adds insult to injury with "The response was cold"; they don't even recognize their own hypocrisy when it's thrust in front of them.

I can't buy C. P. Snow's assumption that the scientific illiteracy of the artist somehow justifies the artistic illiteracy of the scientists for a number of reasons.

First of all, the initial hypothesis that the twain of literature and science never meet in any one man is demonstrably false: Bacon, Pascal, and Descartes are three names that come readily to mind.

Second, knowing the particulars of a field is not necessarily a proof of one's literacy in that field. Robert Frost might have known what the Second Law of Thermodynamics is, but I wouldn't have wanted him to help me with my physics.

Third, what is important is that each discipline respect the product of the other. I too become provoked when I hear someone attack science "with considerable gusto," if only because this person is holding science and the scientist up to contempt. His offense may be compounded by his ignorance, but he is still no better than the scientist who ridicules the humanities.

3

I assume from "standards of the traditional culture," and from the title, *The Two Cultures,* and from his seeming to name scientists as one culture, that he is comparing the "scientific culture" with the "anything but scientific culture." But surely, anyone who can be looked upon as "highly educated" wouldn't use the absoluteness of "illiterate" in his description of scientists. Once, perhaps, through a slip of the tongue; but Snow says this has happened "a good many times." I rather think that Snow is either exaggerating the term "good many times" or the use of "illiterate." After I have received this feeling in the first part of the paragraph, I find it hard to dismiss in the rest of the paragraph. "Once or twice I have been provoked. . . ." Right away I am sure it has happened only once. The "twice" has been put in to get the reader to think that it has happened more than once, and thus to give Snow more sympathy. It seems as though this is a person who has had his feelings hurt, so he exaggerates the facts to try to get the reader on his side. Finally, to top off his "argument," he equates the Second Law of Thermodynamics with a work of Shakespeare's. Is this a "pears equals apples" statement, or does it show some kind of equivalence between "derivatives" of his terms? For instance, it would be hard to equate a Buick and Boeing 707 in themselves; but, by taking a kind of "first derivative," it might be possible to come close to a basis for comparison. Relative speed, passenger accommodation, or fuel consumption could, perhaps, be linked together to get some kind of equation; but how are you going to do this with the Second Law of Thermodynamics and a work of Shakespeare's? Feelings regarding the two subjects, importance in their respective fields, study necessary to comprehend them—these might be examples of "first derivatives," but they are just as inequitable as our initial functions. It seems as if you would need to take a "second" or "third derivative" in order to make an equation, but by that time you would be so far from the primary field of interest that all accuracy would be lost in whatever conclusions you drew.

226   "Dan, what did your group conclude about what these three writers have in common in their attitudes toward Snow?"

"We felt that none of them like Snow very much."

"Do they all dislike him for the same reason?"

"No, not exactly. Well, in some ways they do, though. They all think he's trying to play some kind of game. They all seem to think that there's something fishy about what he's doing."

"Specifically, in, say, the first paper?"

"Well, the writer there makes the point. . . . I guess I better not talk that way any more. The guy who wrote the first paper seems to feel Snow has a bad argument."

"Simply because he didn't know what the Second Law of Thermodynamics was?"

"Partly that. I had to look it up, too. I wondered why Snow picked it. But it's more that the guy thinks Snow is just getting into a lot of name-calling that isn't going to get anybody anywhere."

"Is the writer of the paper right, by the way,"—I moved from Dan to the class as a whole—"when he says he thinks that a lot of you didn't know about the Second Law of Thermodynamics?"

He was.

"Why do you think Snow picked it, then, Dan?"

"Because he wanted to make damn sure nobody would know it."

"Would that have anything to do with the writer's argument about name-calling?"

"It would bring him out on top—Snow, I mean. 'All you know is Shakespeare. I know Shakespeare *and* the Second Law of Thermodynamics. That makes me better than you are.' "

"Which would tie in nicely with this writer's point—we can't get away from the word entirely, can we?—about the difference between 'read' and 'describe.' Who hasn't read at least 'a work of Shakespeare's'? Who hasn't been to high school? But to be able to 'describe' the Second Law of Thermodynamics, if, as this writer says, 'describe' really means describe, is going to take a pretty special form of knowledge."

"Is the writer saying that Snow is being unfair, then?" someone asked.

"He's certainly on the edge of saying that, isn't he, that Snow has not just a 'bad argument' as Dan said, but a crooked one? Is that what you meant, Dan, by saying that your group thought all the writers felt Snow was doing something fishy?"

"Yeah, but we talked about the second paper mainly. The guy who wrote that comes right out and says Snow's argument is loaded."

"So does the third paper," said someone else. "That's the one we spent most of our time on."

"OK. Is there any way of seeing the objections that the writers of the last two papers seem to have to Snow in similar terms? That is, do the writers of those papers seem to find him fishy for the same reasons?"

"I think both writers think Snow is putting it on. The writer of paper three says he thinks Snow exaggerates the facts to get the reader's sympathy. And in the second paper, I think the paragraph where the writer says Snow 'sets up his victim' is getting at the same thing."

"You mean neither writer seems to believe that what Snow says happened really happened?"

"They don't seem to believe it happened the way Snow says it happened."

"Do you? You're going to be a scientist. Have you ever heard the kinds of remarks Snow claims he's heard?"

"Sure I have. We all have."

"From whom? And where?"

"In the snack bar. From the kids at Reserve. We're the Casey Dips. We go to bed with slide rules at night."

"They kid you?"

"Sure. They kid us all the time. Then we talk about Ye Olde Western Reverse."

"OK. They kid you and you kid back. Now where would you find a group of people, this 'vast foe' that the second writer sees Snow setting up, who could be counted on over and over again to 'express their incredulity,' as Snow puts it, 'at [your] illiteracy' because you're a scientist, and who would do this with 'considerable gusto,' and do it not kiddingly but seriously? Where would you find a group of people like that?"

"I don't know."

"I don't know either, not this side of a TV situation comedy or a Donald Duck cartoon, that is. Mrs. McSnootem's literary tea. And yet Snow asks us to believe not only that such 'gatherings of people' exist, but that he has been present at them 'a good many times.' (And why, one wonders.) Or does Snow mean 'a good many times' to refer to the frequency with which he has had to endure such insulting behavior (as the writers of both papers two and three seem to think), and therefore to celebrate his own heroic forbearance in refusing to respond to such outrageousness any more often than he does (the 'pat on the

228   back')? Taking it either way, *or* both ways at once, I find myself very suspicious of the existence of this gathering of people, and even more disbelieving when Snow asserts that the group was 'thought highly educated' and 'by the standards of the traditional culture.' I know what the writer of paper three means when he suggests that no one thought 'highly educated' by any standards whatever would behave as Snow claims these people behave. What's all you'd need to know to become a member of this 'highly educated' group Snow talks about?"

"You'd have to know how to be clever about the illiteracy of scientists, for one thing."

"How to sneer, OK. Anything else? I mean according to Snow's paragraph?"

"You'd have to know Shakespeare."

" 'Know,' meaning what? How much would you have to know about him?"

"To join this gathering? Not much really. You could probably get by on just a couple of the plays."

"That you'd simply 'read,' as the writer of the first paper suggests, enough to remember the outline of a plot—a reading that would no more make you somebody who knew Shakespeare or gain you admittance to a traditional culture that amounted to anything, than being able to recite the Second Law of Thermodynamics would make you a scientist."

"It seems like Snow's being as snotty as the people he's attacking."

"Well, 'respect' in the sense that the writer of the second paper uses it, and in the sense that the writer of the last paper we looked at last time did too, wouldn't seem to be Snow's long suit, no—which raises the question of why Snow might have manufactured this little anecdote to begin with. What exactly is he comparing with what and for what reason? So far as the comparison as a comparison is concerned, I should think that the argument of the writer of paper three might have occurred to Snow if all he'd been interested in doing was making a case for the validity of science as a discipline. It would seem obvious that there *is* no 'scientific equivalent of: Have you read a work of Shakespeare's,' any more than there is a literary equivalent of: Do you know what $F = ma$ means? On the other hand, if it's what this writer calls the 'derivatives' that are being compared, we're no better off, because as he says they're 'just as inequitable as [the] initial functions.' So the conclusion I draw is that Snow has concocted this anecdote and set the comparison for no better reason than to get one up on the traditional culture by running it down, and by running it down in the same way he claims 'it' runs down science and scientists. The knife work is nasty enough, but what really bothers me is the covertness of it, the pretense that he's doing something else."

"You mean you think Snow's real purpose was to knife the traditional culture?"

"And to avoid taking responsibility for having done it, yes; I'm afraid that's what I see that set of sentences saying."

ASSIGNMENT 27

The humanities as a requirement at an institute of technology

You are a student at an institute of technology. Although no major is offered by the humanities division of the institute, you are required to take certain humanities courses. Why is this, do you suppose? Is such a requirement desirable so far as you are concerned?

Before you make up your mind just how you are going to address this Assignment, consider carefully whether you are sure that you want to talk about A Balanced Education, or being The Well-Rounded Man in just these terms. (Have you ever wondered what happened to The Well-Rounded Man? What's he doing these days?) What sort of rhetoric is this, by the way: a balanced education? How far do you think it will take you with the problem of this Assignment?

Is there another way of talking?

Assignment 27 I still think is a good one, but I hadn't read very many papers before realizing that it's a harder Assignment than I first thought it was—particularly, perhaps, for science majors. I found myself making a great many comments of the same order on their papers:

Does [Lucretius' theory of atoms, etc.] *help* you with modern physics? Are you sure it doesn't get in the way?

If, using English, you can "apply" science, why couldn't you get from $E = mc^2$ to Hiroshima on Assignment 25?

But *how* exactly can a humanities course make you [tolerant, understanding, etc.], and why should one be *required*?

"The course will give me . . ." Why are you the object of such sentences? What do *you* do?

There *is* a scientific equivalent for having read Shakespeare's plays, then?

Isn't there a way in which education *isolates* you from other people?

That is, the majority of students had little difficulty seeing that the problem of the Assignment involved avoiding the rhetoric of cant, but, to develop "another way of talking," turned out, as it always does, to be another thing again. In any event, it was obvious that I was going to have to try to make the class on the Assignment open what the Assignment hadn't.

The first paper I chose to work with is a curious mixture of commonplaces at the edge of something more than the commonplace. Maybe. For there is some question whether the writer of the paper was aware of what he is at the edge of. Whatever, I figured the matter was certainly worth a conversation:

From my last paper I learned that the criticisms I had previously leveled at the social sciences because they did not answer the questions that I wanted them to could just as easily be leveled at me. I found that I could not explain a scientific law in such a way that a nonscientist felt that the law affected him. I now want to explain why we are required to take Humanities courses at Case. When I look at my C's in Soc. and English while the rest of the grades are A's and B's, I wonder whether the Humanities are really so necessary. To get some idea of the reason the school feels that these courses are important, I went to my Case catalog.

"You will be educated for work in a profession," it said, "but not in a sterile human vacuum. On the contrary, you will be made aware of your relationship to the community, state, nation, and the world. This can be no age of two cultures, the scientist on one side, the humanists on the other. Scientists and humanists are forging a unity of knowledge, wisdom, and practice; and that unity is the foundation upon which Case's educational program is built."

I read this twice and thought about it for a minute. It reminded me of my last English paper. I had tried to show that since forces act on a car every driver should know that $F = ma$. But, as was pointed out in class, every driver could answer, "I've driven all these years without $F = ma$ and gotten along just fine; why do I have to know it now?" No, that way of talking isn't going to take me very far.

I think I see something. As a scientist (or aspiring scientist) I have

232 been so near-sighted that I have been committing the same sins I have been attributing to others. I expected everyone to get excited over $F = ma$ because I did. Then when I tried to explain it to them, rather than make it affect them, I explained it like a small-print-no-pictures physics book. How dull.

But it isn't dull for me. And I suppose that T. S. Eliot and George Bernard Shaw and Shakespeare are interesting to my English teachers. Somewhere I got on a different track and fell into a separate community for scientists. Case is trying to pry me out of this icebox. Unless I know how the humanist thinks, I will suppose that he thinks like me. Or that he doesn't think at all.

As the statement that I quoted said, we cannot have two separate cultures in our world if we want to prosper. Scientists must learn to communicate with humanists. But this dogmatic statement would have had no meaning if I had not realized how illiterate I was when I tried to explain a scientific principle to laymen. Case's policy of requiring Humanities courses provides a means for a student to gain an insight which will in his eyes join the foundation of the worlds of the scientist and the humanist. I think I am beginning to enjoy Humanities.

"At the end of this paper, the writer suggests that he's seen something, that he's come to a realization of some sort. What's he seen? What's he realized?"

Nobody volunteered anything, and the silence didn't feel as though it would be very useful to wait out.

"What about it, Bill?"

"What's he say he realizes? Oh, that we can't have two cultures, and we have to know how each other thinks. The usual."

He wasn't quite sullen, but he was annoyed and he wanted me to know it.

"What do you mean 'the usual'? Come on, man, spit it out."

"I mean it's about the same damn thing I said. What the hell else could you say? This is a hooker assignment. It's like the paper where we had to explain the course, or the one on the scientific principle. You knew right away what you'd be stupid to do, but you ended up doing it anyway."

"You mean the answer was obvious, but how to make the obvious mean something more than the obvious wasn't so obvious?"

"That's about the size of it. So what do I end up doing? I talk about holding hands across the sea and that kind of crap."

"And that's what this writer does? Comes up with a lot of junk talk, catalogese?"

"Well, look at it. 'We cannot have two separate cultures.' 'Scientists must learn to communicate.' I wouldn't call that saying very much. That's the kind of stuff we spent the first three weeks in here beating the hell out of."

"I grant you that that kind of talk isn't an awfully long way from language like A Balanced Education and The Well-Rounded Man. OK. I particularly grant you that about what you quoted from the paper as an excerpt. It's about all I saw when I first read the paper too, maybe because I'd already read fifteen or twenty that sounded very much like it. But I'd like to ask you about something here that stopped me. I don't mean that it turned this paper into something I'd want to bury in a time capsule at the World's Fair, but it did stop me because it suggested a possibility for this Assignment I hadn't seen. Not to be coy about it, it's the writer's use of 'illiterate' in that final paragraph. What's he mean by it?"

"He means he sees he didn't explain the importance of $F = ma$ very well."

"I know, but why not? Because he doesn't know English very well, a language of the humanities very well? Or is it through his experience with something else that he might have realized what he calls his illiteracy?"

"You don't mean that he might have realized that he was illiterate about science, do you?"

"Go ahead."

"Well, I don't know whether I'm following you exactly, but are you saying that this guy might be saying that trying to put $F = ma$ into English, imagining that he could do it the way he tried to do it, showed him that he didn't know as much about *science* as he thought he did?"

"And that if he uses the value of that experience to stand for the value of this humanities course, then maybe a way for a science major to talk about the value of the humanities would be to say that studying it, or them, could make him more aware of himself as a scientist—not because, as you say, Bill, he sees he can 'hold hands across the sea,' but because he sees he *can't,* because he sees that there *is* no way he can put $F = ma$ into English, any more than he can find a 'scientific equivalent' for: 'Have you read a play of Shakespeare's'?"

"Well, if that's so, then doesn't this guy contradict himself when he talks about his 'separate community' as an 'icebox' that Case is trying to get him out of?"

"I think the way *he* puts it, there's a contradiction in the paper, yes.

234   But I'm not sure that he was even conscious of using the term 'illiterate" in the way we've just been talking about it. I wonder if there would *have* to be a contradiction in the notion, though? Is there any way in which realizing that you were in a 'separate community' as a scientist might be a way out of the 'icebox,' might be a way of 'joining the foundations of the worlds of the scientist and the humanist' as this writer concludes by saying? What was the way out of the trap of nonsense?"

"You mean realizing you were in a 'separate community' might be a way of seeing that the humanist was in the same boat, that he couldn't get into your world any more than you can get into his? I guess if you both realized that you'd share something."

"Just the way you and the nonsense writer have to if you're going to get out of the trap of nonsense. If you recognize that all the other professionals of different professions are alone in the same way that you are with yours, then the term 'alone' changes its meaning. In a way you're not alone any more. Either of you. You've communicated by recognizing when and why and how you cannot communicate, by recognizing that neither of you can know where the other is as the other knows it."

"That's what the guy who wrote the paper on the Second Law of Thermodynamics was getting at, wasn't he?"

"Exactly. What I as a nonscientist have got to know about that Law is that a scientist has got to know about it in a way I can't."

"So we're separate but equal."

"Maybe 'equal but separate' would be better. Or equal *because* we're separate."

"Is this why you made fun of the idea of the Well-Rounded Man? Were you saying that that's a stupid ideal?"

"It depends on what's meant by it, doesn't it? It's like that catalog talk 'forging a unity of knowledge, wisdom, and practice.' If it's some slovenly, C. P. Snow-ish mingling of disciplines that's being referred to, the search for a common denominator or 'derivation,' as the writer of paper three last time put it, that turns each discipline into something other than a discipline, then I'd say it was a stupid ideal, yes. I'd say the same thing if I heard it used as a way of defending the notion that you guys ought to slide through a little Shakespeare while I bone up on Newton, just because . . . well . . . because a little learning about a discipline is enough to 'acquaint you,' in the jargon, with the discipline. Knowledge has gotten too complex for anyone even to pretend

that any more—which is why you don't hear that metaphor the way
you used to, I suppose. It was a big term in the thirties and forties."

"But isn't the talk in the catalog pretty much the same sort of thing?"

"Sure it is. And like 'well-rounded,' what you feel about it is a matter of what you understand it to mean, what you make it mean the
way the writer of this paper did; or, depending on how you read it, the
way he might have. Maybe a catalog has to talk in general terms like
that, though I don't like to think it does. At any rate, if that's the only
language I have to explain to myself why I'm taking humanities, I'm
going to be as sore as Bill was any time anyone calls the question. And
I'd be sore for exactly the same reason Bill was. Is. I'd know that such
courses were supposed to be for my own good and all that, but I
wouldn't have discovered a language for making that mean anything
to me as me. Whether or not I see a humanities requirement as desirable, then, is going to depend on what I can make not just you understand but *me* understand that my answer means to me. 'The Well-
Rounded Man' and talk of the sort is not going to take me very far
in that direction.

"Also, there's another way of talking about the inadequacy of 'Well-
Rounded' as a metaphor. Let's look at this last paper:"

I don't really know why the Case catalog states that all students
must take Humanities courses. But I like to think that I would study
the humanities even if I didn't have to, and perhaps if I were determining
curricular requirements for Case I would insist that everyone else study
them too.

Part of the reason is that I'm not able to think just in terms of equations
and cations; I would become bored if all I could study were science.
But there is more to it than this. This "something extra" is the fact that
there is something extra to me. I am more than a human computer, an
equation solver, and to deny this fact, to define myself as some sort of
machine, or even as a single Well-Rounded Man is to create a world
where up is down, black is white, and yes, where every illegitimate
child is an amateur.

I want to go on here. I want to find a way to talk about this
"something extra" mentioned above. But to find words which will tell
about it is difficult. I like to think that part of it lies in: "This story is
like a Cheshire Cat, propounding all sorts of riddles, each of which has
a thousand different meanings and interpretations, and then grinning
at the reader as he tries to fit every possible meaning into one grand
plan. . . ." And I think it can be found in: "Part of the importance
of these laws lies in their relative unimportance. . . ." And now, I

think that even "We were amateurs because our techniques, knowledge, and abilities were not comparable to those of the leaders in the field" reveals something about that something extra.

After reading the paper through, I explained to the class that the three sentences the writer quoted were all sentences he himself had written. The first appeared in a paper we had considered in class as a sample paper addressed to Assignment 24. Both the paper and the sentence had, as they remembered, received a lot of praise. The second sentence had appeared in a paper written for Assignment 25. I hadn't mimeographed the paper, but I had in my marking of it singled out the sentence as having had marvelous possibilities that never came to much. The last quoted sentence the student had written on a paper for Assignment 4.

It was a sentence, as he'd had to remind me, alongside of which I'd written, "spit the marbles out of your mouth."

"Let's begin with that last paragraph. What's he doing there, anyway?"

"He's trying to define this 'something extra' he talks about."

"As what? That is, what do the three sentences he chooses to quote define the 'something extra' as?"

"Well, from what you said about where they come from, isn't he trying to say that now he knows the difference between a good sentence and a bad one? But I'm not really sure that's what he's doing."

"Maybe he's trying to show that he's developed as a writer," said someone else, "but that he knows he's not home free yet, because even though he can write a good sentence that doesn't mean he always writes good papers. I was thinking of your saying that the sentence about the laws wasn't developed in his paper."

"Or," I said, "is he trying to say something about himself as a user of metaphor? Is he saying that at one time he couldn't use it very well, but that now he's becoming more conscious of it as the only way to define the indefinable, as he's trying in *this* paper to define the 'something extra'? Or is he saying simply that in the instance of those three sentences, even in the one he doesn't like—if that's what he means by 'and now, I think that *even*,'—he was three different people, no one of which was just 'a human computer' or just 'an equation solver'?"

"You can't really tell which he means. Maybe *that's* his point, that he doesn't know exactly what the 'something extra' is, but he knows it's there. He's leaving it up to the reader to decide."

"That's what was first said about 'I Saw a Peacock' and *The Wil-lowdale Handcar*. Are you saying that this is another example of nonsense?"

"No. I don't think it is. I don't think he's deliberately trying to hang me up the way the poem and the story did."

"Is he trying to do what the writer of the paper on the Second Law of Thermodynamics was doing, then? Is he trying to demonstrate that he understands something in a way you don't and can't?"

"No, I don't think he's doing that either. Or if he is, I don't believe he does understand something I don't."

"You mean, so far as you're concerned, the writer isn't clear about either what the 'something extra' is or about the way the three sentences define it?"

"Right. All he says is that this sentence has something to do with it, and that that sentence has something to do with it, but he never works any of it out."

"Did he try to, do you think?"

"Well, I guess he tried, but he didn't get very far with it."

"How hard would you say he tried when you remember I had to tell you where those three sentences came from so that you could understand the paper? I had to ask the writer about two of the sentences myself. Suppose he'd explained where they'd come from *in* his paper. Might he have explained anything else in the process?"

"I think it might have given him a chance to see what sorts of connections he was trying to make."

"And that's the important thing, isn't it, that it would have given *him* a chance to see, and, in seeing the connections, a chance to see something about the 'something extra' too maybe? That way the act of writing could, through the putting of words on paper, have become something more than just the putting of words on paper. I admire the writer's implicit recognition that this 'something extra' he speaks of can't just be labeled and amount to very much. I admire also the way he seems to tie it to his development as a writer. But he asks me to do more as a reader than I feel he has a right to because of what he shows he hasn't done that I know damn well he could have tried to do. He asks me to be a writer for him, not only with those three sentences but in working out an obscurity like 'where every illegitimate child is an amateur.' And to be a writer *for* someone else, as this paper makes clear, is to tell him who he is.

"One other thing about this paper that interested me is the way in

238   which the writer dismisses the metaphor of The Well-Rounded Man. To judge from the paper as a whole, why do you think he finds it inadequate? Notice that he specifies that he's not a 'single' Well-Rounded Man."

"Maybe he sees the term as another way of saying he's a machine."

"How do you mean?"

"A machine has just one function; he's saying he has many."

"Maybe I'm making too much of it, but it's the grammar of that saying that I thought might have possibilities. He doesn't say, 'I can function as a computer, an equation solver, a writer.' He says 'I am a computer, an equation solver,' and so on. What's the difference between those two ways of seeing one's self?"

"One way you're saying you're one person with a lot of different functions. The other way you're saying you're different people."

"That's what interested me. Maybe he's throwing away the metaphor of The Well-Rounded Man because it doesn't suggest clearly enough that when he changes his function he changes his identity too, that he is, as you say, different people depending on what language he uses. The value of the humanities for him, then, he might be suggesting, or might be on the edge of suggesting, is to enable him to express, to create, not the 'something extra' that's him, but the someone else, the someones else, he believes himself to be."

ASSIGNMENT 28

The value of studying
the humanities

"What good is that to me, anyway? I'm going to be a [poet, scientist, etc.]."

The attitude that such a remark arises out of you are no doubt familiar with. You have probably heard something of the sort expressed around you at some point in your educational experience. Perhaps you have even said something like it to yourself, and not only about the humanities courses of your curriculum. At most liberal arts colleges, by the way, there is a science requirement about which it is possible to hear much the same sort of talk that you have heard, or maybe used yourself, about the humanities requirement (and other course requirements) here at Case.

Why should I have to take such a course? What good is such knowledge to me? I'm going to be a physicist. I'm going to be a chemical engineer.

This is an opportunity for you to have a look at this attitude in terms of your own experience.

Select an example from your study of the humanities (outside this class) and use it to explain your position on whether such a thing is any good to you. Be as specific as you can in explaining just what the benefits of such a study, of such knowledge, are; or of why such a study, such knowledge, is of no use to you.

I devised Assignment 28 as a way of inviting the students to confront the significance of both the activity and the study of the activity of model-making. More explicitly, I was asking the students to con-

240   sider a model as a metaphor, a formal arrangement of symbols super-
imposed upon the chaos of experience for the purpose of enabling a
metaphor-maker to locate himself. I included the references to the talk
of liberal arts students and the fact that a dismissive attitude might be
taken toward even courses or subjects of supposed relevance to one's
own career ("and not only about the humanities courses of your curriculum") in order to suggest that the problem of the Assignment is
first one of seeing a model as a model (or metaphor), and then one of
how to establish a relationship between that model and one's self as
the maker or user of it. The problem of the Assignment would have
been substantially the same had the students worked with the relevance
of a scientific model to their study of science and themselves as
scientists.

I hoped that the Assignment would put the students into the position of recognizing that, whatever their examples, it was a language
about the world of experience and not the world of experience itself
that they were considering—which would in turn be a way of seeing
that the value of that language, of such a structure, lies precisely in
the fact that it is a structure: autonomous, self-consistent, self-con-
tained; not capable of translation without becoming other than what
it is. The "benefit" to be had from the study of structuring then, particularly when the activity being studied takes place in a discipline
other than one's own, will have to do with one's seeing in the implicit
rebuke of incompleteness by completeness, of the unsophisticated by
the sophisticated, an incentive to make over (in order to make better)
structures of his own—all those millions upon millions of structures
that each one of us creates in order to be who we are. At least this is a
way of speaking of the value of the humanities to a scientist and of
the study of science to the humanist that makes some sense.

As a way of taking us into these matters, I began class with a statement of the traditional argument—pat and bullet-proof:

Thus far, the Social Studies course that I am taking fails to impress
me as having any definite benefit for me as a student in a technical
school. I am sure that the ideas and objectives which lie behind the
Humanities courses at Case are all justifiable and intended to help me as
a student, but I have failed to recognize these ends in the reading
assignments and class discussions that I have encountered, most of them
being dull and uninteresting.

One example which more fully explains my position is a book,
Human Types by Raymond Firth, in particular a section which deals

with the method of canoe-building in a primitive society. Firth devotes ten full pages of print and two pages of illustration to the intricacies of canoe-building—types of materials used, methods of construction, ingenuity of design, and aesthetic value of the canoe's appearance. He goes into such great detail that I used a little ingenuity of my own and flipped the pages to the final paragraph of the section which, as I had suspected, explained the "point" of the preceding ten pages with a minimum of words. I was presented with the amazing fact that canoe-building in this primitive society is a ritual and an important determinant of cultural traits. And contrary to what many believe, the primitive *does* have a "definite system of knowledge and technique, is adaptable, willing to learn, and capable of profiting by the lessons of experience." Somehow this fact is supposed to help me come to a better understanding of *my* society. Again, I fail to recognize what I believe are the objectives of this course. After reading this type of writing, the drug-store philosophy of a Plato looks pretty good.

"The writer follows his summary of what he calls the 'point' of Firth's pages on canoe-building by saying 'somehow this fact is supposed to help me come to a better understanding of *my* society.' What sort of attitude does that sentence seem to have emerged from?"

"Well, it's sarcastic. He thinks the whole idea of the book is silly, that the course has nothing to do with him. And he's mad that he has to take it."

"Who's he mad at exactly? The school?"

"Maybe the school. More likely it's the course or the teacher. And Firth. It's the whole situation he seems p.o.'d with really."

"Himself?"

"I guess he's mad at himself too. He says he's failed to recognize the objectives of the course."

"But he's like a little kid the way he talks," said someone else. "He says he failed and all that, but I don't think he really thinks it's his fault, not the way he sets up Firth. It's like the way Snow loaded the dice against the traditional culture. In the paper I wrote for last time I talked about what the humanities ought to 'give me.' You asked me what I thought it was up to me to give. I think that's this guy's trouble. He can't make anything out of the course, so he's mad at everything and tries to blame it all on the System or something."

"What do you mean when you say he 'sets up Firth' the way Snow did the traditional culture? Have you read Firth?"

"No. We're reading Elkins in my section. But I don't believe Firth is as stupid as this guy makes him. I think he's trying to make him

242   look that way so he won't have to feel so bad about not being able to get anything out of the book."

"Except, put that way, it might sound a little as though you're saying nobody can write a stupid book. Is there anything about what this writer says *about* Firth that would lead you to believe that maybe Firth isn't quite as stupid, and that the whole subject of canoe-building in a primitive society isn't necessarily as irrelevant, as this writer implies?"

"I haven't read Firth either," said another student, "but would it have anything to do with the way Firth talks about canoe-building in this society as a ritual and as a determinant of cultural traits?"

"How do you mean?"

"I'm guessing, but it looks as though Firth might be doing a little more in those pages that this guy skipped than showing that the members of this society are able to learn. If canoe-building is a ritual and a determinant of cultural traits, then maybe Firth is using it somehow to talk about what kind of society this is, what kind of people these are."

"What good is that to you and me here in the center of Cleveland? Even if we did build canoes, we probably wouldn't build them ritualistically. So why read about it? Why study someone who is studying it?"

"That way, of course there isn't any connection. But maybe it would be possible for me to look at something in my society that determines some of my cultural traits and see it as a ritual. If I could see that, then wouldn't I have a better understanding of my society?"

"That is, if you looked not at canoe-building but at the way Firth looks at canoe-building, the way he sees it as a ritual, as 'an important determinant of cultural traits,' and then took *that* way of seeing and looked at something in your culture—such as how you build friendships, or meet girls, or go about getting an education—and tried to see *those* things as rituals, then this might give you a way of looking at your society that you hadn't seen before?"

"Yes. What might be valuable in Firth is his approach, his technique."

"The process of it. His approach seen as an activity. It's not the vocabulary of his study that could be of much value, which is all the writer of this paper chooses to look at; it's the syntax of it, maybe, which could provide me with a way of renaming and reconnecting what I see around me in order to see things I hadn't been able to see before.

"I'd like to go on with the implications of this as a way of talking

about what could be seen as a 'benefit' of the study of the humanities
by looking at two sections of two different papers. The first is the last
two-thirds of a paper. The second is only the writer's final paragraph:"

1

It certainly doesn't make me a well-rounded individual, bubbling over
with well-rounded conversation to spring on someone. It didn't do me
much good while I was stranded for twelve hours in a bus twenty-nine
miles outside of Buffalo. The conversation didn't seem to lend itself to
a consideration of national character; the topic of snow came naturally,
and I could have handled that without *People of Plenty*. *People of Plenty*
didn't enable me to tell why the people on the bus behaved as they did
or why I behaved as *I* did (for ten of those twelve hours I was a real
boy scout). If I gained any psychological insight from reading the book,
it didn't help me then.

But sitting there I had a lot of time to think about this paper, and
after a while it struck me that I might as well be complaining that
People of Plenty couldn't get the bus started either. Nobody in his right
mind would pretend that it should have been able to. It's not so much
that the humanities course I'm taking tells me anything new or useful,
but rather that a book like *People of Plenty* makes me aware of things
I take for granted. The humanities do not cause me to lose sight of my
scientific surroundings. I am not reading sociology books to get new
terms for the same old ideas. I am taking humanities so that I remember
that another, more human, condition exists amidst the scramble of
equations, pulleys, and chemicals. Then, when I can perceive how the
nonscientific and the scientific are related, I will be able to make my
step forward as a scientist.

2

The benefits of my political activities are doubtful; I don't think that
I can change the course of history by talking on street corners. The real
benefit comes from my battle with the language. In this I am forced
to understand both myself and my ideas in the fullest sense possible
in order to express them to other people.

"What is it, exactly, that the writer of the first paper claims is the
benefit of a book like *People of Plenty*?"

"Well, he seems pretty clear, the way the guy in the last paper we
looked at wasn't, that the book isn't a cure for cancer or anything like
that. I like that first paragraph."

"So do I. That's a nice touch there the way he holds back the title of the book for as long as he does. He's able to take a position like that of the writer of the first paper, at the same time he's able to make fun of it. So much for what he says the book won't do. What *will* it do, though?"

"In the last part of his paper he really doesn't get all that specific, does he? About all he says is that the book makes him aware of things he takes for granted."

"I know what you mean. All that stuff about becoming aware of the human condition and stepping forward as a scientist strikes me as terribly obvious, derivative in all the wrong ways. What interests me, though, is the way this writer follows saying that the benefit of a book like *People of Plenty* is to make him aware of things he takes for granted with the statement that he's 'not reading sociology books to get new terms for the same old ideas.' My question is, how do you do one without doing the other? How do you get a new term for an old idea?"

"You couldn't. You can't. It's a contradiction."

"How?"

"It's like what we were just talking about. If you see something in your culture as a ritual that you hadn't seen as a ritual before, that's a new term; but it's a new term that makes you see what before you were just taking for granted. So you see something new. The old idea has become a new idea. I don't see how you can separate terms and ideas."

"I don't see how you can separate them either. And not only are the two inseparable, but to judge from the way the second writer of these two samples speaks of his experience, it would seem possible to specify the connection between them even further. What I found arresting there was the way in which the writer sees the real benefit from his study and interest in politics coming not through a change he makes in 'the course of history,' but through a change he makes in himself, a change which takes place as a result of what he calls his 'battle with the language.'"

"You mean because he's constantly looking for 'new terms' to explain his political ideas to other people, *he* gets clearer on what *he* believes."

"Exactly. His 'new terms' change his 'old ideas' into new ideas in that, as he says, they 'force' him to understand them in the 'fullest sense possible,' force him to become aware, that is, of what he had earlier understood in a lesser way, or, in the first writer's terms, 'taken for granted.' So it's not just that he sees his awareness as inseparable from his use of 'new terms'; he implies that his awareness depends on them—on them, on the search for them, on what he calls his 'battle with the language.' Without that, he suggests, he wouldn't have the awareness that he does."

With that we turned to the final paper:

"Right order is nothing but the working out of free actions." The speaker is a soft-spoken man with a disarmingly polite way of being angry. He is speaking on university freedom and order at the Allen Memorial Library Auditorium. His name is Paul Goodman.

On the first day in Introduction to Humanities we were given a reading assignment in a book that seemed to me dry, dull, and pointless. In it, Clark Kerr told how useful the university was, is, and always will be. World without end. After being bored by Kerr's endless "bullet-proofing," I was overjoyed to find that the second book was a caustic attack on the premises of the first. Although it gave no solution, the second book exposed the major faults in Kerr's university, as well as those in modern society. Although I could find some faults in the second book, I enjoyed its dissection of the first. For that dissection I respected Paul Goodman, the author.

Paul Goodman calls himself an anarchist. He says, "Order is chaos; property is theft." I can reply that order and property hold society together, but that is his point also. I agree with most of his views. So now I am looking at the term anarchist. Do I ask, what is a semi-anarchist?

Had I not taken HS–4 I would probably never have heard of Paul Goodman. And, more important, I would probably still regard anarchists as wild-eyed fanatics with illogical ideas.

"How would you say 'new terms' that can bring about an awareness of what one has earlier taken 'for granted,' in the sense that we've just been using these phrases, are important in understanding what happens in this paper?"

"He comes to understand 'anarchist' in a way that he didn't."

"As what, finally? He can't any longer define 'anarchist' as a 'wild-eyed fanatic with illogical ideas'; that's clear. How does he define it?"

"Maybe as somebody 'soft-spoken' the way he says Goodman is. And somebody who's logical."

"In other words, he once saw anarchists as bad guys and now he sees them as good guys?"

"No," said someone else. "It isn't that black and white. I don't think he knows exactly what an anarchist is any more. That's why he puts in that question, 'Do I ask, what is a semi-anarchist?'. He's looking at the term, and he's looking at Goodman, and he's not sure about either one."

"What do you mean he's not sure about Goodman?"

"Well, he likes Goodman, the way he took Kerr apart; he respects his doing that. And he seems to like the way Goodman handles himself too. He says he had 'a disarmingly polite way of being angry.' But it's the way Goodman defines things. ' "Order is chaos; property is theft." ' The guy wants to say that's wrong because 'order and property hold society together.' But then he imagines Goodman's saying 'that's right, they hold society together and that's why they're wrong.' So he doesn't know where he is with Goodman. That's why he thinks maybe he ought to call him a semi-anarchist."

"OK, because he doesn't know where he is with 'Goodman,' he doesn't know any more where he is with 'anarchist.' And he doesn't know where he is with either of those terms because he doesn't know where he is with 'order,' 'chaos,' 'property,' 'theft,' 'society,' and 'hold together.' All of these 'old terms,' through the experience of Goodman, which as you say, Sam, isn't a black and white thing, have suddenly become new. He can say what anarchist isn't now, but for him to say now what it *is*, would be to cop out of his 'battle with the language.' Seen this way, what does a 'battle with the language' involve? Why does he end up saying that what's happened to his definition of anarchist is 'more important' even than his having heard of Goodman?"

"Because Goodman was only the way he came to his new awareness."

"The new term for the new idea. Awareness of what?"

"Of the fact that there're a lot of things he thought he understood that he sees now he doesn't."

"That he has a lot of definitions, as we all do, a lot of names in which he's locked the world; the world, and as a consequence, himself. A 'battle with the language' is a matter of seeing that the old definitions won't hold any more and that one has to develop new ones. It's not a place to stay—or that one can. 'So now I am looking at the term anarchist,' as this writer says so beautifully. What the writer's done here is to turn a key; he's unlocked a world. And, in the process, he's unlocked himself as a locker."

ASSIGNMENT 29

You as a student of technology and of the humanities

On the basis of what you have written, read, and talked about for the last four Assignments, what do you conclude about the relationship between you as a student of technology and you as a student of the humanities?

The papers addressed to Assignment 29 were good in such a way as to make me aware of how much better they might have been had I been a little more thoughtful in the way I'd worded the problem of the Assignment. If, instead of asking the students, as I did, *"what* do you conclude . . ."* (a demand for a production, really, rather than a performance), I had asked them *"how* with this aspect of the subject do you locate yourself as . . . ,"* I'd have given them more of a chance than I do to use the writing of their papers as a way of discovering connections I seem to be asking them simply to assert. But a still better assignment would have been one I didn't see even the possibility for until a student's paper gave me the idea—and an idea that I needed our class discussion to help me formulate fully. This paper I saved to deal with toward the end of our period. I wanted to spend the first part of class on two other papers, neither of which touches on much we had not already raised, but both of which I would call imaginatively fresh in their putting together of what no one had put together in quite that way before:

248   On the basis of what I have written in my last four papers I can
hardly *conclude* anything about the relationship between the student of
technology and the student of the humanities; I only wish I could. Either
such a relationship does not exist, or it is too complex and far-reaching
for me to appreciate. I can, however, piece together what I have learned
so far from the papers of my fellow students and the class discussions.

Originally I had taken the position of opposing the study of the
humanities here at Case, but now I find myself questioning my initial
judgement. I find myself being pulled by the objectives and ideals of
the Case handbook on the one side, while my disappointment in and
dislike for the humanities pulls just as hard on the other. I am dissatisfied,
but maybe this dissatisfaction is a product not of the humanities course
but of my misconception of it.

Perhaps I already recognized my own fault in a previous paper,
though I don't think I knew what I was saying then in the way that I
do now. I said, "an understanding is not always best achieved by looking
for simplicity—in fact, an understanding is not always achieved by
looking for anything in that sense." What I have been doing is "looking . . .
in that sense" for the objectives and ideals of the Case handbook to
come along some day in my humanities course. They don't exist that
way. I have been asking to be taught like some kind of an animal,
rather than trying to learn the way only a human can do. I was
"looking" for simplicity in complexity.

Now I think I understand. Of course the study of humanities has no
value to me as a student of technology, but it does have value to me as
a student of the humanities. The relationship between the student of
technology and the student of the humanities is a relationship between
two students; but both students are me. If I had not studied the
humanities, I don't see how I would have seen this.

"In the first paragraph of this paper, the writer says that he 'can
hardly *conclude* anything' on this subject, but that he can 'piece together what [he has] learned so far.' To judge from what he goes on
to do in the paper, what does this 'piecing together' consist of?"

"Well, he does mention a lot of the things we've talked about. The
language of the Case handbook and the way he has to make it mean
something. The way he has to make a course mean something for
himself. We also talked about the way the humanities and sciences
are separate and how you can't join them. And where this guy ends
up saying that he's two students, two people; that's like the paper
where the writer said he was an equation solver but someone else too,
the one where the guy used the three sentences from his other papers
that we couldn't figure out."

"So this paper's a rehash, then? He not only talks about things

we've talked about before, he even uses techniques we've seen before.
You mentioned the paper in which the writer quotes from his earlier papers, for example. So 'piece together' means scissors and paste? A Scotch tape job?"

"I think the guy's done more than that. I know you're going to ask me how, and I don't know how. But I think he's done more than just stick things together."

"I know what you mean, Bill. You've got a good ear. I think he does more than that too. And you're right, the 'how' is damned hard to show. Maybe we could close in on that another way. Is this paper boring?"

"I'm not bored by it. Maybe, as you say, I wouldn't want to send it to the World's Fair, but I don't think it's boring."

"I don't either, and that would be one of the things I'd use to say, 'Scotch tape job' wasn't the metaphor for the paper. Not as it reads. If it were just a mechanical putting together, nothing more than a rehash; if all it were were all he says it is, then it would be boring. But it isn't. What I'm pushed into seeing then, is how much the paper depends on the effect of voice, on the illusion of some *one's* handling all this stuff. In other words, the thing that I hear in the paper that I don't know how I hear and can't describe very well, is one of the things I'd use to say that for me the totality here is more than the sum of its parts, that this is a piece of writing done by *somebody*. There are other ways to come at the aliveness here too. For instance, the things this writer mentions he says we've talked about before: which classes did he get them from?"

"From a lot of different classes."

"And not just one, or from the discussion of just one paper. And the sentence he quotes from his earlier paper: I don't care whether or not we've seen somebody else do that before so much as I care about how he uses what he's making use of."

"And he *does* make clear how he's using it," said someone else, "the way the writer that Bill was talking about didn't, the one who used the Cheshire cat sentence and the other two."

"And not only does he make it clear, he pushes it beyond itself by playing with the term 'looking.' That's another way I'd argue my sense of the person behind all this. 'I used it then to mean one thing. I'm using it now to mean another. I was one person. I'm another person. But because I can see both I'm a third person; I'm someone right here, now, in this writing.'"

"One thing I like is the way the guy says the whole study of the

250 humanities shows him that it *doesn't* connect with science. That's pretty neat."

"*It* doesn't, no, but it does connect with him and he connects with both. Neat it is."

We turned to the second paper:

Constant Day—Something Lost

In the past four assignments I have thought about my relationship to my studies and the relationship of two parts of my studies, technology and humanities, to each other. One of the main things I've gained is that I've modified my ideas about what a student is from this exercise. A subject of study does not do something to me; it enables me to do something for myself. I could memorize the Bible and be irreligious, just as I could know every structural formula of organic chemistry and not be a scientist. Information in itself must not be knowledge, then. It's the application of a subject to one's self that makes a student a student. I feel uneasy calling it an application; it's more than that, but also more than I can describe. I can study a subject and gain from it in more than one way. I may come to understand or appreciate my studies. I may come to regard them with a mixture of feelings that I could never hope to enumerate. So there must be more to a student than studying and more to a study than information; and there must be more than one way of being a student of any one study.

I don't claim to be the same kind of student of social science I imagine a humanities major would be if he were taking the same course I am. On the other hand, he can't be the same student of physics that I am. I take social science with a different purpose from what I do chemistry. I won't go around analyzing my colleagues' thought processes, at least the way a psychologist might, but I do plan to analyze chemical processes and I owe it to myself to find out as much about what it means to analyze as I can. Also, I think I would be missing something if I didn't know that there were people who do try to analyze thoughts and habits. It would be like living your entire life in daylight. You would get along all right; but you would never know that darkness exists, or whether or not you could enjoy it. So I, as a student of technology, say, "I am working to understand this," and as a student of the humanities say, "Well, there is another way of looking at things." I'll go back to my analogy with light and darkness. My technology may be more clear to me in the light, but at least I know that the world looks different in darkness. And maybe there's a way in which my knowing about darkness can make my day brighter.

"Would you call that paper one in which things are 'pieced together'?"

"Yes, I would; but I'm not bored by this paper any more than Bill was by the other one. I guess what I mean is no, I wouldn't say that 'pieced together' was the metaphor, as you put it. He *puts* things together in the same way the writer of the other paper did."

"In the same way?"

"Well, it's a different putting together, but he says some of the same things the first writer did, and most of them are things we've talked about before. I mean he says too that he has to do things for himself, for example."

"How is the paper any different from the first one, then? And you still haven't said why it isn't boring."

"He touches on different points from the first writer, for one thing. He talks about the process of analysis being important because it's a process. The first writer doesn't mention that at all."

"The way we talked about process in class when we were seeing canoe-building as a ritual. OK, go ahead."

"But that was just last period that we talked about canoe-building," said another student. "This guy had written his paper before that. He saw all this on his own. And another thing. Even when he does use what the first writer uses, he uses it differently. When he talks about having to make courses do something for him, he connects that with how he's changed his ideas about what a student is. The first writer implies that, I guess, but this guy goes on to talk about the different ways he can be a student of the humanities, the different ways he can get things."

"And," I said, "I admire how, when he does try to talk about those ways, he's conscious of his terminology. He realizes, for example, that terms such as 'information' and 'application' are not going to explain very much. I don't believe that ten weeks ago this writer would have been at all 'uneasy,' as he puts it, with a term like 'application.' In fact, I know he wouldn't have been. It's the display of that kind of consciousness that I'd use to argue that there's a voice in this paper too."

"Also there's that stuff about darkness and light. We didn't use that before."

"No, we didn't. Do you mean you admire it because it's a metaphor we haven't used?"

"Well, it's a way of showing the paper's more than Scotch tape."

"Simply because the metaphor is new? A new one for this subject for us in here, I mean?"

"It's not just that it's new; he works on it."

"OK. It isn't just used for its own sake. 'He works on it,' as you say,

252   pushes it, develops it—not altogether successfully maybe—but in such a way as to make me sympathetic to his saying earlier that what makes a student a student is more than he can describe. When he reaches for terms to try to explain that, terms we haven't used before, I find myself saying 'It's important to this writer not just that I understand, but that he does.' Also, there's one notion that the using of those terms takes the writer to that I don't know whether he could have got to another way, with other terms. What's he mean by that last sentence: 'And maybe there's a way in which my knowing about darkness can make my day brighter'?"

"He seems to mean that knowing about the humanities can make him better as a scientist."

"Which came up in one other paper this term, or at least the possibility of it did. I'm thinking of the paper in which the writer said that the attempt to translate $F = ma$ made him aware of what he called his 'illiteracy' as a scientist. At any rate, it's a notion that fascinates me: that the function of the study of the humanities for a scientist might be to enable him to become a better *scientist,* to see more in *science* than he saw before. Let's look at how the writer of this last paper plays with the notion:"

In attempting to explain a scientific concept to a nonscientist I found it necessary to simplify and approximate even what little knowledge I have to the point of misrepresentation. Now I wonder if I even have the right to say that I was describing anything to anyone. Who was my audience? I don't know. When I reread that paper I feel as though I'm talking only to myself, and to myself as though I were someone else. It reminds me of C. P. Snow, except that it lacks his fluency in the use of language. I'm trying to find common ground between science and the humanities, but all I see around me is quicksand and I can't decide where to step.

When pressed to state or to create a relationship between science and the humanities and to express its significance to me, I felt and still feel inadequate. I can stammer around and talk about "a well-rounded personality" and "preparation for leadership," but that's just avoiding the issue. I know it's hard to do, because even the Case catalog resorts to that kind of talk; but I also know it can be done because I've seen it done—in the paragraph from Darwin that we worked with, for example. Darwin is a scientist in those sentences, but he is also able to present a scientific concept in a way that the nonscientist is able to understand. His use of language in some indefinable way lets the reader feel and even share his enthusiasm. Darwin is so successful that if I had not known who the author of that paper was, I couldn't have said whether he was a humanist or a scientist. I could have said he was interested in talking to me and that he knew what he was talking about. I think Darwin approaches some sort of ultimate in combining scientific and humanistic qualities in his paper.

Even as a student at an Institute of Technology, I am beginning to see closer and closer relationships between science and humanities through the few holes in the stone wall separating the two. Sure, there is lack of effective communication between them, but doesn't the same thing hold true within science itself? A nuclear physicist and a molecular biologist have very different vocabularies, and difficulty in expressing to each other basic ideas of their respective specializations.

I am uncertain of the relationship between me as a student of technology and me as a student of the humanities, but I am certain there is a relationship. It's a closer relationship than I realized before.

After reading the paper through, I had the students turn back to the paragraph from Darwin that the writer had referred to:

> It is interesting to contemplate a tangled bank, clothed with many plants of many kinds, with birds singing on the bushes, with various insects flitting about, and with worms crawling through the damp earth, and to reflect that these elaborately constructed forms, so different from each other, and dependent upon each other in so complex a manner, have all been produced by laws acting around us. These laws, taken in the largest sense, being Growth and Reproduction; Inheritance which is almost implied by Reproduction; Variability, from the indirect and direct action of the conditions of life, and from use and disuse: a Ratio of Increase so high as to lead to a Struggle for Life, and as a consequence to Natural Selection, entailing Divergence of Character and the Extinction of less-improved forms. Thus, from the war of nature, from famine and death, the most exalted object which we are capable of conceiving, namely, the production of the higher animals, directly follows. There is grandeur in this view of life, with its several powers, having been originally breathed by the creator into a few forms, or into one; and that, whilst this planet has gone cycling on according to the fixed law of gravity, from so simple a beginning endless forms most beautiful and most wonderful have been, and are being evolved.

"The writer says that if he hadn't known it was Darwin who had written the passage, he wouldn't have known whether its author 'was a humanist or a scientist.' What is there about the passage that might have suggested a humanist to him?"

"I think it's the way Darwin talks about this order he sees, the terms he uses to describe it. I remember we talked in class about the feeling of wonder Darwin seems to have."

"Which terms specifically seem to generate the sense that Darwin has such a feeling?"

"Well, he calls the production of the higher animals 'most exalted,' for example. And at the end he talks about forms that are 'most beautiful' and 'most wonderful.' And the way he speaks of God, 'the Creator,' breathing life into this whole thing. It's reverence. I remember that was another term we used in class."

"What would such terms ordinarily be used to describe: forms that are 'most beautiful and most wonderful,' and the like?"

"Oh, a sunset maybe. Or a person you felt a special way about. Or a statue. A painting."

"Art, in other words. Or what there is in nature that strikes one as artistry, as a creation. Yet Darwin uses such terms to talk about evolution, both the process and the theory, or the two in some mysterious way having become each other."

"You mean Darwin's looking at evolution as though *it* were a work of art. He's *seeing* it as a work of art."

"Which maybe he learned how to do through having studied works of art, through having studied the humanities. And when he'd become the kind of professional he became—maybe this is the way he was *able* to become that kind of professional—his field of science had begun to have the sort of beauty, the kind of aesthetic effect and value, that we ordinarily associate with a work of art. Further, in becoming an art for Darwin, or in becoming the art he made it into, maybe science—and I mean 'maybe' too; this is all speculation on my part, which the writer of this paper is responsible for—maybe science, or in our terms, Darwin's study of science, came to bring with it everything, every benefit, that the study of the humanities is traditionally said to bring."

"Do you mean that if you make science art it can bring you everything art is supposed to bring you?"

"Well, that's the question that the example of Darwin raises for me, Jim; I'm not sure. I can show what raised it even higher than this paper did though, raised it and complicated the notion even further. The first thing I did after reading this paper was to go back to the paragraph from Darwin we just read over. When I read it through listening to Darwin as a humanist, as somebody appreciating art, I remembered a passage from his *Autobiography*, one that I think I have a way of understanding now that I didn't when I first read it:

> In one respect my mind has changed during the last twenty or thirty years. Up to the age of thirty, or beyond it, poetry of many kinds, such as the works

of Milton, Gray, Byron, Wordsworth, Coleridge, and Shelley, gave me great pleasure, and even as a schoolboy I took intense delight in Shakespeare, especially in the historical plays. I have also said that formerly pictures gave me considerable, and music very great delight. But now for many years I cannot endure to read a line of poetry; I have tried lately to read Shakespeare, and found it so intolerably dull that it nauseated me. I have also almost lost my taste for pictures or music. Music generally sets me thinking too energetically on what I have been at work on, instead of giving me pleasure. I retain some taste for fine scenery, but it does not cause me the exquisite delight which it formerly did.

"Now, in the light of what we've just been talking about, is there any way of explaining what might have happened to Darwin after 'the age of thirty'—beyond saying that that's the point at which people cease to know anything? Is there any other way of explaining why he may no longer have been interested in art in the way that he had been?"

"How old was Darwin when he wrote *Origin of Species*—do you know?"

"I know because I got thinking along the same lines I think you are. I looked it up. Darwin was fifty when the *Origin* was published. It came out in 1859. But I *also* found out that Darwin had formulated his theory of evolution maybe twenty years before that."

"Which would make him about thirty. OK. Maybe it's possible that Darwin began to lose interest in art when science started to be art for him."

"Which is a way of saying that maybe he didn't really lose interest in art at all, even though he thought he had. Maybe what he did was to lose interest in some forms of it, because he'd become so deeply involved in others. In other words, maybe from another point of view Darwin's sentences could be describing a process of growth rather than one of decay. We saw that Gorey was able to take a number of different languages and put them together in such a way as to suggest that he was larger than they were. Is Darwin then an example of someone, of a certain kind of professional, who has put together a language of the sciences with one of the humanities so as to have achieved something like what Gorey did? Like and unlike. Because Darwin is not only larger than what he has put together, he's complete as a result of it. In putting together a language of the sciences with one of the humanities, he's put together those two parts of himself, or those selves, as we had it said in here a couple of periods ago."

"Yes, but Darwin says that when he tried to read Shakespeare again

256   it was so dull that it almost made him sick," someone said. "Are you saying he grew out of Shakespeare? Can you do that?"

"Again, I'm not sure. There's an awful lot here I'm not sure of. Can there be an aesthetic to science as powerful as the aesthetics of art? Can the aesthetic force of one negate the aesthetic force of the other, so that, at least in some contexts, it's possible to speak of someone's growing out of Shakespeare? Or would it be better to say that the value, or a value, of reading Shakespeare to begin with might lie as much *through* that reading in something outside it as it does in what one reads? And if that should be true of the study of Shakespeare, does it hold also for the study of science? These are real questions. I wish we had a few more assignments to open them up."

A "few more assignments" wouldn't have begun to do that, of course, but when class ended I did see a way that I might have written Assignment 29 so as to have raised what seemed to me the key question of our discussion. Here's the Assignment I wish I'd used:

> *Although the Well-Rounded Man is not listed in the most recent issue of the Manhattan Telephone Directory, the idea that the study of the humanities (and not just for future scientists) will result somehow in some sort of self-improvement is a notion that retains a good deal of contemporary popularity. Perhaps this is because, among other things, the notion is one of considerable antiquity. Music hath charms, and so on. At any rate, we are all of us familiar with the argument that the study of philosophy will teach us to live, that the study of Great Writers will teach us to . . . write? That the study of art will teach us to . . . what? Paint? Draw? See?*
>
> *Now, here is a True Story:*
>
>> *A Famous Teacher at a Great University was attending a dinner given by the Board of Trustees to honor him on the eve of his retirement. His dinner partner, who happened also to be the wife of the Chairman of the Board, at one point remarked to the Famous Teacher that she had always believed the study of the humanities to be beneficial. Those were her words: "the study of the humanities" and "beneficial." "But who is to say," replied the Famous Teacher, his tone making clear that the question was rhetorical, "that you can't be benefited the same way by the study of something else?" Whereupon the woman quickly changed the subject of conversation.*
>
>> *End of True Story*
>
> *This assignment is to give you, as a student of science, an opportunity to make what you can of this Famous Teacher's assertion in terms of your*

own experience. For the purpose of this paper, you may assume that the teacher was not simply lacking in social grace and also that his remark was more than a wisecrack. That is, this Famous Teacher was not called a Famous Teacher for nothing.

What are the benefits that a study of the humanities is traditionally said to bring?

Is there, so far as you are concerned, a way in which the study of the discipline of science might be said to carry with it the opportunity for someone to receive these same benefits?

Has such a thing ever happened to anyone you know or know about? Has it ever happened to you? Do you believe that such a thing could happen?

Why?

That has some tone, I think; some style to it. More importantly, it raises a question that would have given the students an opportunity to reach beyond themselves, a question that seems to me the central question to raise in speaking of the relationship of the sciences and the humanities: Can the study of a discipline other than those traditionally associated with the humanities, specifically one of the disciplines of science, be seen as bringing with it all of the "benefits" that the study of the disciplines of the humanities is popularly supposed to bring? That is, if the study of the humanities may be said to provide an opportunity for one to broaden his horizons, to know himself and other people better, to develop his aesthetic faculties, to enrich his sensibility, and so forth—whatever may be understood to be meant by such ways of talking—does it then follow that someone who does *not* study the humanities loses the opportunity to obtain such benefits another way? Second, if it is noticed that the "Man," for which the subject of "Mankind" is said to be the proper study, is no less a hypothesis, no less a postulation, than $E = mc^2$, then has not the study of science the possibility of becoming another way to the benefits claimed to result from the study of the humanities? There is a way of saying "no," of course, to all these speculations. But not an easy way. The question, as I said in class and as I still believe, is a real one.

ASSIGNMENT 30

Putting things together

We shall not cease from exploration
And the end of all our exploring
Will be to arrive where we started
And know the place for the first time.

T. S. Eliot

This is the last writing Assignment you will address yourself to this term. The class meeting in which we talk about what you do with this Assignment will be our last class meeting.

Look back over the Assignments given you this term, the papers you have written addressing yourself to them, and the papers mimeographed for discussion in class. Recall any conversation you may have had about the course, either in class or out of it.

Where did you start this term? Where do you seem to come out?

Do not simply arrange the Assignments in chronological order. Put things together in a way that will enable you to say what for you the real subject of the course has been.

Perhaps a convenient place for you to begin would be with the paper you wrote on the first day of class which has just been returned to you. The subject there, too, you will remember, was that of change. To judge from what you said about yourself in that paper, who were you? Who are you now?

I invariably conclude a sequence of assignments for a semester with
some form or other of the problem posed by Assignment 30: Where
did you start this term? Where do you seem to come out? It's my
way of inviting the students to enact in their own styles whatever
sense they may choose to make of things, and to see in that enactment
the only way of talking about the "real subject" of the course that can
mean anything. I'd done what I could with the assignments and in
our conversations to involve us in seeing writing as a matter of language using and language using as a way of talking about writing. I'd
tried to maintain as the audience for both the best of what I believed
the students capable. It seemed fitting, then, that for the final paper
I offer the students the opportunity to say only what they could say
for themselves about where they had been, what they had come from,
and where they were going. I wanted them not to say what they
thought they had learned in a term, but to show what they had. For
better or for worse then, the final paper, in being the expression of
what each student had made his experience with the course mean to
him, would be the expression also of each student's understanding of
the relationship of his writing and his language to himself. It was on
the quality of that awareness as the students enacted it in their sentences that I intended to judge what they wrote.

A couple of writers came uncomfortably close in their papers to
suggesting that the course had washed them in the Blood of the Lamb,
and in general there was a heavier leaning on such terms as "the self"
and "how to think" as ways of talking about "the real subject" than
I would have liked to see, but it was heartening how many of the
students did better with the final paper not only than I had expected
they would, but than *they* had expected. What I mimeographed for
us to talk about, therefore, was what I hoped would represent a spread
of accomplishment, a spectrumlike sense of improvement for the class
as a class. I did up five sections of five different papers and a sixth in
its entirety—each written by a student whose work had been publicly
criticized at one class meeting or another during the first two weeks of
the course. I planned in each case, first to read over that earlier writing,
and then to read what the writer had done with Assignment 30. I
planned, that is, to talk about growth as both an individual and a
collective phenomenon.

The class didn't go exactly as I had planned it.

We were just about to break for the Christmas holidays. When I'd
passed out Assignment 30, someone, noticing that it was the last regu-

260   lar writing assignment for the term, had said that maybe we ought to
have a Christmas party or something. In the same spirit I'd said OK
and that we'd sing some carols. The students hadn't forgotten.

There were two clarinets and a guitar that came to class that last day
along with a mimeographed sheet the students had persuaded our
secretary to do up for them:

ASSIGNMENT 69
"What good *are* Christmas carols, anyway? Besides, I'm going to the Baha-
mas for the vacation."

Have you ever heard anybody say anything like that? Maybe you know
somebody who heard somebody say it. Then again, maybe you don't.

Have you ever said anything like that?

Have you ever said "Bah"?

Have you ever said "Humbug"?

Who was your audience? Did they stay for the next show?

Who were you?

Now, regardless of how you wrote the Assignments for this semester, and
after talking it over with your roommates, the Dean, and the girls at Western
Reserve, *and* after singing the following in a loud clear voice, address yourself to this statement:

It is impossible to say that not singing Christmas carols will be unbeneficial
because the benefits from singing them do not always turn out to be benefits.

● ● ●

Here is "the following": (please see above or behind or something):

STEVE, LIKE JAZZ, GOES TO COLLEGE (to the tune of *Jingle Bells*)

1ST VERSE
Dusting off a Theme, keeping words just right,
Down the page I go, writing through the night.
Write the intro. first; turn the body, too,
Exeunt with a flourish and it's off to bed I'm through. Oh—

CHORUS I
Steve and Sue, Thomas too, the rest are friends you know;
Here comes every one of them, All Butt C. P. Snow;
The peacock too, old Saccoo, Nellie and the rest;
I don't know what it could mean, it's just a Gorey mess.

2ND VERSE
I got a lot of calc., and physics work to do,
And so I'd better dust this theme, or go to O.S.U.

I think I'll weave a rug, add magic just for kicks;
What good will English be to me, a budding scientist? Oh—

CHORUS II
"Bulletproof, bulletproof," that's my teacher's cry;
He's not seen the likes of this—not since junior high.
This is slop, throwing rocks, a weak and bloody dodge;
Without an ear you'll hear no voice, you need some good advice.

Even to the yodel of "Jingle Bells" it would have been a pretty ill woodwind to have blown no good in that situation. We sang. I was presented with a pocketbook done up in silver paper: *Short Cuts to Effective English* ("Experience shows that people who speak and write correctly get ahead faster. If you doubt this I suggest you read the introduction to this book written by an executive of General Electric."), and with a new red Pentel pen to which a note was attached by a ribbon: "This pen is guaranteed to write on the belly of an alligator, even if it should be submerged." Whether they meant the pen or the alligator didn't seem to matter. There was a lot of that unmanufacturable, warm, and laving sort of laughter, indescribable to someone who has never heard it in a classroom, unforgettable to anyone who has. I was moved and they knew it.

The festival didn't leave us time for the class I'd planned. So after explaining how I'd intended to run things (I told the class also that the writers of the first four samples we were going to look at were students to whom I'd given C's at midterm), I settled for saying that I'd read through what I'd mimeographed and explain what it was I admired in each case. Anything in the way of disagreement or a question that anyone wanted to throw in along the way they could stop me for.

1

The writer of this selection wrote the third paper addressed to Assignment 1 (see pp. 23–24):

When I first started writing I used bad words. I was always making vast generalizations. I made the judgments of a moralist. Now, I am better prepared to find the point and the deep meaning of a literary work. Whereas before I was frequently unclear and incoherent, I am now becoming more clear and coherent. I do not know any formula for writing except to write. I am now able to write better than I was, because I can often tell intuitively if I have written a good paper or a bad one.

That first paragraph is an attempt to show a number of the things

262 I did as a writer without knowing there was anything else to do. I might still write such sentences (if one is so liberal as to call them sentences), but I know I couldn't write them now with a straight face.

I read just that first paragraph to a roommate of mine after he had read the assignment. His response was, "That's great! It'll make the Prof. think you liked his course." Somehow at that moment a feeling of satisfaction, a feeling that the working and slaving had really done me some good, came over me.

What I admire in the opening of this paper, I explained, is the writer's attempt to express indirectly, by means of metaphor, what the resort to metaphor demonstrates would be inexpressible any other way. The first paragraph is a metaphoric description of what was; the third, which develops the metaphor of an outsider's response to what was, is a description of a certain kind of now. But the writer arbitrates between the was and the now in such a way as to suggest that he is both linked to them ("I might still write such sentences") and apart from them ("I knew I couldn't write them now with a straight face") at the same time. The two metaphors intersect to create an image of an expanded sensibility, one that, in knowing what it was and what its roommate's is, knows more than both and so is somewhere else: "Somehow at that moment a feeling of satisfaction . . . came over me." The terms of the paper define "feeling of satisfaction" so as to make the writer's claim that he has done himself "some good" believable to a reader. But the defining is an action that will not translate into the easy equivalents of a definition—sense of superiority, sense of achievement, etc.—without the loss of something.

"To explain all he seems to mean by 'feeling of sataisfaction' at the end there," one student said, "I'd have to write a paper myself."

2

The writer of this selection wrote the third paper addressed to Assignment 3 (see p. 40):

I got my first complimentary comment on Assignment 10. It was the first assignment on which I knew I had something. My second compliment was on Assignment 17. It was getting so I didn't like newspapers the same way any more. The Assignments numbered in the twenties, and my work was getting harder.

Here I am learning in a course which couldn't be taught, using a skill which couldn't be given to me, following rules which don't exist. You might call it irony, but I can't say I haven't gained by the course.

Like the paragraphs from the paper used as the first example, those above are not Great Writing, but they are, first of all, a real achievement for the student who produced them; and second, admirable I think in their attempt to express some complexity of attitude toward an experience which, whatever it may or may not have been for the student, was at least not simple. I like particularly the way he plays off against the numerical progression of the assignments his responses as both a writer and a person, responses which are anything but numerically progressive. Is not liking "newspapers the same way any more" a gain only? Why after the compliments on 10 and 17 didn't the assignments get easier? It's a technique that sets up the paradoxes of the final paragraph and prepares also for the ambiguity of attitude expressed in the hesitant, reluctant, maybe even slightly grudging admission of "benefit": "I can't say I haven't gained." Change that is really change, and even when it can be seen as growth, is hardly a steady march to serenity.

3

The writer of this selection wrote the first paper addressed to Assignment 2 (see pp. 27–28):

We started out with the simple subjects of professionalism and amateurism (they weren't really so simple) and progressed to such complex things as the Gorey story and the Sacco letter. The odd thing is that if we had reversed the order, I would probably be saying now that things started simply with Sacco and Gorey and grew more complicated as we moved to professionalism and amateurism. On the other hand, I don't think that I would be writing as I am now if we had taken the course in reversed order. I think I needed to learn how to read to learn how to write. But I had to see I couldn't write before I learned to read. At least that's the way I see it now.

My private reason for using the paragraph above was to acknowledge the courage of its writer, a student who had had difficulty all term extending himself beyond the safety of doing what he already knew how to do. I wanted to praise the fact that in trying to make sense as he does of the interdependence of reading and writing and of the paradox of the order of the assignments' making no difference at the same time it made a difference to him, the writer runs the risk of painting himself into a corner. I also wanted to praise (publicly) his taking such a risk by suggesting the value of what it brings the writer to recognize, not only about his position in relation to the course, but about his position as a student in relation to his education. To assume the responsibility of shaping his experience with the course by making an order of the assignments for himself ("I don't think that I would be writing as I am now if we had taken the course in reversed order"), and yet to understand at the same time that that order is as arbitrary as the order of the assignments may have been originally ("The odd thing is that if we had reversed the order, I would probably be saying now that things started simply . . . and grew more complicated"), and is as unfinal as he is ("At least that's the way I see it now")—to do these things is to have a jump on recognizing that the necessarily artificial *process* of education need not be artificial in its result.

4

The writer of this selection wrote the first paper addressed to Assignment 4 (see pp. 43–44):

So where do I finally stand amidst my first vain attempts, my confusion, and my last attempts? In terms of papers, I estimate that of thirty times at bat, I've scored four hits, a few "nice tries," a couple of "not bads," and the rest have been strike-outs. They're strike-outs in the sense that I could have done better, but they're not in the sense that every mistake I made told me something about my writing. My use of clichés and trite expressions, and the general ambiguity which generally accompanies my papers, show that I do not carefully compose what I want to say, but rely often on words and expressions aimed at amusing the reader. Sometimes I have not convinced myself of a point, and yet have tried to convince a reader. I've learned to beware of "Steve," and also to avoid "drugstore sociology," and the cartoon type flair. Obviously, though, I haven't, and I can't, learn writing the way I learned my multiplication tables. Not writing as writing. So what am I left with? I just try to say what I want to say? How much does *that* say?

There seems to be one thing, however, that comes with the course that is not necessarily connected with writing or composing, and that is a way of thinking. If I had seen the "Bedford Incident," or had heard someone try to define amateur or professional before I had taken the course, I probably would have taken it for granted. Now, when I hear someone try to define professional or amateur, or advice, or knowledge, or for that matter anything, I remember the trouble I had with making a definition for something when a definition did not exist in the way I thought it did. When someone tells me that a professional is a certain thing or that I should study the humanities for a certain reason, I find myself asking "Why?" in almost the same sense that the reader of my papers asked "Why?" in the margins. Not only have I found myself asking "Why?" just for the case of definitions, but for a good many other things. The Assignment about why I was studying the humanities gave me a good chance to think about why I *was* really studying the humanities. It wasn't necessarily because someone at one time or another has said that it would make me a "well-rounded" person, but it did tie in somehow with the intriguing questions of what it means to know and of what is worth knowing.

I have found myself asking a lot more questions, but I haven't always been finding the answers. It's almost like being asked thirty questions about what is the difference between an amateur and a professional without ever finding an answer. Whether or not an answer is immediate, however, I find that when I ask "Why?" of a statement which I have read, or a statement which someone has written, or for that matter a statement which I have written, I find myself looking for an answer. I don't know whether or not this is an anticipated outcome of the course, but I'm not going to argue about it: I now have a way of seeing things which involves being conscious of the composition of what I think as well as of what I write. In short, I have a new way of looking at myself. As you would say, I guess that's been worth the price of admission.

Like the writer of the last paragraph, the writer of those above was never a student who had had any difficulty demonstrating what is called "proficiency." His difficulty as a writer was that he was generally too damned Proficient for his own good. He had never had anyone demand of him that he write a sentence that was *about* anything, and he responded to the demand initially as though he had been asked to drop his pants. Ordinarily, I don't work very well with that sort of student, but along about the time we were finishing up with the assignments on nonsense, for some reason he got interested, and his papers began to show it. Unfortunately, he'd done his best papers on assignments that I'd used the papers of other students to work with in class. The real reason I mimeographed the section of his paper above was that I simply hadn't had a chance to acknowledge what had happened to him at a public level. The paper is marred by generality, I think, but for me it's saved, maybe just saved, by voice. I'd still take exception to the way in which he opposes writing with "a way of thinking" at the opening of his second paragraph, but I was happy to be able to admire the student's attempt to see writing as an activity that carried beyond itself, and I praised also his recognition that the problems with which we had concerned ourselves (definition; what it means to know) were more than artificial.

The writer of this selection wrote the first paper addressed to Assignment 5 (see pp. 51–52):

The paradox, I have to call it that, involved in trying to find a way of talking about the concepts of amateur and professional is connected with something that only opened up for me in about the last five or six assignments. In Assignment 25, the directive stated that we were to try to explain a scientific law or principle in terms which a nonscientist could understand. I thought about it for a while, and decided that I really couldn't explain something to a nonscientist without having to use the same types of definitions and meanings which had condemned my previous papers. Apparently the reader agreed, or at least thought I had stumbled onto something, when he wrote on one of my papers, "Do you speak as just a scientist here or as something more? Does this open up 'professional' at all?" The comment didn't open up my understanding of the meaning of professional exactly, but it did open it up as a way of seeing things. Suppose that instead of having to find a language to write about professionals and amateurs at the start of the term, we had been asked to find a language with which to write about scientists and nonscientists, or for that matter, science and the humanities. I would probably have had as much trouble explaining a "work of Shakespeare's" or defining the Second Law of Thermodynamics as I did in trying to distinguish between professional and amateur. But I didn't see this at first.

It seems now that the thirty assignments might not have been to have us find a relationship between professionals and amateurs or between the humanities and the sciences, so much as they were asking us to find a relationship between the writer and the reader in trying to distinguish between professionals and amateurs or the sciences and the humanities. For that matter, the problem wasn't restricted just to "finding" a language. The problem was how I, as a writer, could use that language to talk about $F = ma$ to a nonscientist; and as a reader, how I could use a language to help me hear the Gorey story. If language consisted simply of definitions, meanings, and explanations, as I had originally thought, then why couldn't I just stop with definitions and meanings for amateur and professional? Apparently, language consisted of something more than what you could just "find" as in the case of understanding "I Saw a Peacock," or describing the difference between amateur and professional, or even understanding the question about what is worth knowing. The ability to use that language is "out there somewhere," just as is the meaning I kept looking for in the poem, or the voice I heard in the Sacco letter, or the difference which seemed to exist between amateur and professional. It's there, but how to grasp it, how to use language, seems to be the challenge the course leaves after the last assignment.

I don't always know how I do use language successfully even when I do. I don't know how I used language on Assignment 29 to get a "not bad." Do I have to know? I don't need an explanation to say why I felt good when one of my papers came back with a "Bloody fine" written on it. I don't need a way of explaining to mys   why I feel like an amateur after I squawk out a few notes on   nor sax and then listen to a few bars by Stan Getz. The probl m omes in finding a way of conveying the way I feel to a read   his would seem to me to be the need for a language, to get what I feel or think to the person who is reading what I have written.

No matter how I've tried to write about it, the problem of the amateur and the professional still remains as paradoxical as the Gorey story and as unattainable as the language needed to write about it. Just as I fashioned a somewhat "meaningful" explanation for the anonymous poem, the relationship between amateur and professional can become anything I make it. If I called an amateur a "clumsy bastard," then I could also warp this definition into that of a professional, as in the case of Sacco, whose clumsiness made him a professional. I could say that a professional was a person who earned a salary, but even so, there is a great deal of difference between the garbage collector and the president of General Motors. No matter what I say about the relationship between them, I can make it fit. The trouble comes when I try to make this relationship mean something to a reader. It was then that I saw everything go to pieces. I saw the relationships I had made losing their meanings in the same way Gorey's story did in my retelling of it. I never found the right language, which I don't know whether I can ever do, but which doesn't seem to me as important as something else. The value of what I've been doing is in knowing that one needs a language a reader can understand before he writes anything.

Here again, it's the voice of that paper, which for me makes its sentences readable, the sensibility created by them interesting. The order the writer makes of the assignments, I think, would have been fuller, of more final value to him as a student, had he made the one final turn necessary to see *himself* as his most important reader, and writing, therefore, a means of self-clarification. But the range of mind in the paper, its gathering of the seeming disparateness of the assignments into, if not a solution to the problems raised, at least the suggestion of a position from which to acknowledge the problems as problems, has little in common with the sensibility that on Assignment

268   5 could see professionalism only as a matter of "high quality skill" and the activity of writing as no more than a recording of what Already Is.

6

The writer of this complete paper wrote the first paper we considered in class, paper one of Assignment 1 (see pp. 19–20):

The first paper I wrote for this course is a convenient place to begin all right, because it shows me more than where I started the term. It shows me something about who and what I was. And who I am still. In that paper I *did* think I was being asked why I came to college, and I thought that the answer to "where do you locate yourself at the present time" was: "at Case, of course." In the paper I said things like "the world of science is one of constantly expanding horizons." In a way, I'm still the same person as the one who looked at things that way, but I think I can see now that talking about the "expanding horizons" of science isn't going to get me very far, and that the answer to "where are you" isn't just a place."

So where did I start this term? I started "generally," "in my mind," and "usually" had an answer for every question. I started by seeing everything clearly. I knew what was going on, and I could "help and advise" others. Then about the tenth paper, I began to realize that this whole thing wasn't just some kind of joke; I was actually supposed to get something out of these seemingly ridiculous and repetitive assignments. It was at this time that I *think* I began to "think," but by thinking I became confused. I was surprised to find, however, that when I faced it, this confusion wasn't a detriment to my papers; it actually became a kind of partner in my writing them. Whenever I entered this state of confusion, it seemed that I was able to get past my initial readiness with or loss of words and sometimes get a glimpse of that which was causing my confusion. And this I found to be an excellent thing to write about.

"Where do you seem to come out?" I am still mixed up by the assignments. For some reason, I have had a kind of faith that whenever we came to the end of this course everything would fall together, and it would be possible to turn and see the road by which I had come. We were told Monday that this is the end; so, I'm turning. At first all seems dark, but then I think I can recognize a little light. My main hope is that this light is the beginning of dawn and not just moonlight. Maybe, as one writer said, "my knowing about darkness can make my day brighter."

Look at this "hedging." Where *have* I come out? What has the course been all about—writing, learning, seeing, thinking, understanding? I looked at these words after writing them and wondered why I had written them in the -ing form. I could just as easily have said "how to write, learn," etc.; but I didn't. I guess this would have made it sound as though I had definitely learned something; for instance, you can "learn" how to ride a bicycle. I haven't learned anything in this manner. I guess that I would have to say that I have learned enough to automatically put these examples (writing, learning, etc.) in the -ing form rather than some other way. I have only begun to learn things.

I think I am coming close to saying something in this paper. I don't know whether "close" is as far as I can get or whether I could go all the way and describe "close to knowing"; but "close to knowing" is where I want to come out, where I think I am coming out, in this course.

I seem to be writing this paper in the same manner that I have tried to write the last fifteen or twenty, but now I don't seem to be getting anywhere. Does this make it the hardest assignment that I have yet addressed, or could it be that I am no longer content with writing "assignments"? I have been led so far, and I have found a way to adjust to this leading and to be able to get something out of it; but I can't be led all my life. I think this assignment is making me kick myself out of the nest. I can use the things that I have learned in this course, but any further learning that I'm to do is going to have to be on my own. I'm going to have to make my own assignments. I'm going to have to teach myself "what is worth knowing," instead of having someone sort it out and feed it to me.

It's tempting to try to sum up my paper and this course by saying something like "this has been a course in learning" or "seeing" or, better yet, "living"; but I'm not going to do it. At the beginning of the year, I wouldn't have said anything like this either; but about a month and a half ago I would have. However, this doesn't mean that I'm back where I started. At the beginning of the year, I wouldn't have used the words learning, seeing, and living in connection with this course, because I was ignorant of the fact that they could even exist in an English class. And I certainly wouldn't have used the -ing form. After I became confused, I tried to take the attitude that writing was seeing and living and used it as a solution to my problem; but it didn't take me long to find out that this was wrong. Now I realize that these things are present in this course; but at the same time, I know enough not to say that this course has been *about* these things.

What about amateurism and professionalism? This is the path that we have taken to learn about writing. We were told at the beginning of the year that this set of assignments represented a "fresh progression in thought and expression." I am sure that this is so, but I am equally sure that students who have taken this course in previous years have come out at approximately the same place I am now. They might not

270   have had to struggle with help, advice, amateurs, and professionals; but whatever their "progression in thought and expression," I am sure that through it they saw the complexity of writing, and that in writing they had a key that could open—at least part way—any door that it was set to.

That paper no one had any trouble understanding why I reproduced in its entirety or why I used it to conclude the class. It would have been a marvelous paper with which to suggest how the end of the course is but its real beginning, but in the time that was left us after I'd read it through, I didn't get a chance to do more than state a tithe of what I admired it for: the manner in which the writer refuses to disown completely his first-day-of-class naiveté, the way he speaks of making a "partner" of his confusion, his seeing that "readiness with" a certain kind of language is the same thing as a "loss of words," his distinguishing between being led and leading himself, his imagining himself as his own assignment maker, and, above all, his consciousness of the activity of writing as an action ("the -ing form") undivorceable from the actions of seeing, thinking, and learning—a fusion which his paper not only makes, but is.

Perhaps more important than anything else, at least to me, is the way in which the paper as a gesture—one in which rejection and acceptance become adjuncts of each other—enacts the most meaningful paradox of teaching and learning. The paper is a rejection of dependency, on the course and its procedures, on an earlier way of seeing, on me as a teacher. What the writer does in his paper, as he is well aware, he has done by and for himself; the triumph of its having been written belongs to him. But as the writer is also aware, this triumph does not belong to him alone, not any more than he is completely separated from the self, the way of seeing, with which he began the course. He could not have done what he did without the rest of us. The rejection in his paper, then, is made as it is made necessary, in the name of a re-creation of himself as an individual whose independence is conditioned by its new and free acknowledgement of its dependence—on both the self from which it came and on the rest of us as well. In the formation of that plural I, each one of us in that class had had a sharing.

—and After

LOOKING BACK ON
THE PLURAL I

Goethe, probably among others, says to be wary of our youthful wishes, for in maturity we are apt to get them. I go back now to [Shillington] Pennsylvania, and on one of the walls of the house in which my parents live there hangs a photograph of myself as a boy. I am smiling, and staring with clear eyes at something in the corner of the room. I stand before that photograph, and am disappointed to receive no flicker, of approval or gratitude. The boy continues to smile at the corner of the room, beyond me. That boy is not a ghost to me, he is real to me; it is I who am a ghost to him. I, in my present state, was one of the ghosts that haunted his childhood. Like some phantom conjured by this child from a glue bottle, I have executed his commands; acquired pencils, paper, and an office. Now I wait apprehensively for his next command, or at least a nod of appreciation, and he smiles through me, as if I am already transparent with failure.

He saw art—between drawing and writing he ignorantly made no distinction—as a method of riding a thin pencil line out of Shillington, out of time altogether, into an infinity of unseen and even unborn hearts. He pictured this infinity as radiant. How innocent! But his assumption here, like his assumptions on religion and politics, is one for which I have found no certain substitute.

John Updike, *The Dogwood Tree*

At this writing it is almost ten years since *The Plural I* was published and over twenty since I worked in the course it ostensibly describes, taking notes as I went day by day, really quite a lot of notes, on what I thought we'd said, on what I

272   hoped we'd be able to say, writing out wishes, filling in dreams. There is no question that some of what Updike describes himself as experiencing in confrontation with his youthful self I feel too in looking back through my pages. It's not the class I remember best, not the students or their papers, not the exchanges we had over them. It's the experience of trying to put that all together, of trying to find a way to make it mean something, that is as clear to me today and as complicated to place my relation to as is Updike's photograph of himself. I worked at the book off and on for a period of over ten years, writing and rewriting mostly in the summers in a converted ice house on an isolated Canadian lake, working early, very early in the morning by the light of a kerosene lamp. I really did want to be a teacher of writing even then, and there were moments when I believed I'd become one. I remember the day the art and science connection became clear to me, the connection made in the chapter on Assignment 29, and how it rolled light back through everything I had written, making it whole, turning the future into a radiant infinity of possibility. I wrote the dedication of the book out of that moment, right then, scrawled it out by hand, and went up to the sunporch with it to where my daughters slept, six and four. And I stood between them, the world tipping into dawn forever, moving and still, still moving, forever, and was anointed, and consecrated in all things.

Am I today what I on that day had in mind for myself?

But I am not just a ghost to the hero narrator of *The Plural I*, and mainly what I feel in locating myself with the book at this remove is an enormous gratitude—for what the book became in spite of what I would have made it, at what the privilege of having worked at the creating of its hero narrator goes on giving me, again in spite of myself.

In first thinking over what I wanted to say in this afterword, my temptation was to apologize. I thought of explaining the ways in which the assignment sequence of the book, my first try at one, is really not very good (and really it is not very good) by comparing it with its revision, published as *Composing II* by Hayden in 1981. I thought of showing how with a chance to do it all again I'd present the students differently, as individuals rather than as simply individuated voices, as

more fully developed characters along the lines of those created for *Seeing Through Writing* (Harper & Row, 1988).
Above all I thought of making excuses for my narrator, of
underscoring the way in which he is only a persona, after all,
no better than the best I could do way back then, and of
expressing my surprise that anyone could ever have imagined
anything else (most recently, William Irmscher in *College
Composition and Communication*, February, 1987: "I get a
clear notion what the instructor is like and how the students
react. All of this is so vivid that I know I don't want to be like
Coles. I don't want to use his approach, and I don't want to
treat students as he does."). My temptation, in other words,
particularly with my hero narrator, was to patronize myself,
to beg a penny for the Old Guy by showing in how many ways
I've outgrown him.

In a sense, of course, the teacher of *The Plural I* never was
any more than a persona, and in a way I have outgrown him—
as suggested by the teacher-speakers of *Composing II, Seeing
Through Writing*, and in the essay following this one. But in
another sense he's a good deal closer to me and a lot more
important than a term like "persona" can suggest, and it's at
my own peril that I forget that.

Case-Western Reserve University Press rejected the first
version of *The Plural I* in the fall of 1968. It was a tract then, a
kind of a diatribe on what was wrong with the teaching of
writing in the United States cast in the form of an explanation
of how to do things right. The manuscript was filled with the
use of the first person singular, but there was no dialog in it.
"Arrogant" they called it. "Self-aggrandizing." Neither term
was in a subordinate clause and both were more than deserved. I rewrote the book completely, toning down what
seemed to need it, and it was again rejected, by two publishers this time, in 1969, and for pretty much the same reason
Case-Reserve had turned it down originally. I took two years
to rewrite the book still again, as a set of carefully choreo-
graphed classroom scenes, but again nobody would touch it. I
rewrote the book a third time—for rejection by five publishers in 1974. It had been in a file drawer for three years when,
after the modest successes of *Composing* and *Teaching Composing*, Holt, Rinehart and Winston agreed to publish it—

274 contingent on another revision and at 2% royalty. I never even made permission fees. Holt decided to let the book go out of print in 1985 without ever having had to send me a dime.

Self-aggrandizement, when it comes to my early relation to *The Plural I*, would not be a bad way of describing a lot more than the first manuscript versions of the book—if one were feeling charitable about it. It's tempting of course to use my knowing now that there was an unforseeable consequence to all that revising to argue that my real motives for taking on the project must have been larger and less mean, and that part of me then must have been aware of them. But an argument is all it would be, and self-serving in precisely the way Frost in "The Road Not Taken" so slyly suggests such arguments always are. No sir. The truth is I wouldn't have worked at the book fifteen minutes longer than it would have taken me to accept the first offer to print it, not in that first seven years or so anyway, and had that happened I'd have been stuck, and with a lot more than a bad book, maybe for the rest of my life.

Because though I really did want to be a teacher of writing when I began *The Plural I*, I also really didn't think I had that much further to go to get there. I was fresh from five years of having worked with some of the best teachers I've ever known—Ben DeMott, Bill Pritchard, Roger Sale, and above all Ted Baird at Amherst College—people that had sealed my belief in the generative power of an approach to teaching writing that worked in a classroom and with student writers even when I couldn't figure out why. I had quite a repertoire of moves. I had a lot of charismatic energy. I'd never met a student I couldn't provoke into making an effort. But though I'd have been furious at the accusation, my measure of good teaching finally was praise. What I thought I needed most as a teacher was fame.

The successive rewritings of *The Plural I* involved me at first then only in a very superficial attempt to eliminate what other people had found offensive in it. I worked to purge my pages of the appearance of arrogance and self-aggrandizement while at the same time trying to hang on to my image of myself as outsider, as the lone wolf professional, tough but fair, directing a learning process in which he himself never really participated.

It didn't work of course, the attempt simply to tone this notion down, and that failure is what pushed me, stumbling, into the dialogic, novelistic form of the book. I had to create something to play against the all-consuming voice of my narrator. My students, in other words, had to get a hearing.

And then I found I had to create my teacher as someone who could listen to them.

Drama, the necessity of developing some believable drama, is what I think saved the book, or rather turned it into one. I couldn't create the students as just sticks without having the papers they wrote explode that as a fiction. And the only way I could create a narrator teacher who had a chance of being seen as anything other than someone seeking domination and control for its own sake was to try to imagine him as someone tough *and* fair, as someone, that is, who served something larger than his own ego and whose behavior therefore could point to the importance of his belief in something bigger than he was. This shifted the focus of conflict in the book. The teacher became less the adversary of the students and more their ally, the advocate of their better selves, someone whose main responsibility was to establish a community of those who through it could experience the miraculous individual transformation that seems always to attend any genuine training discipline. It is the sort of transformation, as Vicki Hearne notes, that can lift all participants in the process, trainer and trainee, teacher as well as students, "out of the moral life and the comforts of its patent goods into the life of art, a life of uncertain value but characterized by genuine risks and diamond-hard responses and unprecedented responsibilities."* I was forced, in short, into trying to imagine the teaching and learning of writing not as *other* than heroic but as a different *kind* of heroic enterprise than I thought it was, as that which demanded not just a hero, but heroes. I was forced to imagine the classroom as a place in which all of us *together* were involved in combat, with the

*Vicki Hearne, *Adam's Task: Calling Animals by Name* (New York: Alfred A. Knopf, 1986), p.245.

276   same shabby equipment always deteriorating, in communal alignment against the same things.

I never thought of *The Plural I* in such terms back then of course, not when I was working on it, not even in the years immediately following its publication. And I can cheerfully acknowledge how for a lot of readers, and I am one of them, I was not completely successful in what I now think I was trying to do. I'm not a good enough novelist for one thing. For another, I was a large part of my subject and there is a limit to what even art can transform. In fact, in my successive rewritings of the book I was conscious of doing no more than trying to solve a writing problem. My point, however, is that in working at trying to create the image of a teacher's doing what he was doing in the context of what structured the universe for him, and in having him insist that the students do the same thing for themselves, I was given a way of seeing what it could mean to belong to one's self as a teacher. In working to create someone not that I *was* like or believed I one day could be like, but whom I knew I was *not* like and could never be like, I was obligated, at the same time I was left free, to work out my own ways of serving the idea that the teaching of writing is about something more than just me. I was myself responding to what I had created in just the way that in the introduction to *The Plural I* I suggest other teachers respond to the same thing. I was responding to "a style performed in such a way as to enable others to make for themselves, or to make better, styles of their own." Not that I was aware of it. As I say, I was trying only to solve a writing problem. But in changing my understanding of the meaning of what I was doing as a teacher, working on *The Plural I* began to change what I did as one.

I don't mean that I became a different kind of a hero or was given humility as a result of *The Plural I*, but doing the book did enable me to understand the value of acting as though I believed in these things, and I began to work harder at the *craft* of teaching in consequence, harder on shaping my assignments into more useful speculative instruments, for example, harder on transforming what I had simply lifted from other teachers into an approach of my own, harder on listening better, on doing more as a result of having to prove less. I became vulnerable as a teacher. I could afford to because I'd discovered a way of going on forever. And this is why I am grateful to the book, particularly to the example of its hero narrator, who freed me in spite of the warden's role I would have cast him in. He made me work to belong to myself as a teacher. And he does so still.

Because, like Updike's photograph of himself, he remains a testament to what's possible. Only as I dreamed it then, yes indeed, but as I have the chance to continue to dream it in new terms, and again and again and again, and must if I am to stay alive as a teacher. For it is not that I have found no certain substitute for that hero narrator's assumptions about teaching. For me there isn't one. So at times of course I feel uneasy in my relation to him, apart, as though we'd been amputated from one another, and at such times he smiles past me, through me, as does Updike's youthful self, for he is always looking to the journey which often I desert. At other times, however, when I give some evidence, as for him I believe I do in the following essay, of understanding that outgrowing him—or rather growing out of him—was the whole point of his having been created to begin with, it is straight at me that I imagine he smiles, as if to say, "Why, yes, that's it. That's just the sort of thing I had in mind."

Pittsburgh, Pennsylvania
1987

WRITING AS LITERACY:
AN ALTERNATIVE TO LOSING*

If we concentrate our attention on trying to solve a problem of geometry, and if at the end of an hour we are no nearer to doing so than at the beginning, we have nevertheless been making progress each minute of that hour in another more mysterious dimension. Without our knowing or feeling it, this apparently barren effort has brought more light into the soul. The result will one day . . . very likely be felt in some department of the intelligence in no way connected with mathematics. Perhaps he who made the unsuccessful effort will one day be able to grasp the beauty of a line of Racine more vividly on account of it. . . . Every time that a human being succeeds in making an effort of attention with the sole idea of increasing his grasp of truth, he acquires a greater aptitude for grasping it, even if his effort produces no visible fruit. An Eskimo story explains the origin of light as follows: "In the eternal darkness, the crow, unable to find any food, longed for light, and the earth was illumined." If there is a real desire, if the thing desired is really light, the desire for light produces it. There is a real desire when there is an effort of attention.[1]

Simone Weil

All the race track people fished. Gibson fished for stripers, as did Slaughterhouse Red and the grooms and some of the jockeys, and Creed fished for trout, up in the Sierras, and Bob Hack fished whenever he got a chance. Optimism, pursuit of slippery creatures, the

*Published originally as "Literacy for the Eighties: An Alternative to Losing" in R. W. Bailey and R. M. Fosheim, eds., *Literacy for Life* (New York: The Modern Language Association of America, 1983), pp. 248–262. Copyright © 1981 by William E. Coles, Jr.

desire to connect with forces beyond your control. Driving back to the Terrace one evening I passed a backwater slough growing spiky reeds and long fingers of grass, perfect habitat for catfish, and thought, *I bet there's horses in there.*[2]

Bill Barich

The question "Who am I?" obsesses the mind and all human activity provides answers, ever changing, uncertain, risky. Grammatically, it would seem that "I" am a user of prepositions. "I" see something as above or below, to the left or to the right, before or after, but the thing itself ever eludes me. And "I" myself turn out to be a maker of patterns, of orders, a constructor of worlds.

Theodore Baird

Most of the people who come out here don't see it my way and that's OK by me. Most of the time anyway. They just don't come out here to handicap horse races, that's all. They're not serious and they know it. I wouldn't call them losers. Plenty of guys come out here who are serious and are still losers, but most of the people here come out here just for fun and that's OK by me. You want to go to the track a couple of nights a season, have dinner, bring the kids, watch the horses run, fine. I can understand that. Bet on the names or the numbers, show bet the favorite, gamble a little, the way you'd do with a wheel in Las Vegas. Fine. It used to bother me the way they never even look at a program really, or the field either, the way they never *see* anything, and it still bothers me when they think what I do is bet a system. But OK. They're just not out here to handicap. They're straight on that. They're not serious and they're straight on that too. It's one of the first things you want to get straight about coming out here because. . . .

. . .One of the first things you want to get straight about the teaching of writing is the vital importance of the question of what you're going to make the whole thing mean, for your students as writers, for yourself as a teacher of writing—what you're going to make it mean and how you're going to keep that central. Against what sea of troubles do you see yourself taking arms as a teacher; in the name of what do you fight? And if there is no sea of troubles for you, no fight to fight, why bother? Why not just sell shoes?

I mean what are you going to make the whole thing mean specifically too, as an idea rather than as some easily labelled

280   ideal: Well, I want my students to be Good Citizens, or Wise Consumers, or whatever. And by how you're going to keep the idea central, I mean how day by day, with what sorts of materials and writing activities, moving from what kind of here to what kind of there, are you going to put your students in the position of seeing what good writing is good for, and in what senses it can be said to be worth someone's while to work at—particularly when you know it's not something most people are going to enjoy doing very much, or do very much of, or ever become very good at? And now, right now at the beginning of your teaching career, is as good a time as any to see why, however you go about addressing this question, the answer to it is not one you can simply take for granted or be supplied with in any form that is likely to do you much good. It's important that you get clear. . . .

    . . .It's important that *you* get clear on what the whole thing means not just for the sake of the other addicts you're going to be working with, but for your sake. If *you're* not clear on what getting clean is all about, you can't work with them, and if you don't work with them you're going back to drink and drugs, you're going back to die. That's the way it is with addiction. So you start there, with addiction, with what it means to be hooked—and with trying to understand how that's the last thing in the world an addict understands, which is one of the primary reasons we become addicted to begin with. And that we stay that way. What did you and I know when we finally asked for help? All I knew when I came to this program was that I hurt and that I didn't want to hurt anymore. I didn't come here to change my life or to save my soul. I came to save my ass. If I thought about it at all I'd have said that the problem was drink, or that the problem was drugs. What I didn't begin to see was how drugs and booze are the solution to problems for people like us and that that was the problem. The real problem was I didn't know how to do life. I didn't know how to live. And I didn't know I didn't know that and that that was the root of things, because I'd found something that made me think I could live without my having to go through the pain of learning how to do it and of needing other people to be able to continue to do it. It's not just chemicals that hook us, see. It's the promises they make.

You'll be all right. You can do it alone. It's all going to be all right. That's why it takes us so damned long to get here. Everybody else, and years before we do, can see what the stuff does *to* us, but nobody else sees what it does *for* us. What it does for us. My God, if I'd known what liquor would do for me, I'd have had a shot on the way to kindergarten. It made me dead to life sure. It made living dead to life too. But at the same time it made both of us into something I couldn't live, or do what I called live, any other way. That's why I could *get* clean, or could seem to, but I could never stay that way. You're addicted when you're somebody who cannot not use death to live life, sooner or later. No wonder addiction is the only disease the primary symptom of which is to convince you that you don't have a disease. You've got to understand this in order to. . . .

. . .You've got to understand the importance of your having to create a meaning for the activity of writing for your students in the context of what can be said to have happened to the teaching of writing in the United States—I mean what can be said to have happened historically, or at least by the pattern I have made of what I would call history in order to locate myself with what I believe to be worth doing as a teacher.

In a world—that is, in a culture or a society—where the meaning of writing is in some sense a given, where teachers can behave as though they believed that their students believed what they believe—that good writing is necessary to, say, godliness (as it was for Emerson in 1836), or to moral rectitude (as it was for Adam Sherman Hill and Genung in the 1890s), or to good manners (as it was in the 1920s and 30s), or to success (as it was in other than a last ditch way for all of us not more than forty years ago)—then the activity of writing can be offered to everybody as that which it can be taken for granted has importance to everybody as a somebody. In such a world, substantive knowledge *about* writing—the terminologies with which the activity is described and all that they imply about how the activity is to be taught and learned—all this can be understood by everyone as a vital inheritance, as the organic link of the individual with a living tradition, as a legacy, a kind of trust fund of the spirit, rather than the dead weight accumu-

282   lation of a thousand thousand rag and bone shops of as many foul hearts. In such a world there is no divorce, in other words, between substantive knowledge *about* the activity of writing and the activity of writing itself, no divorce between substantive knowledge and the agreed upon importance of such knowledge, the shared understanding of why it matters. With such a cultural frame for things, to focus on the relationship of the writing and its intended audience is as natural as it is effective.

In a world where the meaning of writing is *not* a given, however, in a world such as the world we're living in, where nothing can be taken for granted in our classrooms about what it means to write a sentence in English, this meaning must be in some sense created. When it is not, when in such a world the focus remains fixed on the relationship of writing to its audience without being widened to include the relationship of a writer to that writing, the activity becomes ever increasingly an exercise—which is what I think happened with the teaching of writing through the 1940s, the 50s, the 60s, bottoming out finally in the phenomenon known as the literacy crisis in the 1970s—the direct as well as the indirect result of teachers of writing not realizing that what could once be counted on as the vital knowledge of a living tradition had petrified into a dead metaphor for a world that no longer existed. Clung to more and more desperately by teachers, however (as though an inherited tradition would do for us as a profession what there would then be no need for us to have to do for ourselves), this knowledge became more and more internally elaborated, more and more systematized, dogmatized, theologized, at the same time it grew less and less in touch with anything outside itself. With anything or with anybody. Writing, in fact, became a mechanical action rather than an activity, that which anybody could be taught to teach to anybody or that anybody could learn from anybody else, but within which nobody, teacher or student, could find himself as a somebody. Hence the literacy crisis, the inevitable consequence of teachers of writing refusing to take into enough account how at the level of teaching and learning it is the frame for substantive knowledge about writing, what the activity is offered in the name of, that makes both that knowledge and the activity of writing substantive for students. It is neither the knowledge nor the activity all by itself. Seen this way, "the literacy crisis" is the result less of a failure of knowledge *about* writing than a failure of the imagination *with* what knowledge we already had. It is the consequence, in Henry Adam's metaphor, of our remaining a nineteenth century profession trying to operate in a twentieth century world—but with no sense of our need for a different spool on which to wind history. Not to understand this. . . .

. . .Not to understand what handicapping is all about is to have nothing to hang on to yourself with out here. And unless you're out here just to screw around, and are clear about that, without something to hang on to yourself with, you're not just going to lose, you're going to be a loser. You don't want to kid yourself about that either, that not being a loser is just a matter of being careful or being serious. Like I say, there are plenty of guys come out here that are serious, real serious. But they're losers. They're not handicappers. The big score. Money. That's what they're after, and they take it seriously all right. They're here night after night, with six, ten different trifectas boxed in every lousy $2,500 claimer. Race after race. They got systems, see, and that's what they bet. They bet systems, not races. They don't even see the horses anymore. They got pocket calculators to read the program. Slide rules. Honest to God. When they win it's all them. When they lose they got a bad drive, or the horse is a plug, or the fix was in. They don't see anything anymore. All they believe in is luck or some kind of magic they call science. They believe in it but they don't trust it so they don't even know that luck is all they believe in, like those screwballs with the Zodiac. That's not handicapping. They never worked out, or maybe they don't even care anymore, that the track is set up to make money on people who are out here to make money that way, particularly when they win races they haven't figured out. There's nothing can make you a loser faster than that—take it from me, I've been there.

All you got to do is win once on some crazy long shot, 40 to 1, with your last five bucks at the end of a bad night where everything you do right comes out wrong, and it happens that way sometimes, and so you say what the hell, and you start to look for some gimmick like a month old speed fraction or blood-

284   lines, but you're really looking only at the odds on the tote board, not at the field, not at the program, and by God in he comes, by a couple of lengths maybe, in a suck-along race, and something happens to you. Something happens way down deep, way down past what you know, where you start to think that maybe there isn't anything *to* know. You start to think that maybe what you know, because it's never good enough, isn't any good at all. Maybe luck is all there is. Maybe magic is all there is. And you're hooked, Mister, and that's what a loser is, somebody hooked that way. Split up and hooked just that way. You become a loser not because you never win, sometimes you do, and not because you don't win over the long haul, maybe nobody does that, not big anyway. You're a loser because of how you see things. You lose when you don't have to lose, and you always end up losing more than you have to, and you quit learning from when you do lose. You spoil everything for yourself. You let the track make you crazy. So part of what handicapping is about is self-protection. It's a way of hanging on to yourself out here, a way to keep from going crazy. It's a way of knowing where you are when. . . .

       . . .Part of the way you know where you are as a teacher of writing then, is to know where you're not, where none of us is, not any more. For better or worse, that is, it's no longer possible for us to be very effective as teachers by defining writing or the benefits of it in traditional terms only. It's no longer possible for us to get very far by offering writing to our students as a predominantly mechanical activity the importance of which we assert only with the half-truths of predominantly negative arguments: if you *don't* write well then you will not be thought nicely-mannered or well-rounded or decently-educated. If you *don't* write well then you will not be successful, you will not obtain a high-paying job, etc. For it is no more difficult to see how people could fail to care very much about writing conceived of primarily as a set of conventions or rules to be mastered than it is to see why they might have troubles believing that such mastery is a necessary condition for professional survival or even advancement—let alone an indicant of knowledge, intelligence, or character. Not just on *your* say-so, thank you very much. Not any more. Besides, to whatever extent such assertions were ever reasons for anybody's learning to write, they are still more an explanation of how an ability to write is valuable than they are an explanation of why the ability should be valued in the first place. Only in a very limited way do they suggest that there can be something in the activity of writing for the *writer*, for the writer as student, let alone for the writer as anything other than a student.

So OK, if we're not where we're not as teachers of writing, then where are we? Or more to the point, where am I? Where am I and what do I do?

I guess I start with my own private vision of how in the beginning was the word, with why I value writing in the first place. Just for myself. Just for me. I value it for myself as a uniquely powerful instrument for learning, as a special way of thinking and coming to know. I value it as a form of language using, language using understood as the primary means by which all of us run orders through chaos thereby giving ourselves the identities we have. Looking at writing from this point of view gives me a way of seeing the ability to compose in sentences as an ability to conceptualize, to build structures, to draw inferences, to develop implications, to generalize intelligently—in short to make connections, to work out relationships—between this idea and that idea, words and other words, sentences and other sentences, language and experience. And from this point of view also I have a chance of offering writing to students as an activity of language using that can enable them to become better composers, better conceptualizers, better thinkers in whatever other languages they may work with: mathematical formulae, chemical equations, pigments, gestures, speech. Thus, I have a way of offering writing as an avenue to a very special kind of power, the only power I know that is uncorrupting and for my money that it therefore makes any sense to have: the power to choose with awareness, to change and adapt consciously, and in this sense to be able to have a share in determining one's own destiny. And I have a way of suggesting that this power is available not just to those students who *become* writers, whatever we may mean by that, but even to those who are willing to do no more than work at it, to work at imagining what they could do if they were writers. I value writing in the first place because powerlessness is an invitation to victimization. . . .

286   . . .An addict, you got to understand, is a victim of himself,
and that's why he's a loser, just the way you and I were. You
can't *be* an addict and be anything else. I made up a world to
live in with booze and pills at the center of it, a world where
everything supported everything else. I could even diagnose
myself. Hell man, I'd been diagnosed, upside down and back
nine ways to Sunday. I was a paranoid neurotic with schizo-
phrenic symptoms subject to attacks of anxiety, acute depres-
sion, feelings of alienation and despair. Why a guy like that
would just have to have something to get through a day,
wouldn't he? Some anti-depressants, or mood elevators with
antiseptic sounding names like meloril or thorazine? Or I had
my California Kung Fu group therapy talk: I needed Positive
Reinforcement and Support. My trouble was that I engaged
in Suicide Ideation. I was Uncomfortable with my Feelings. I
had a Negative Self-Image. I just couldn't deal with what was
coming on down, baby. It was a goddam circle is what it was,
a circle of talk, bad talk. The wrong names. That's what I was
really addicted to. Sure everything propped up everything
else in my world. The only trouble was I couldn't live in the
world I'd made. Nothing could get to me, but I couldn't get
out of where I was to anything else. I was Genesis 1:1 but
without any power. The King Kong-sized monkey on my back
was both the only thing that made things bearable and my
Cross-Eyed Bear, is how I saw it. I was damned, I said of
myself. I was doomed. Talk about your one-way ticket on a
midnight carousel. And I had no way to get off, no way to
stop, and there sure as hell was no brass ring. There was
nobody anywhere in the world, not so far as I was concerned,
that knew my name. Including me. Especially me.

   I mean that's how I saw it before I did what you did too. I
asked for help, just the way you did. And they came to see
me, just like I went to see you. Jesus, I'll never forget that.
You know what they said when I told them I was damned?
They asked me what made me think I was that important. I
went through my diagnosis number, and you know what they
did? They laughed. That's not what your trouble is, they said.
You know what your trouble is? Your trouble is the same as
ours. We lived it, same as you. The real trouble is that you're
a self-centered, arrogant sonofabitch who never once, not for

one minute, ever raised his head long enough to think about anybody in the world except himself. There *is* no King Kong that's separate from you, Mister, not until you make the separation, and you can't begin to make the separation until you realize how you're one and the same. What's on your back is your own self-pity, your own dishonesty. King Kong isn't drugs. He's got your face and your name and address. It's yourself you're going to have to deal with, but not just with yourself anymore. You're going to need us just the way we need you. That's how things are going to be different. You're not going to be fighting alone any more. If you work with us you won't be able to give King Kong his old names anymore because we got that sucker's number. I didn't understand much of all that of course. You know how damned sick you are. But I heard them. They broke the circle. And that was the start. . . .

. . .Seeing the activity of writing as involving the development of the kind of power that can be an alternative to losing is what allows me to start to restore an Emersonian frame to teaching and learning it. Good writing, good use, using language well, literacy: this for Emerson, and he says it again and again, was intimately a matter of character, involved a vital and dynamic connection of the human with the divine. Hence, as he says in *Nature*, "a man's power to connect his thought with its proper symbol, and so to utter it, depends on the simplicity of his character, that is, upon his love of truth and his desire to communicate it without loss." Further, Emerson says, this power "is at once a commanding certificate that he who employs it is a man in alliance with truth and God."

It is an equation with which his audience seems to have had no trouble.

And writing that was not so good, the disheveled use of language, what then was that a certificate of; with what, by implication, would an inept user of language have to be in alliance?

Neither the speaker nor his audience, apparently, had any trouble here either.

But of course for us, with our students, there's going to be a hatful; we're going to have to write the equations differently.

288   I do not mean that we must find a new way of defining and
specifying illiteracy for our students as a form of Emersonian
ungodliness, but I do think we have got to find a way of
designating illiteracy both literally and as a metaphor with
terminologies that can for our students have an equivalent
significance and the same kind of transforming force. We
have got to find a way of defining and specifying what illiteracy is and is a matter of in terms that matter, and to do this in
as many different ways as we can. I am talking about the need
to imagine illiteracy in the terms that Paulo Freire saw it in,
as an instrument of oppression. I am talking about seeing
what we would call the un-right use of language in the sort of
political context someone like George Orwell gives it. I mean
discussing clichés as Hannah Arendt describes their marching
Jews to gas chambers. I mean seeing the problem of sentence
subordination as a problem with how to put the world together. I mean making use of the whole ragged reticule of
English teacher concerns such as vocabulary, syntax, even
punctuation in the sort of frame that Richard Mitchell provides for them in his ironic contemplation of the social consequences that could attend someone's knowing how to use
language well:

> Just think what happens in the mind of the person who knows the
> difference between restrictive and nonrestrictive clauses. Anyone who
> understands that distinction is on the brink of seeing the difference
> between simple fact and elaborative detail and may well begin to make
> judgments about the logic of such relationships. He may start bothering
> his head about the difference between things essential and things
> accidental, a disorder that often leads to the discovery of tautologies.
> Furthermore, anyone who sees the difference between restrictive and
> nonrestrictive clauses is likely to understand *why* modifiers should be
> close to the things they modify and thus begin to develop a sense of
> the way in which ideas grow from one another. From that, it's not a
> long way to detecting non sequiturs and unstated premises and even
> false analogies. . . .
>
> A fluent command of English cannot exist as an isolated skill, a
> clever stunt. A person who speaks and writes his native tongue clearly
> and precisely does so because of many other abilities, and those other
> abilities themselves grow stronger through the fluent manipulation of
> language. The simple matter of being logical is a function of language.
> A million high school graduates capable of fluent English would be a

million Americans capable of logical thought. What would we do with them, especially if they were black? You think *they're* going to buy those lottery tickets and lamps in the shape of Porky Pig? You think they're going to hang out on the corners and provide employment for everybody from the local social worker to the justices of the Supreme Court?[3]

I'm talking about the necessity of making students aware of the un-right use of language as easy and as addictive—bad language as 40 to 1 shot horse. Bad language as a standing invitation to your own beheading, as the real toad that swallows every imaginary garden. Bad language as the ticket down the river that you sell yourself. Bad language as prison argot, the mumble of the slave corrals. . . .

. . .Don't get me wrong. When I say you got to bet a race and not a system, I don't mean you can come out here and do it all by feel or something—not any more than knowing what a loser is will keep you from turning into one, or than it makes you a winner. Besides, it's losers who think there's such a thing as a winner. You'd better know what you're doing when you come out here. You *got* to know what Andrew Beyer says about speed fractions. You *got* to know how Chapin shows you to figure the horse least likely to lose. You *got* to know what Ainslee says about pace rating, even if you think he's wrong. Because you got to know how to *study* a performance record. You got to know how to read a program, because you got to know how to use it to tell you what's going on out there.

See, it's like this. There are rules. You got to know the rules because you got to know when they won't work, when to break them. You got to have a way of making sense of things out there, but things don't always make the same kind of sense. Early money on a horse, for instance. Sometimes it's stable money, smart money, and sometimes it isn't. It depends on the horse, the race, the conditions. Lots of things. Or, say, you see a horse bolted his last race. That means he's out of shape, right? Not necessarily. Not if you know how to read a performance record. Not if you know how to use it to see what you watch. So you got to pay attention to what's going on, but you got to know how not to pay attention to certain things too, things that don't mean what they look like

290 they mean, things that aren't going to matter the way they're
supposed to matter.

At least the way you figure it. You can never know for sure
and right along with knowing the rules you got to know that
and you got to remember that. You can never know for sure
and neither can anybody else. The best handicappers in the
world make maybe 15, 20 percent of their bets. And that's the
best in the world. They don't make a lot of money, but they
come out ahead. And that's what handicapping is about, coming out ahead in the long run. It's not a way to win races. It's
how not to be a loser. You're like a hockey goalie see, who can
never *win* a game, but you can keep one from being lost. You
can beat a race, but you can't beat the races. You ever hear
that? Really, it's the other way around. Anybody can get beat
by a race. Anybody. But if you can't *beat* the track you can
stay with it; you can make expenses anyway; you can stay in
the game. And, like I say, you've got to remember that because you're going to need it.

You can come out here every Friday, for instance, the way
I do, for four or five weeks, and if you're playing right, you
play maybe no more than eight or ten races. That's two a
night, maybe three, on a ten race card. You stay out of all the
garbage stuff in between. Let's say you bet every one of those
ten races just the way you know you should have, for just as
much money as you figured they were worth. And you got ten
losses in a row. I had that once, ten in a row. Then here's the
eleventh race. You know you ought to be in it solid. And the
board has two favorites against you. You better have rules to
get you where you are then, but when you're there you're
going to need more than somebody else's rules to do what you
ought to do. It's then you need something of your own that
you can believe in, because without that. . . .

. . .Defining illiteracy as a form of powerlessness for our
students, and showing in what ways powerlessness is an invitation to victimization, will not in itself be enough, of course.
Indeed, without providing students with some vision of the
transformation that can attend the attempt to become more
responsible to one's self as a user of language, it is worse than
unprincipled to encourage them to see the inability to use it
well as a kind of addiction, addiction as a kind of despair.

Addicts are not better off simply for seeing themselves as addicts. The Good Samaritan left money with the innkeeper not to make sure that the injured man would be comfortable, but to prevent the possibility—it was so stipulated by Judean law—that the man would be sold into slavery for being unable to pay the innkeeper's bill. And by "vision of transformation" I'm talking about providing students with something more than a description of the kind of miracle that seems to happen only to other people. Saint Augustine, Helen Keller, Richard Rodriguez, Viktor Frankl. What's wanted is a way of making clear to students the availability of such seeming miracles to them, the presenting of transformation in terms that it is possible to help students see they can have a share in. Take the revisions of these three student sentences, for example:

My mother used to love my father, but she left him when he became an alcoholic and wouldn't admit it.
My mother loves my father; she had to leave him because he's an alcoholic who can't admit it.

My high school math teacher was tough but fair.
My high school math teacher was tough and fair.

There were four main causes for the War Between the States.
What are seen as the four main causes for the Civil War seems to depend on the point of view of the historian.

None of these sentences in either its first or its revised form is immediately arresting. There is even a point of view from which the sentences as a group could be said to scrape the edge of banality. And because it could be done accurately, I suppose it would be possible to imagine one were doing the sentences justice by describing the changes in them with no more than English teacher terminology: as a matter of altered punctuation, supplied connectives, changes in tense, differences in vocabulary, and so on. But from another point of view—and no one has to suppose any more here than that the sentences can have contexts—from another point of view what can be said to have "happened" in each revision is something that cannot be described completely without some reference to the reviser, at least as we imagine him or her. From this point of view, the revisers of those sentences, in changing how they have put the world together, have changed their relationship not just to the world, but to themselves—and not just to themselves as writers, but to themselves as more than writers. In the sense that life is, as John Gardner puts it, "all conjunctions, one damn thing after another, cows *and* wars *and* chewing gum *and* mountains," the revisers of those sentences are no longer life's victims. In the sense that art, what Gardner calls "the best, most important art—is all subordination: guilt *because of* sin *because of* pain,"[4] the revisers of those sentences have become artists. No longer, at any rate, is the world that which simply happens to them. They have begun to happen to the world.

It is a change, so far as I am concerned, no less momentous in its implications than the "deliverance" that Walker Percy argues attended Helen Keller's famous learning experience at the water pump with her teacher Anne Sullivan. Before the event at the pump, Helen Keller had been using words for some time, but she had been using them as what Percy calls "signals" rather than "symbols":

When her teacher, Miss Sullivan, spelled out *water, mug, drink* in her hand, she "understood": she responded by drinking water, going to water, fetching the mug, etc.—that is to say, she interpreted the word in a signal context and *did* something. What Miss Sullivan could not make her understand was that the word water was not a command to *do* something with water, but *meant*, denoted water. Then at last and in a sudden flash of insight, Helen understood that the gesture in her hand *meant* the water. It was an experience of tremendous excitement. Having learned that this "is" water, what she had to know immediately was *what everything else was!*[5]

So it is that the mind is awakened, that a being becomes human. From an understanding of language as signal only, and in consequence of herself as responsible only to adapt to signals of various kinds, Helen Keller moves to the seeing of language as symbol and in consequence to the seeing of herself as a maker of meaning, someone who through the power of symbolization has gained what Percy calls "possession" of the world. And something analogous to this awakening, this "deliverance," this thrust from victimization to freedom, I would argue, is implicit in the direction being taken by the

revisers of those three sentences—an implicitness that were
it made explicit would be for the writers of those sentences to
come into "possession" of themselves as more than being just
the writers of those sentences. . . .

. . .The biggest problem I had with getting clean, and you
can count on this being the hump anybody you work with is
going to have to get over too, the biggest problem I had was
one of belief. I don't mean just believing it was going to be
possible for me to get clean to begin with, particularly the
way they told me I was going to have to work at it, which
made absolutely no sense. I mean beyond that. Suppose it
did work. That's what I had trouble with. Suppose I could
stay clean. I couldn't believe there was any way it was going
to be worth it. I couldn't see what was supposed to *make* it
worth it, not as a way of life. All they told me was that everything was going to look different. Nobody promised me a new
car, or a steady job, or that I'd get my family back. In fact,
they said that that didn't matter. None of it. Nobody promised me I wouldn't feel afraid any more ever either. And I
thank God that nobody promised me any of that psychiatrist
crap about getting myself back for myself, which I didn't want
anyway. In fact, that's exactly what I used the booze and pills
to get away from. They just told me that things were going to
be different. And it came up that very first day.

The same guy that told me about King Kong told me something else. He told me I was going to have to learn how to
believe in something bigger than I was, more than I was.
That's just how he put it too, "you'll have to learn how to."
But of course I didn't get it. I figured he was a Christer or
something, a candy-ass, and I got nasty. Not too nasty, understand, you know how sick you feel, but quiet nasty, scared
nasty. "Tell me," I said. "How do you pray to a God you don't
believe in?" I'll never forget the way he handled that. "Son,"
he said, "I think if I were you I'd just pray anyway." And then
he said something else. "Look," he said, "nobody in the Program you'll be in will ever ask you to do anything like that, to
believe anything that way. All we ask is that you act as though
you wanted to, as though getting well could have something
in it for you. You don't even have to act as though you *did*
believe it. Just act as though you wanted to." And then he

294   said, "You do that, and I'll guarantee you something. I absolutely guarantee you that if you stay clean *our* way, everything in your life will get better."

It was crap to me then, of course, even what I understood.
He didn't convince me of a thing. But you know what I
couldn't get away from? I couldn't get away from how sick I
knew I was and from knowing he'd been there too and from
seeing he wasn't there any more. I mean the way he talked
about his own life I knew he'd been there. And he'd been
clean for ten years, he told me that right off and I could see it.
So I didn't believe what he told me, but I did believe that he
believed it, and that's what I hung onto. I wanted what he
had. I wanted to be me the way he was him. That's why I did
what he told me to do. And it was only through that, through
doing what he told me to do, that I found out what he meant.

All those things they told me to do, none of which had
anything to do with anything, like writing out a moral inven-
tory of myself—can you imagine me doing that?—and asking
for help in the morning, from a Power Greater than Myself
they called it, and even if I didn't believe in it—talk about
craziness—and attending meetings, and working with new
people, and trying to straighten out my past, not one bit of
which ever made any sense to me, not one bit of which ever
felt natural to do, except that all those things, doing those
things I mean, somehow they gave me a way of living life that
gave me a life to have. In the Program we fight a mystery with
a mystery, they told me. And by God things got better. Not
perfect understand, but they got better, and in a totally different way from the way I thought they would. I was becoming
somebody new. I never did get my family back, as you know.
I still feel afraid a lot. But it's OK in a way it never was. What
the guy couldn't tell me that first day, see, was that the me
that getting clean was going to be worth it to wasn't here yet.
Understand, all the rest of me is still here too. I'm not *brand*
new. I'm going to be an addict till the day I die, right along
with all the things that make me one. Nothing changes that.
But I've got a me I never had before. I'm not what I was. . . .

. . .Offering what the activity of writing involves in the
name of what it is about and for can enable a teacher of
writing to invite students to participate in an activity with

meaning—whatever forms of discourse we may ask our students to experiment with, whatever conventions we may expect them to master. Very simply, we have a better chance of getting better sentences from our students when they have some understanding of what composing a sentence can be a matter of, and of what it can mean for someone to compose them, than when they don't. It's in this sense that Richard Lanham suggests writing can be seen as an "act of socialization" plus; and "it is," he says,

by repeated acts of such socialization that we become sociable beings, that we grow up. Thus, the act of writing models the presentation of self in society, constitutes a rehearsal for social reality. It is not simply a question of a pre-existent self making its message known to a pre-existent society. It is not, initially, a question of message at all. Writing is a way to clarify, strengthen, and energize the self, to render individuality rich, full, and social. This does not mean writing that flows, as Terry Southern immortally put it, "right out of the old guts onto the goddam paper." Just the opposite. Only by taking the position of the reader toward one's own prose, putting a reader's pressure on it, can the self be made to grow. Writing should enhance and expand the self, allow it to try out new possibilities, tentative selves.

The moral ingredient in writing, then, works first not on the morality of the message but on the nature of the sender, on the complexity of the self. "Why bother?" To invigorate and enrich your selfhood, to increase, in the most literal sense, your self-consciousness. Writing, properly pursued, does not make you better. It makes you more alive. This is why our growing illiteracy ought to distress us. It tells us something, something alarming, about the impoverishment of our selves. We say that we fear written communication will break down. Unlikely. And if it does we can always, as we do anyway, pick up the phone. Something more fundamental is at stake, the selfhood and sociability of the communicators. We are back to the basic peculiarity of *writing*—it is *premeditated* utterance, and in that premeditation lives its first if not its only value. "Why bother?" "To find out who I really am." It is not only what we think that we discover in writing, but what we are and can be.[6]

And such a frame for the teaching of writing is as necessary for teachers, or at least for me as a teacher, as it is for students. I thought for a long time that I was unique in being as good a teacher as I know I am and in being as unsuccessful in teaching writing as I know myself to be. Few of my students

296 learn what I think they ought to have learned; few of them come so far as I begin every course supposing that they can and will, and that I end every course knowing that they have not. And it's only in a sense that the particular achievements of particular people help very much, for there are many, many more particular people who, for a variety of reasons, not all of them bad by any means, simply turn off to writing, or worse choose to have no choice with it, find the price of freedom, involving as it always does the sacrifice of one's immediate sense of his own well-being, just too damned high to pay.

But I do not believe that I am as unique as I once thought I was in concluding that no teacher of writing teaches writing very well. I do not believe that I am alone in having worked out that for this reason my primary obligation as a teacher is to preserve myself from what I would call the besetting sin of the profession: unacknowledged self-contempt, that form of existential despair the precise quality of which, as Kirkegaard noted, is that it ceases after a time to be able to experience itself as despair. The junkie's nightmare and the junkie's dream. I no longer believe that I am alone as a teacher in knowing that I've got the temptations of my own kind of addiction to deal with, and that it's a lot more than fragments, in the form of the newest logarithmic, clinically validated, heuristical, deconstructive, ultimately-problem-solving-quick-fix of a system I want to shore against that kind of ruin I can tell you. A deliberate belief is what Conrad's Marlow calls it, when techniques and even principles won't do. A deliberate belief. . . .

. . .Because finally, see, handicapping as something you can believe in, as a way for yourself, is all you've got to put against all of this out here, to stay in the game. And I mean all of it too, the color, the noise, the money going every which way, the hustlers, the touts, the creeps and the losers, the odds changing on the tote board every 15 seconds, the whole goddam mess out here. You've got to have a place for yourself, see, some place to come from, somewhere to stand in the middle of all this action. You've got to have something to hang onto.

But you know, I'll tell you something. When you got that,

everything changes out here. Everything. You *see* everything out here different. It's not a place where just anything can happen anymore; it's a place where things are possible. Every race is new then, the first and last time in the history of the world. It'll never be again, not in the history of the world. You watch the bets go up on the board, odds up odds down, everything changing every 15 seconds. By God it's *like* the history of the world, the dinosaurs out there underlaid to hell, 1 for 10, 1 for 15 maybe, and here's the caveman, 80 to 1 at first, then he's out of the cave at 10 to 1, 8 to 5, then he's even money, and then it's the race, bottom line time, and in two minutes it's all over.

But you got a place in that, a chance to be with the final flick of the board when it's all over: win, place, and show and you count your money, and you know just where you are. It can be wonderful that way, wonderful, because win or lose, when you do it right—well it's all a question of how you feel on the way home I guess, and that's what keeps me coming out here. I don't mean to say I don't get bad nights and feel lousy. I do. I act like a loser sometimes too and I feel even lousier about that. But when I pay the right kind of attention, and figure things out the best I can, and don't sucker myself into races I shouldn't be in or into wrong bets, too much or too little, when I keep my goddam ego out of the way—well, it's like nothing else in the world. I'm alive on the way home then—not a big gambler or the guy who beat the system, because I don't even have to win to feel what I can feel sometimes. I mean I'm me alive. I'm just me but I'm some-body. I can see what kind of night it is. I'm glad to be going home. And even if I don't feel like it right then, I know I'll want to come back. . . .

. . .What I do for my students, I'm saying, I do for myself, and *vice versa*. Taking arms against a sea of troubles, as you will recall from the metaphor in context, is more than a com-plicated way of describing a simple conflict. Can it be that there are troubles that are ended, rather than defeated or resolved, by the action of certain kinds of opposition only? To judge from how I can feel sometimes on the way home at night, I just guess I'd say that there can be. At any rate, in dealing as a teacher of writing with writing not as a way to be

298 a winner, or even as a way to win, but as an alternative to losing, I obligate myself to make alive for my students what can keep me alive as me, and alive in the face of the fact that my students may never *become* writers, not any more than every addict gets clean, or than the horse has to win.

Notes

1. Simone Weil, "Reflections on the Right Use of School Studies with a View to the Love of God," in *The Simone Weil Reader*, ed. George A. Panichas (New York: David McKay Company, Inc., 1977), pp. 45–6.

2. Bill Barich, *Laughing in the Hills* (New York: Penguin Books, 1981), p. 97.

3. Richard Mitchell, *Less Than Words Can Say* (Boston: Little, Brown and Company, 1979), pp. 154 and 159–60.

4. John Gardner, *On Moral Fiction* (New York: Basic Books, Harper & Row, 1981), p. 6.

5. Walker Percy, as quoted by Robert Coles, *Walker Percy: An American Search* (Boston: Little, Brown and Company, 1978), p. 82.

6. Richard A. Lanham, *Revising Prose* (New York: Charles Scribner's Sons, 1979), pp. 105–06.